Athanasius

Peter J. Leithart

Baker Academic
a division of Baker Publishing Group
Grand Rapids, Michigan

Published by Baker Academic
a division of Baker Publishing Group
P.O. Box 6287, Grand Rapids, MI 49516-6287
www.bakeracademic.com

Printed in the United States of America

Library of Congress Cataloging-in-Publication Data

Leithart, Peter J.
    Athanasius / Peter J. Leithart.
       p. cm.
    Includes bibliographical references and index.
    ISBN 978-0-8010-3942-3 (pbk. : alk. paper)
    1. Athanasius, Saint, Patriarch of Alexandria, d. 373. I. Title.
BR65.A446A84 2011
270.2092—dc22   2011001593

11   12   13   14   15   16   17   7   6   5   4   3   2   1

To Matthias Ehud

"Pursue, for Yahweh has given your enemies into your hands."

Judges 3:28 (author's translation)

Contents

Series Preface

Recent decades have witnessed a growing desire among Orthodox, Catholics, and Protestants to engage and retrieve the exegetical, theological, and doctrinal resources of the early church. If the affirmations of the first four councils constitute a common inheritance for ecumenical Christian witness, then in the Nicene Creed Christians find a particularly rich vein for contemporary exploration of the realities of faith. These fruits of the patristic period were, as the fathers themselves repeatedly attest, the embodiment of a personally and ecclesially engaged exegetical, theological, and metaphysical approach to articulating the Christian faith. In the Foundations of Theological Exegesis and Christian Spirituality series, we will explore this patristic witness to our common Nicene faith.

Each volume of the present series explores how biblical exegesis, dogmatic theology, and participatory metaphysics relate in the thought of a particular church father. In addition to serving as introductions to the theological world of the fathers, the volumes of the series break new ecumenical and theological ground by taking as their starting point three related convictions. First, at the core of the Foundations series lies the conviction that *ressourcement*, or retrieval, of the shared inheritance of the Nicene faith is an important entry point to all ecumenical endeavor. Nicene Christianity, which received its authoritative shape at the councils of Constantinople (381) and Chalcedon (451), was the result of more than three centuries of ecclesial engagement with the implications of the incarnation and of the adoration of Father, Son, and Holy Spirit in the liturgy of the church. Particularly since the 1940s, when Catholic scholars such as Henri de Lubac, Jean Daniélou, and others reached back to the church fathers for inspiration and contemporary cultural and ecclesial renewal, *ressourcement* has made significant contributions to theological development and ecumenical discussion. The last few decades have also witnessed growing evangelical interest in an approach to the church fathers that reads them not only for academic reasons but also with a view to giving them a voice in today's discussions. Accordingly, this series is based on the conviction that a contemporary retrieval of the church fathers is essential also to the flourishing and further development of Christian theology.

Second, since the Nicene consensus was based on a thorough engagement with the Scriptures, renewed attention to the exegetical approaches of the church fathers is an important aspect of *ressourcement*. In particular, the series works on the assumption that Nicene theology was the result of the early church's conviction that historical and spiritual interpretation of the Scriptures were intimately connected and that both the Old and the New Testaments speak of the realities of Christ, of the church, and of eternal life in fellowship with the Triune God. Although today we may share the dogmatic inheritance of the Nicene faith regardless of our exegetical approach, it is much less clear that the Nicene convictions—such as the doctrines of the Trinity and of the person of Christ—can be sustained without the spiritual approaches to interpretation that were common among the fathers. Doctrine, after all, is the outcome of biblical interpretation. Thus, theological renewal requires attention to the way in which the church fathers approached Scripture. Each of the volumes of this series will therefore explore a church father's theological approach(es) to the biblical text.

Finally, it is our conviction that such a *ressourcement* of spiritual interpretation may contribute significantly toward offsetting the fragmentation— ecclesial, moral, economical, and social—of contemporary society. This fragmentation is closely connected to the loss of the Platonic-Christian synthesis of Nicene Christianity. Whereas this earlier synthesis recognized a web of relationships as a result of God's creative act in and through Christ, many today find it much more difficult to recognize, or even to pursue, common life together. A participatory metaphysic, which many of the church fathers took as axiomatic, implies that all of created reality finds its point of mutual connection in the eternal Word of God, in which it lies anchored. It is this christological anchor that allows for the recognition of a common origin and a common end, and thus for shared commitments. While the modern mindset tends to separate nature and the supernatural (often explicitly excluding the latter), Nicene Christianity recognized that the created order exists by virtue of God's graciously allowing it to participate, in a creaturely fashion, in his goodness, truth, and beauty as revealed in Christ through the Spirit. A participatory metaphysic, therefore, is one of the major presuppositions of the creed's articulation of the realities of faith.

In short, rooted in the wisdom of the Christian past, the volumes of the series speak from the conviction that the above-mentioned convictions informed the life and work of the church fathers and that these convictions are in need of *ressourcement* for the sake of today's theological, philosophical, and exegetical debates. In light of a growing appreciation of the early Christians, the series aims to publish erudite introductions that will be of interest in seminary and university courses on doctrine and biblical exegesis and that will be accessible to educated lay readers with interest in how early Christians appropriated and passed on divine revelation.

Hans Boersma and Matthew Levering, series editors

Acknowledgments

I have many people to thank for their assistance on this project. Above all, I am grateful to Hans Boersma and Matthew Levering for their invitation to contribute to the series and for their helpful feedback on the first draft of this book. One of the pleasures of writing a volume in this series was that of being able to work again with Rodney Clapp and the rest of the staff at Baker Academic. Even before I had signed on to this project, I had worked through several Athanasius texts with graduate students in a seminar in Christology. Thanks to Brad Littlejohn, Justin Hughes, Anna van den Broek, Lisa Beyeler, and Ahn Jung Jin for their questions, challenges, and discussions. Anna also prepared indexes. Donny Linnemeyer proofed the first draft of the manuscript and caught many infelicities and errors; it is a better book because of his assistance. My oldest son, Woelke, hosted me during a research week in Durham, drove me to the Duke Divinity School library, and found productive ways to spend his time while I hunkered over a musty copy of Migne's Patrologia Graeca and worked slowly and with exuberant delight through the *Discourses against the Arians*. Throughout the project, Woelke was an invaluable research aid, providing copies of articles to which I had no access in northern Idaho.

As I studied the life and treatises of Athanasius, I often marveled, and occasionally winced, at his violent intensity. On the whole, I think Athanasius was on the side of the angels, a salutary antidote to the wilting cowardice that has too often passed as piety in the modern world. Athanasius possessed, or was possessed by, zeal of biblical proportions, the zeal of an Elijah, a Moses, one of the judges. Matthias Ehud Leithart, Woelke's second son and my second grandchild, bears the name of one of those zealous judges—Ehud, the left-handed assassin of Eglon of Moab—and I dedicate this book to him in the hope that he may grow to find Athanasius as inspiring as I have and so live up to his name.

Introduction

Scripture and Metaphysics (in the Augustinian Mode)

What is the nature of things? What are things, ultimately and in their most basic structures and essence? You, O Lord, know, for you made them all, sustain them all in existence, direct and guide all things to your good ends. You know every thing, love every thing, are good to every thing. You know them all more nearly than they know themselves. But how shall *we* know?

Should I even ask, O Lord? Should I even ask? You have spoken, and you have acted, and you have called us to believe. You have taught us that we walk by faith and not by sight, by trust in your good promises of goodness, and not by understanding. It is enough that you know the nature of things. Should I ask?

If I ask, will I receive an answer? You are beyond all my thoughts, greater than all that I can say, incomprehensible in your eternal communion as Father, Son, and Holy Spirit. You cannot be encompassed with any concept, bounded by anything greater than yourself, since you are greater than all. All my efforts to encompass you are acts of idolatry and not true worship. And you made all things and all things shine with the bright radiance of your glory. Your world seems as incomprehensible as you yourself.

Should I even ask? Can I ask? Dare I ask?

Have not some of your servants turned to such idols? Have they not bound you in forms and substances and concepts of their own imagining and bowed to worship what their own hands have made? Have they not turned your glory, the glory of the incorruptible God, into idols more ethereal than four-footed beasts and crawling creatures, and worshiped and served the creature rather than you, their Creator? Have not your servants all but denied that you were Creator, following vain philosophers who spoke of eternal matter and changeless forms? Have they not said that you are subject to time and development, denying that you are eternally complete and fulfilled? Have they not danced and sung before other gods? They asked, what is the nature of things? And were they not turned from your ways?

Dare I ask?

Yet, I cannot escape the question, for others have spoken before me. Others have asked, what is the nature of things? and have given answers. Are their answers true? Should I, O Lord, ignore their questions and answers and devote myself to prayer and service to the poor? Or shall I seek to answer? Shall I seek to determine if they speak the truth? How can I not? Can I tell whether their answers are true without asking the same questions? If a philosopher says that all things exist by participation in forms, should I, O Lord, believe him? If another says that matter is eternal, shall I, O Lord, accept that? If yet another says that all substances are informed matter, shall I receive that? If another says that we can know nothing of things beyond their phenomenal appearances, what shall I say? If the philosophers are correct about the nature of things, do they also describe your nature, O God? Are you one of the things whose nature these philosophers describe?

If you would not have me believe these philosophers, I would know why. And if they are false, I would know what truth to speak in place of their falsehoods.

Blessed be God. You have not been silent but have spoken too about the nature of things. You have said that in the beginning you made the heavens and the earth, and all that is in them. You warn that we do not know the activity of God who makes all things, just as we do not know the path of the wind or how bones take shape in the womb. You give to all life and breath and all things. You cause all things to work together for good to those who love you. You have said that you were with your Word in the beginning, your Word that is God and yet also with God, and that you made all things through this Word, so that nothing is made without him. You have said that he is the light that lightens every man, the light that shines in all that you have made. You have said that in you we all "live and move and have our being." You have said that Christ is before all things and that in him all things consist, and that you will put all things under his feet, and that you will sum up all things in Christ, who fills all things. You have handed over all things to your Son, even judgment and life, and all things are put in subjection under him. You have given us the Spirit of your Son, the Spirit that "searches all things, even the depths of God." You have promised that at the end you will be all in all, and you have taught us to receive all things with thanks.

What is the nature of things? Can I say more than this, O Lord, that from you and through you and to you are all things? Need I say more? Dare I?

This is what you taught your servant, Athanasius. You taught him that exploring the nature of things was exploring the truth that is Jesus the Christ. You taught him concerning the eternal Word, who is your living will and your eternal "plan," the radiance of your glory, the river of living water that flows from you, the never-barren fountain. You taught him that you were never speechless or without reason. You taught him that every created thing, and all the rationality, pattern, and harmony of things, comes from that Word. You taught him that when we look rightly at your creation, we look not at a portrait of some unnamed and unnamable God but at the traces of your Logos. You taught him that everything shines with glory, and the glory is the eternal radiance that is the eternal light that is the Father. Human beings are *logikos*, rational, but you showed Athanasius that we are so because we are made in the image of your Logos. You taught your servant Athanasius that when the world descended into corruption and the image of God was tarnished, when death dragged the human race toward the grave, your living Logos became man to transform creation from the inside, to overcome death on the cross and to rise again so that your light might shine within and through our flesh. You showed Athanasius that through your incarnate Son and Spirit, you are forming new, stable human beings, a deified human society, where death and the fear of death are overcome.

You taught your servant Athanasius that Christ unites Scripture and all things, for Scripture, as much as the world and human existence and history, is all about Christ. Scripture everywhere teaches about Christ. His life, death, and resurrection are the hinge on which the drama of Scripture turns, and you taught Athanasius to find shadows of Christ in the Old Testament, shadows that break forth in light with the fulfillment of the New. And you taught that Christ is the pattern not only for the Scriptures but for all things. You taught Athanasius that Christ impresses his form on Old Testament institutions and persons, and that those forms are revealed in their fullness when he manifests himself in the flesh. You taught him to see that same pattern within creation, for the Logos is the exemplar of created reality as he is of Scripture.

Through your servant, you have taught us metaphysics as "christic metaphysics," which we might also call "typological" metaphysics—just as we can call his interpretation of the Scriptures with equal justice both "christic" and "typological."

What is the nature of things? What is ultimately true of things? Shall we listen to Athanasius, O God? Shall our final answer be not forms, and substances, and hylomorphic unions, and possibility and actuality, but finally only this: from eternity to the eschaton, it is all about Christ?

Is that not the answer to my questions, O Father? Is that not the sum of all questions about Scripture and metaphysics? How could I speak more or other than the Word that is the first Word and the last, the beginning and the end, Alpha and Omega?

Should I say more? Dare I?

1

Evangelizing Metaphysics

Battle in Alexandria

Even before the controversy over Arius broke out around 318, the church scene in fourth-century Alexandria, Egypt, was tumultuous. Escaping the Diocletianic persecution (c. 303), Bishop Peter of Alexandria had fled from his city more than once.[1] During one of his absences, one Melitius found the city bereft of pastoral care and promptly ordained some men to fill the vacuum. Peter returned and wondered what had happened to his bishopric. It was the beginning of what we now know as the Melitian schism.

In part, this was another battle, like the Donatist schism to the West, about the proper response to persecution, and the question was whether to encourage or discourage what some regarded as the imprudent zeal of voluntary martyrs. Peter, like the anti-Donatist Bishop Mensurius of Carthage, urged moderation and was mild toward those who lapsed by offering sacrifice to the emperor; Melitius was of Donatist stripe. In Alexandria, the division was so acute that, according to legend, Peter and Melitius were not even able to cooperate when they were, ironically, forced to share a prison cell. Peter hung a curtain down the middle of the cell and urged his supporters to remain on his side of the curtain.[2]

Despite his prudent escapes, Peter died a martyr in 311. Achillas briefly followed him as bishop, but he soon died, and Alexander was installed in 313. Sometime around 318, he and a local priest, Arius, came into conflict over Christology. Ancient church historians give differing accounts of the origins of the controversy, but the most likely explanation is that of Socrates, who recorded that Arius objected to a sermon of Alexander that so stressed the

1

unity of Father and Son that it seemed to verge toward the Sabellian or modalist heresy by denying distinctions among the persons.[3]

A charismatic preacher, Arius was tall, stooped, and curved—as one ancient historian put it—like a snake. He wore the garb of an ascetic and a philosopher and oversaw a large number of devoted virgins within the Alexandrian church. He had a reputation as an acute logician. Possibly a student of Lucian of Antioch (as Arius's ally Eusebius of Nicomedia definitely was), Arius was in some respects a traditional Alexandrian theologian. Like Clement and Origen, the great Alexandrian theologians of the previous centuries, Arius was devoted to more speculative theology and taught mainly a small band of devoted disciples. He was not, like Alexander, responsible for a large congregation of lay believers. The conflict between the two is in part a conflict of different theological styles: catholic versus academic.[4]

Arius aligned with Origen in another respect too. On the issues that came to the forefront in the Arian controversy, Origen's position was ambiguous. On the one hand, Origen taught that the Son was eternally and timelessly generated by the Father, but on the other hand, he implied that the Son was secondary and ontologically subordinate to the Father. Arius joined with Origen in stressing the subordination of the Son to the Father, but unlike Origen, Arius cut through the ambiguity and denied the eternal generation of the Son.[5]

Arius's precise views are hard to come by. Very few of his writings still exist in complete form, and we are, in the main, forced to rely on his opponents, mainly Athanasius, who quoted fragments and often put them in the worst possible light. Yet several of Arius's basic ideas and emphases can be reconstructed. One of the few extant works from his own hand is a letter to Bishop Eusebius of Nicomedia, in which he complains that he is being persecuted for teaching that the Logos exists "by will and counsel," that "before he was begotten, or created, or determined, or established, he did not exist," and that he "derives from non-existence" (*ex ouk ontōn estin*).[6] To be sure, the Logos is not a creature as other creatures are, but neither is he unbegotten, since there can be only one unbegotten, the Father.[7]

Another letter to Alexander, preserved by Athanasius in his treatise *On the Synods*, provides a fuller explanation of Arius's viewpoint. Claiming that he is only summarizing the "faith from our forefathers,"[8] Arius confesses "One God, alone Ingenerate, alone Everlasting, alone Unbegun, alone True, alone having Immortality, alone Wise, alone Good, alone Sovereign, Judge, Governor, and Providence of all, unalterable and unchangeable, just and good." The repeated "alone" is revealing, since it highlights Arius's claim that he is confessing the "one God" of Scripture, which, in his view, necessarily excludes any notion of a Son who is, "along with" God, ingenerate, everlasting, unbegun, true, immortal, wise, good. He claims to be worshiping the "God of Law and Prophets and New Testament," a God who "begot an Only-begotten Son before eternal times," through whom he made all things. This Son is begotten "not in semblance but in truth," and this means that God "made Him subsist at His own will, unalterable and unchangeable" as a "perfect creature of God, but not as one of the creatures" and as "offspring, but not as one of the things begotten." Carefully distancing himself from earlier heretics—he names the gnostic Valentinus, the Manicheans, and Sabellius among others—he describes the view of the Son that he and his allies ("we") held.

> For when giving to him [the Son] the inheritance of all things [Heb. 1:2], the Father did not deprive himself of what he has without beginning in himself; for he is the source of all things. Thus there are three subsisting realities [*hypostaseis*]. And God, being the cause of all that happens, is absolutely alone without beginning; but the Son, begotten apart from time by the Father, and created [*ktistheis*] and founded before the ages, was not in existence before his generation, but was begotten apart from time before all things, and he alone came into existence [*hypestē*] from the Father. For he is neither eternal nor co-eternal nor co-unbegotten with the Father, nor does he have his being together with the Father, as some speak of relations, introducing two unbegotten beginnings. But God is before all things as monad and beginning of all. Therefore he is also before the Son, as we have learned also from your public preaching in the church. (*On the Synods* 16)[9]

Arius also summarized his views in a poem, known as the *Thalia*, whose original form is notoriously difficult to reconstruct. Athanasius provides two summaries of Arius's beliefs, which he claims are taken from Arius's own writings. Some quotations are from the *Thalia*, but scholars still puzzle over whether Athanasius is quoting verbatim or slicing a few juicy pieces from the work.[10] The first is found in Athanasius's treatise *On the Synods* and bears the heading "The Blasphemies of Arius":[11]

> God Himself then, in His own nature, is ineffable by all men. Equal or like Himself He alone has none, or one in glory. And Ingenerate we call Him, because of Him who is generate by nature. We praise Him as without beginning because of Him who has a beginning. And adore Him as everlasting, because of Him who in time has come to be. The Unbegun made the Son a beginning of things originated; and advanced Him as a Son to Himself by adoption. He has nothing proper to God in proper subsistence. For He is not equal, no, nor one in essence with Him. Wise is God, for He is the teacher of Wisdom. There is full proof that God is invisible to all beings; both to things which are through the Son, and to the Son He is invisible. I will say it expressly, how by the Son is seen the Invisible; by that power by which God sees, and in His own measure, the Son endures to see the Father, as is lawful. Thus there is a Triad, not in equal glories. Not intermingling with each other are their subsistences. One more glorious than the other in their glories unto immensity. Foreign from the Son in essence is the Father, for He is without beginning. Understand that the Monad was; but the Dyad was not, before it was in existence. It follows at once

that, though the Son was not, the Father was God. Hence the Son, not being (for He existed at the will of the Father), is God Only-begotten, and He is alien from either. Wisdom existed as Wisdom by the will of the Wise God. Hence He is conceived in numberless conceptions: Spirit, Power, Wisdom, God's glory, Truth, Image, and Word. Understand that He is conceived to be Radiance and Light. One equal to the Son, the Superior is able to beget; but one more excellent, or superior, or greater, He is not able. At God's will the Son is what and whatsoever He is. And when and since He was, from that time He has subsisted from God. He, being a strong God, praises in His degree the Superior. To speak in brief, God is ineffable to His Son. For He is to Himself what He is, that is, unspeakable. So that nothing which is called comprehensible does the Son know to speak about; for it is impossible for Him to investigate the Father, who is by Himself. For the Son does not know His own essence, for, being Son, He really existed, at the will of the Father. What argument then allows, that He who is from the Father should know His own parent by comprehension? For it is plain that for that which has a beginning to conceive how the Unbegun is, or to grasp the idea, is not possible. (*On the Synods* 15)

Early in the first of his *Discourses against the Arians* (sometimes known as *Orations against the Arians*), Athanasius cites a collection of fragments. Mocking Arius's "effeminate" meter and tone,[12] he quotes Arius's claim to be summarizing the "faith of God's elect" that he has learned from "partakers of wisdom," so that he might be "accomplished, divinely taught, and wise in all things." Athanasius follows with a catena of "repulsive and irreligious" teachings:

"God was not always a Father"; but "once God was alone, and not yet a Father, but afterwards He became a Father." "The Son was not always"; for, whereas all things were made out of nothing, and all existing creatures and works were made, so the Word of God Himself was "made out of nothing," and "once He was not," and "He was not before His origination," but He as others "had an origin of creation." "For God," he says, "was alone, and the Word as yet was not, nor the Wisdom. Then, wishing to form us, thereupon He made a certain one, and named Him Word and Wisdom and Son, that He might form us by means of Him." Accordingly, he says that there are two wisdoms, first, the attribute co-existent with God, and next, that in this wisdom the Son was originated, and was only named Wisdom and Word as partaking of it. "For Wisdom," says he, "by the will of the wise God, had its existence in Wisdom." In like manner, he says, that there is another Word in God besides the Son, and that the Son again, as partaking of it, is named Word and Son according to grace. And this too is an idea proper to their heresy, as shown in other works of theirs, that there are many powers; one of which is God's own by nature and eternal; but that Christ, on the other hand, is not the true power of God; but, as others, one of the so-called powers, one of which, namely, the locust and the caterpillar, is called in Scripture, not merely the power, but the "great power." The others are many and are like the Son, and of them David speaks in the Psalms, when he says, "The Lord of hosts" or "powers." And by nature, as all others, so the Word Himself is alterable, and remains good by His own free will, while He chooses; when, however, He wills, He can alter as we can, as being of an alterable nature. For "therefore," says he, "as foreknowing that He would be good, did God by anticipation bestow on Him this glory, which afterwards, as man, He attained from virtue. Thus in consequence of His works fore-known, did God bring it to pass that He being such, should come to be." (*Discourses* 1.5)

Rowan Williams provides one of the most careful and charitable summaries of Arius's theology. For Arius, "God alone is self-subsistent" and does not have "any kind of plurality or composition." Because he is not eternally and intrinsically related, "He is entirely free, rational and purposive." To create the world, he freely and voluntarily brings "the Son into being, as a subsistent individual truly [*alēthōs*] distinct from himself." Though this occurs "before all ages," yet, in a sense, "the Father exists prior to the Son, since the Son is not eternal, that is, not timelessly self-subsistent." The Son remains what he was created to be, "a perfect creature," and as such he receives "all the gifts and glories God can give him."[13]

The Councils Begin

Alarmed not only at Arius's teaching but also at his popularity, Bishop Alexander summoned a synod of one hundred Egyptian bishops, who roundly condemned Arius. Banished from the city, Arius journeyed to Nicomedia, where he knew he would gain a sympathetic hearing from the powerful Eusebius, an intimate of Constantia, the wife of the eastern emperor Licinius and sister of Constantine. Arius had chosen a good ally. Eusebius summoned a council in Bithynia, which reversed the decision of the Egyptian council by finding Arius orthodox.[14] Another council was held at Caesarea, presumably headed by another Eusebius, the bishop of Caesarea and author of the first *Church History*, and this too found Arius innocent of heresy, though it recommended that he return to Alexandria to attempt a reconciliation with his bishop. Arius returned, but reconciliation did not happen; instead, Arius's presence in Alexandria only provoked further quarreling. Meanwhile, a council held in Antioch condemned and excommunicated Eusebius of Caesarea in 324.[15]

Resolution of the controversy was made more difficult by Licinius's prohibition of Christian assemblies in 322 (which may have been a response to the controversy), and so it was not until Constantine took over the East in 324 that the bishops could safely meet to resolve the question. Constantine's inclination was to settle the dispute by negotiation. He rapidly dispatched his advisor Ossius to Alexandria, bearing an imperial letter, but Ossius found the situation far worse than he had expected. Soon after his mission failed, Constantine summoned the bishops of East and West, together with several from outside the empire, first to Ancyra, and then to Nicaea, to put the issue to rest once and for all. It was the first ecumenical council in the history of the church.

Athanasius was thrust into this controversy in his early adulthood.[16] Born sometime between 295 and 299 into a pagan household in Alexandria, Athanasius rose to prominence as a young man. According to legend, Alexander found Athanasius on the beach playing bishop with his friends on the anniversary of the martyrdom of the previous bishop, Peter, and Alexander "construed the coincidence as an omen and took the boys into his household to give them an education."[17] Under Alexander's tutelage, Athanasius received a smattering of classical education, but the focus of his training was on Scripture.[18] As Gregory Nazianzen describes it in his oration in praise of Athanasius,

> He was brought up, from the first, in religious habits and practices, after a brief study of literature and philosophy, so that he might not be utterly unskilled in such subjects, or ignorant of matters which he had determined to despise. For his generous and eager soul could not brook being occupied in vanities, like unskilled athletes, who beat the air instead of their antagonists and lose the prize. From meditating on every book of the Old and New Testament, with a depth such as none else has applied even to one of them, he grew rich in contemplation, rich in splendor of life, combining them in wondrous sort by that golden bond which few can weave; using life as the guide of contemplation, contemplation as the seal of life. For the fear of the Lord is the beginning of wisdom, and, so to say, its first swathing band; but, when wisdom has burst the bonds of fear and risen up to love, it makes us friends of God, and sons instead of bondsmen. (*Oration* 21.6)[19]

Though he was able to use the philosophy he knew in anti-pagan apologetics and anti-Arian polemics, Athanasius remained throughout his life mainly a Bible teacher, his most basic convictions, passions, instincts, beliefs, and views shaped not by Plotinus or Stoicism but by Scripture.

Athanasius's life was one of epic proportions—a biblical epic, to be precise. He consistently viewed his opponents and his circumstances through the lenses of the biblical narratives that he had learned so thoroughly at the feet of Alexander. For example, he opens an encyclical letter describing the circumstances of the Alexandrian church with a lengthy comparison to the account of the Levite and the concubine in Judges 19–21. "My object," he writes, "in reminding you of this history is this, that you may compare those ancient transactions with what has happened to us now, and perceiving how much these last exceed the other in cruelty, may be filled with greater indignation on account of them, than were the people of old against those offenders." In his view, "the calamity of the Levite was but small, when compared with the enormities which have now been committed against the Church." In fact, "such deeds as these were never before heard of in the whole world, or the like experienced by any one." In the time of the judges, "it was but a single woman that was injured, and one Levite who suffered wrong," but "now the whole Church is injured, the priesthood insulted, and worst of all, piety is persecuted by impiety." Then, "the tribes were astounded, each at the sight of part of the body of one woman; but now the members of the whole Church are seen divided from one another, and are sent abroad some to you, and some to others, bringing word of the insults and injustice which they have suffered." He ends the analogy by exhorting his readers to throw themselves into the battle, "lest shortly ecclesiastical Canons, and the faith of the Church be corrupted. For both are in danger, unless God shall speedily by your hands amend what has been done amiss, and the Church be avenged on her enemies" (*Encyclical Letter* 1).

Defending the onetime bishop of Alexandria, Dionysius, against the charge of Arianism, Athanasius compares the Arians to the nations of Psalm 2 that take counsel against the Lord and against his anointed (*On the Opinion of Dionysius* 1). In a later letter to the bishops of Egypt, he styles the Arians as the false teachers of Jesus's Olivet Discourse (*Letter to the Bishops of Egypt* 1.1; cf. Matt. 24:11, 24), and charges that the heretics are fools who build on sand (*Bishops of Egypt* 1.4; Matt. 7:26–27). He invokes the examples of Achan and Saul, both of whom seized Yahweh's plunder: "As it is written in the Book of Joshua the son of Nun, when Achan was charged with theft, he did not excuse himself with the plea of his zeal in the wars; but being convicted of the offense was stoned by all the people (Josh. 7). And when Saul was charged with negligence and a breach of the law, he did not benefit his cause by alleging his conduct on other matters (1 Sam. 15). For a defense on one count will not operate to obtain an acquittal on another count" (*Bishops of Egypt* 1.11).

He frequently compares the Arians to the Jews who opposed Jesus. Arian doubts about the incarnation make them similar to the views of the high priest Caiaphas, who found Jesus guilty of blasphemy (*Discourses* 3.27). The Arians are like Judas, betraying God, though they attempt to hide their treachery (*Discourses* 3.28). On their premises, Athanasius argues, the body that the Son assumes promotes the Son, rather than being promoted by the Son, a conclusion that Athanasius denounces as "Jewish" (*Discourses* 3.39). Arians consider the body of the Son, along with the body's passions, and conclude that the Son is less than the impassible Father (*Discourses* 3.35). Arian arguments against the Son imply an attack on the Father, and these are Judaic: "Cease then, O abhorred of God, and degrade not the Word; nor detract from His Godhead, which is the Father's, as though He needed or were ignorant; lest ye be casting your own arguments against the Christ, as the Jews who once stoned Him. For these belong not to the Word, as the Word" (*Discourses* 3.41). Arians are "unthankful Jews" (*Discourses* 3.55).

Athanasius and the Arians

Whatever his original connection with Alexander, Athanasius had by 325 become a deacon in the Alexandrian church and went with the bishop as a secretary at the Council of Nicaea. Again, later legend embellished his role. Despite his youth, Alexander probably relied on him as a theological expert, but he did not dominate the proceedings of the council by any means.

Alexander died on April 17, 328, and Athanasius was elected bishop on May 9, in an election that was later challenged as shady and underhanded. Some claimed that Athanasius was too young to be elected, under the required age of thirty. As bishop, Athanasius became the focal point of the ecclesiastical politics of Alexandria, the largest church in Egypt and one of the major churches of the East. His duties brought him into regular contact with the new Christian emperor, Constantine. If the emperor's relations with Alexander were strained, his spars with Athanasius threw off sparks. Both were domineering personalities—Athanasius, for all his reputation for piety and theological acumen, was a tough, skillful infighter, a community organizer and rabble-rouser, willing to use intimidation or other tools in pursuit of his aims. Above all, the clash was one between an emperor whose main hope for the church was peaceful concord and a bishop who wanted no part of a consensus not based on truth.[20]

Constantine had been working to reconcile Arius to the Alexandrian church since the Council of Nicaea, and once Athanasius was made bishop, Constantine renewed those efforts. When Athanasius refused, Constantine threatened to depose him. The situation was exacerbated by the side conflict between Athanasius and the Melitians, who accused Athanasius of trying to impose a levy on Egyptian linen, and of bribery and sacrilege. The latter charge rested on allegations about the actions of one of the bishop's agents, Macarius. The Melitians claimed that Macarius burst in on Ischyras—whose right to priestly office Athanasius contested—while Ischyras was celebrating Mass, overturned the altar, burned a book, and broke a eucharistic chalice.[21] Hoping to stamp down that fight, Constantine summoned bishops to Nicomedia in 332, where Athanasius produced a letter in which Ischyras admitted that the charge was false. Athanasius was exonerated, but the Melitian bishops were not satisfied with the outcome and appealed again to Constantine, repeating the charge that Athanasius was responsible for breaking the chalice and adding a charge that Athanasius had murdered a man named Arsenius. A burnt hand was produced as evidence, allegedly the only surviving limb of Arsenius. At another council in Antioch, the story goes, Athanasius produced Arsenius, who had been hiding in a monastery, and the charges were again dropped.[22]

Arius was still eager to be vindicated, and he found allies among the Melitians. In 334, Constantine called yet another council, this one at Caesarea. Athanasius refused to attend, and Constantine backed down. The following year, the bishops assembled at Tyre, Athanasius among them, and he again had to answer the charge of breaking the sacred chalice. In the meantime, Ischyras had retracted his retraction and added the claim that Athanasius had imprisoned him on the false charge that he, Ischyras, had stoned a statue of the emperor. Five other Melitian bishops complained that they had been flogged on orders from the bishop of Alexandria. Recognizing that the council was set against him, Athanasius slipped away one night in disguise and was condemned by the council in absentia.[23]

Athanasius sailed to Constantinople, where he confronted the emperor in disguise, in one of the most dramatic scenes in this series of events. Constantine recalled,

> As I was making my entry into the city which bears our name, in this our most flourishing home, Constantinople—and it happened that I was riding on horseback at the time—suddenly the Bishop Athanasius, with certain ecclesiastics whom he had around him, presented himself so unexpectedly in our path, as to produce an occasion of consternation. For the Omniscient God is my witness that at first sight I did not recognize him until some of my attendants, in answer to my enquiry, informed me, as was very natural, both who he was, and what injustice he had suffered. At that time indeed I neither conversed, nor held any communication with him. But as he repeatedly entreated an audience, and I had not only refused it, but almost ordered that he should be removed from my presence, he said with greater boldness, that he petitioned for nothing more than that you might be summoned hither, in order that in our presence, he, driven by necessity to such a course, might have a fair opportunity afforded him of complaining of his wrongs.[24]

Constantine was persuaded and dashed off a blistering condemnation of the proceedings at Tyre. Within a few days, a delegation of Athanasius's enemies arrived in Constantinople to see the emperor, including Eusebius of Caesarea and Eusebius of Nicomedia, and they persuaded the emperor to reverse himself. The bishop of Alexandria was not deposed, but he was suspended from exercising his duties as a bishop, and he was exiled—for the first but not the last time—to Trier.[25]

Contra Mundum

In the Easter letter written as he was leaving for his exile, Athanasius again exhibited his penchant for reading his life through biblical categories. He assured the people of Alexandria that his tribulations were consistent with what the apostle Paul had predicted about the life of Christians (Rom. 12:12). He cited Psalm 119:143, "Though afflictions and anguish have come upon me, your commandments are my meditations," and took comfort in the beatitude that

Jesus promised to the persecuted, finding assurance in the fact that "affliction shall not befall every man in this world, but only for those who have a holy fear of Him" (*Festal Letter* 11.12). As usual, Athanasius turned the occasion into an anti-Arian polemic. Since the Arians did not worship the incarnate eternal God, they could not take assurance from the resurrection. Like all the orthodox, Athanasius was a servant of the risen Son of God and therefore knew that death held no power. He went into exile without fear.

Arius, meanwhile, continued his appeals to the emperor. He professed to accept the orthodox faith in a letter to Constantine, and Constantine, ever eager to reunite the church, accepted his profession. It was not to be. Reportedly while on his way to church to be readmitted, he suffered a bizarre death, perhaps by poisoning, in what James Joyce called a "Greek watercloset" where "with beaded mitre and with crozier, stalled upon his throne, widower of a widowed see, with uplifted omophorion" he died "with clotted hinderparts."[26] According to later sources, no one used the seat again for some time, and it is said that Theodosius set up a statue of Arius in Alexandria so that the citizens could amuse themselves, and affirm their orthodoxy, by spattering it with feces and urine.[27] Athanasius found Arius's end entirely fitting, an act of divine justice. Arius was a Judas, and so it was right that he die by "being burst asunder" (*History of the Arians* 7.51; cf. Acts 1:18).

The controversy over Arius's views did not end with the heretic's death any more than it ended with Nicaea. If anything, the debate intensified. Many of the most dramatic events of Athanasius's life and ministry took place after Arius's death. When Constantine died in 337, his three sons, Constantinus (Constantine II), Constans, and Constantius, agreed to recall exiled bishops to their sees. Athanasius returned to Alexandria during that year and resumed his position as bishop. His enemies were far from satisfied, and soon they brought the old charges against Athanasius before the emperors, adding the claim that he was "personally appropriating funds that were generated by the sale of wheat and intended for the benefit of widows."[28] Athanasius fought back, convening a council in Egypt that produced a circular letter in his defense, and traveling to Cappadocia to appear before Constantius. He enlisted the help of the already famed hermit Antony, who traveled from the desert mountains to Alexandria to silence supporters of Arius who claimed Antony took their side of the debate:

> Having entered Alexandria, he denounced the Arians, saying that their heresy was the last of all and a forerunner of Antichrist. And he taught the people that the Son of God was not a created being, neither had He come into being from non-existence, but that He was the Eternal Word and Wisdom of the Essence of the Father. And therefore it was impious to say, "there was a time when He was not," for the Word was always co-existent with the Father. Wherefore have no fellowship with the most impious Arians. For there is no communion between light and darkness. For you are good Christians, but they, when they say that the

Son of the Father, the Word of God, is a created being, differ in naught from the heathen, since they worship that which is created, rather than God the creator. But believe that the Creation itself is angry with them because they number the Creator, the Lord of all, by whom all things came into being, with those things which were originated. All the people, therefore, rejoiced when they heard the anti-Christian heresy anathematized by such a man. And all the people in the city ran together to see Antony; and the Greeks and those who are called their Priests, came into the church, saying, "We ask to see the man of God," for so they all called him. For in that place also the Lord cleansed many of demons, and healed those who were mad. And many Greeks asked that they might even but touch the old man, believing that they should be profited. Assuredly as many became Christians in those few days as one would have seen made in a year. (*Life of Antony* 69–70)

Despite these defensive measures, the Council of Antioch of 339 reiterated the decision of the earlier Council of Tyre, deposed Athanasius, and placed Gregory of Cappadocia on the episcopal throne of Alexandria. Athanasius was sent away into a second exile, this time in Rome. By Athanasius's account, Gregory's seizure of the see was not peaceful.

Constantius at once writes letters, and commences a persecution against all, and sends Philagrius as Prefect with one Arsacius an eunuch; he sends also Gregory with a military force. And the same consequences followed as before. For gathering together a multitude of herdsmen and shepherds, and other dissolute youths belonging to the town, armed with swords and clubs, they attacked in a body the Church which is called the Church of Quirinus; and some they slew, some they trampled under foot, others they beat with stripes and cast into prison or banished. They haled away many women also, and dragged them openly into the court, and insulted them, dragging them by the hair. Some they proscribed; from some they took away their bread for no other reason, but that they might be induced to join the Arians, and receive Gregory, who had been sent by the Emperor. (*History* 2.10)[29]

Attacks on churches were, Athanasius thought, desecrations similar to Uzzah's desecration of the ark as it was being brought into Jerusalem (2 Sam. 6:1–8; cf. *History* 7.57).

During his Roman exile, Athanasius began writing his great anti-Arian treatise, the *Discourses* (or *Orations*) *against the Arians*,[30] and established alliances with sympathetic Western church leaders, including Pope Julius and Marcellus of Ancyra, who had been deposed in 336 for teaching modalism and was in the West to appeal the decision to Julius. Julius attempted to restore Athanasius with a council in Rome in 341, but in the East the council was regarded as the act of an interloper. Yet progress was being made, and Constantius invited Athanasius to a face-to-face meeting shortly after Gregory's death in 345. Constantius permitted Athanasius to return to Egypt in 346, a triumphant return that one scholar described as being "less the return of an exiled bishop than the *adventus* of a Roman emperor."[31] He remained bishop of Alexandria for the next decade, the longest uninterrupted period of his entire forty-six-year episcopacy.

Despite the reconciliation with Athanasius, Constantius remained a supporter of the Arian cause. During the early 350s, he summoned two councils in the West that pressured Western bishops to adopt an explicitly anti-Nicene doctrinal standard. Having orchestrated the theological opposition, Constantius moved against Athanasius directly, ordering his agent in Alexandria, Syrianus, to seize the bishop. Just after midnight on February 8, 356, soldiers attacked the church at Theonas and moved against Athanasius. As Athanasius described the incident,

> the Arians were mixed with the soldiers in order to exasperate them against me, and, as they were unacquainted with my person, to point me out to them. And although they are destitute of all feelings of compassion, yet when they hear the circumstances they will surely be quiet for very shame. It was now night, and some of the people were keeping a vigil preparatory to a communion on the morrow, when the General Syrianus suddenly came upon us with more than five thousand soldiers, having arms and drawn swords, bows, spears, and clubs, as I have related above. With these he surrounded the Church, stationing his soldiers near at hand, in order that no one might be able to leave the Church and pass by them. Now I considered that it would be unreasonable in me to desert the people during such a disturbance, and not to endanger myself in their behalf; therefore I sat down upon my throne, and desired the Deacon to read a Psalm, and the people to answer, "For His mercy endures for ever," and then all to withdraw and depart home. But the General having now made a forcible entry, and the soldiers having surrounded the sanctuary for the purpose of apprehending us, the Clergy and those of the laity, who were still there, cried out, and demanded that we too should withdraw. But I refused, declaring that I would not do so, until they had retired one and all. Accordingly I stood up, and having bidden prayer, I then made my request of them, that all should depart before me, saying that it was better that my safety should be endangered, than that any of them should receive hurt. So when the greater part had gone forth, and the rest were following, the monks who were there with us and certain of the Clergy came up and dragged us away. And thus (Truth is my witness), while some of the soldiers stood about the sanctuary, and others were going round the Church, we passed through, under the Lord's guidance, and with His protection withdrew without observation, greatly glorifying God that we had not betrayed the people, but had first sent them away, and then had been able to save ourselves, and to escape the hands of them which sought after us. (*Defense of His Flight* 24)

Athanasius again saw his experience through biblical lenses. Like Jesus passing through the crowds at Nazareth who wanted to kill him (Luke 4:30), Athanasius safely escaped the troops of the emperor. When Athanasius defended himself to Constantius, he thought of himself as an imitator of Paul: "To your Piety I answer with a loud and clear voice, and stretching forth my hand, as I have learned from the Apostle, 'I call God for a record upon my soul'" (2 Cor. 1:23; *Defense before Constantius* 3). Constantius was Saul slaughtering priests at Nob (*History* 8.67; 1 Sam. 21). Athanasius depicts Constantius as, in fact, a conglomeration of all the worst kings and rulers in Scripture:

> Ahab himself did not act so cruelly towards the priests of God, as this man has acted towards the Bishops. For he was at least pricked in his conscience, when Naboth had been murdered, and was afraid at the sight (1 Kings 21:20) of Elijah, but this man neither reverenced the great Hosius, nor was wearied or pricked in conscience, after banishing so many Bishops; but like another Pharaoh, the more he is afflicted, the more he is hardened, and imagines greater wickedness day by day. And the most extraordinary instance of his iniquity was the following. It happened that when the Bishops were condemned to banishment, certain other persons also received their sentence on charges of murder or sedition or theft, each according to the quality of his offense. These men after a few months he released, on being requested to do so, as Pilate did Barabbas; but the servants of Christ he not only refused to set at liberty, but even sentenced them to more unmerciful punishment in the place of their exile, proving himself "an undying evil" to them. To the others through congeniality of disposition he became a friend; but to the orthodox he was an enemy on account of their true faith in Christ. Is it not clear to all men from hence, that the Jews of old when they demanded Barabbas, and crucified the Lord, acted but the part which these present enemies of Christ are acting together with Constantius? Nay, that he is even more bitter than Pilate. For Pilate, when he perceived (Matt. 27:24) the injustice of the deed, washed his hands; but this man, while he banishes the saints, gnashes his teeth against them more and more. (*History* 8.68)

Constantius is, in short, a Herod (*History* 7.52).

Athanasius's biblical dramatizations of his life thus support a political theology. As we have seen, he regularly charges that the Arians are like the Jews who rejected the incarnate Son and sold themselves out to Caesar (that is, to Constantius; *History* 4.33; *Discourses* 1.7; 1.10). Like the Jews, the Arians will be punished for their unfaithfulness: "The Jews then have the penal award of their denial; for their city as well as their reasoning came to naught" (*Discourses* 2.42). Their fear of the emperor is the only thing that keeps them from letting their true theological colors show: "Let them openly confess themselves scholars of Caiaphas and Herod, instead of cloaking Judaism with the name of Christianity, and let them deny outright, as we have said before, the Savior's appearance in the flesh, for this doctrine is akin to their heresy; or if they fear openly to Judaize and be circumcised, from servility towards Constantius and for their sake whom they have beguiled, then let them not say what the Jews say; for if they disown the name, let them in fairness renounce the doctrine" (*Discourses* 3.28). With the Pharisees, the Arians cry out, "No king but Caesar" (*History* 4.33). The orthodox, by contrast, know a King greater than any creature, the incarnate Word of the Father, exalted now to a heavenly throne. As a result, they have the courage to despise earthly kings.

Athanasius often combines political and apocalyptic themes. Constantius's expulsion of bishops is "an insurrection of impiety against godliness," and thus his zeal for Arianism is "a prelude to the coming of Antichrist, for whom Constantius is thus preparing the way" (*History* 6.46). Constantius exhibits every mark of Antichrist himself: "And does not the vision of Daniel (7:25) thus describe Antichrist; that he shall make war with the saints, and prevail against them, and exceed all that have been before him in evil deeds and shall humble three kings, and speak words against the Most High, and shall think to change times and laws? Now what other person besides Constantius has ever attempted to do these things? He is surely such a one as Antichrist would be" (*History* 8.74).

After escaping the troops sent to arrest him, Athanasius fled to the desert and spent the next six years among the Egyptian monks. Some charged him with cowardice for abandoning Alexandria, as Athanasius had himself mocked Arian leaders who fled from a Roman synod as men who were guilty "like Cain" (*Letter to the Church of Alexandria*), but Athanasius defended himself with biblical precedents:

> He who censures me in this matter must presume also to blame the great Apostle Peter, because though he was shut up and guarded by soldiers, he followed the angel that summoned him, and when he had gone forth from the prison and escaped in safety, he did not return and surrender himself, although he heard what Herod had done. Let the Arian in his madness censure the Apostle Paul, because when he was let down from the wall and had escaped in safety, he did not change his mind, and return and give himself up; or Moses, because he returned not out of Midian into Egypt, that he might be taken of them that sought after him; or David, because when he was concealed in the cave, he did not discover himself to Saul. As also the sons of the prophets remained in their caves, and did not surrender themselves to Ahab. This would have been to act contrary to the commandment, since he says, "You shall not tempt the Lord your God." (*Defense of His Flight*, 25)

Constantius placed George over the church of Alexandria, and, like his predecessor Gregory, he violently persecuted the orthodox faithful of Alexandria. When George was lynched by an angry mob in 361, Athanasius returned to the city, holding the episcopacy for a brief period between February and October 362, before the pagan emperor Julian forced him again to flee into the desert. Julian died shortly afterward, and Athanasius returned a year later, this time with the support of the emperor, Jovian. When Jovian died in February 364, Athanasius found himself again opposed by an anti-Nicene Eastern emperor, Valens, who arrested and exiled Athanasius for the fifth and last time. He was back in Alexandria before 364 was over, and he remained bishop until his death on May 2, 373.

Through most of the history of the church, Athanasius has been regarded as both a theologian of superior ability and a theological warrior of the first order. He is a Christian hero, standing with his Lord *contra mundum*. Even Edward Gibbon, who found little to admire among early Christians, commended Athanasius for his "superiority of character and abilities," though the bishop of Alexandria was, like all early Christians, "tainted with the contagion of fanaticism."[32] Harnack too believed that he was not "ignoble or mean" by the standards of the time, and, despite his flaws, he "saved the character of Christianity as a religion of the living fellowship with God." In Harnack's view, Athanasius eschewed the philosophical speculation that had corrupted the church, and he returned to the simplicity of Scripture.[33]

Recent historians have been less impressed. Timothy Barnes compares Athanasius to a modern gangster and a mafioso, though he also recognizes the bishop's stature, albeit one that depended on an absence of Christian virtues.[34] R. P. C. Hanson finds him a deeply ambiguous figure. There is no doubt that Athanasius was a tough customer, and he employed methods to combat heresy and to shore up the Nicene settlement that would make modern bishops blanch. His self-defenses are often evasive. A recently discovered papyrus contains a letter from the Melitian Callistus, written around 335, which complains about "adherents of Athanasius" who terrorized the Melitians.[35] It belies Athanasius's frequent claim that the Arians were the ones who, like the devil, broke "down the doors of those who do not receive him" (*History* 33). Athanasius was not the kind of man you would want as an enemy.

Without excusing his errors and sins, we should recognize that only a tough man, a man of extraordinary determination, could have so single-mindedly fought off Arian views that he regarded as dangerous blasphemies threatening the foundations of the gospel and the church. Only a very determined man could have stood against emperors and councils of bishops, endured five exiles, and fought off numerous false accusations, all in defense of the gospel. It is testimony to the sincerity of the appeals to love and gentleness (especially evident in his *Festal Letters*) that by the time he died, he was reconciled to nearly all his remaining opponents.

"Arian" Diversity, Arian Unity

What was at stake in the Arian controversy? To answer that question, contemporary scholarship has shown that we need to be precise about what "Arianism" is and even ask whether it ever existed at all.

Many recent scholars have concluded that "Arianism" is a misnomer, a rhetorical construction that was mainly produced by Athanasius.[36] They offer several reasons for this skepticism. Arius certainly had allies, both in Alexandria and elsewhere, but Arius himself played a comparatively minor role in the controversy, and his own views were not representative of all those on whom Athanasius attempted to pin the label.[37] Especially after Nicaea, attempts to mediate the dispute between "Arian" and "Nicene" produced a variety of positions. While there are continuities among the various parties, it is misleading to characterize this as a simple two-way debate.

Athanasius knew very well that the "Ario-maniacs" differed among themselves, and he made this an important apologetic point: while the orthodox stand together around the Nicene formula, the Arians fragment into mutually contradictory sects. Some, like Asterius (regularly labeled the "Sophist" in Athanasius's writings), taught that there is an eternal "Wisdom" and "Word" that is "proper" to the Father's essence. This was not the same as the Nicene position, since, for Asterius, the Father's own proper Wisdom and Word are distinguished from the Son, and it is *through* this Wisdom and Word that the Son is begotten. Yet, in Athanasius's view, Asterius was teaching a double "Ungenerate," in contrast to Arius's own insistence on the singularity of God's ungeneratedness.

Another subtle difference is evident in "Arian" views of the Son's knowledge of the Father and the Son's immutability. In the *Thalia*, Arius emphasizes the absolute invisibility and incomprehensibility of the Father. According to Athanasius's summary, Arius teaches that "'even to the Son the Father is invisible,' and 'the Word cannot perfectly and exactly either see or know His own Father,' but even what He knows and what He sees, He knows and sees 'in proportion to His own measure,' as we also know according to our own power. For the Son, too, he says, not only knows not the Father exactly, for He fails in comprehension, but 'He knows not even His own essence'" (*Discourses* 1.6). Later anti-Nicene leaders, such as Aetius and Eunomius, disagreed. Aetius's opposition to the Nicene formula, in fact, depends on the assumption that the Son knows his own essence. In Rowan Williams's summary, "God knows he is by nature ingenerate, the Son knows he is by nature generated, therefore they cannot be consubstantial. The repudiation of the homoousion here actually depends upon the Son knowing whence and what he is."[38] The theology of the *Thalia* was later unpopular among the anti-Nicene bishops, and Williams suggests that Athanasius quotes from it not because it was influential, but in order to embarrass those who had defended Arius.

Differences among anti-Nicene theologians regarding the changeability of the Son are more subtle, probably due more to gradations in theological sophistication than to worked-out disagreements. Arius is clear that the Son is not elevated to his status, but from the beginning possesses all that a creature can possess. Because the Son is a creature, he is "theoretically" changeable and unstable, but Arius insists that the Son remains himself unchangeable due to the gracious will of God his Father. He is not unchangeable *in essence*, though *in fact* the Son never changes. Responding to Arius, however, Alexander returns again and again to the problem of mutability, and this suggests that some of Arius's supporters were "less than completely clear on the admittedly fine distinctions being drawn between essential and *de facto* immutability."[39]

Athanasius was a bishop until his death in 373, that is, for nearly a half century after the Nicene council, and he was fixated on defending the Nicene formula, especially the controversial term *homoousios*, "one substance."[40] Yet, through the middle decades of the fourth century, anti-Nicene theology was fracturing and anti-Nicene parties were proliferating.

During the 350s, the "Anomians" Aetius and Eunomius began to spread the view that the Son was "unlike" (*anomoios*) the Father, apparently in an attempt to address the ambiguity of the earlier compromise "homoian" position, the view that the Son was (in some undefined way) "like" (*homoios*) the Father. Dissatisfied with the hedging and qualifications of the homoian position, the Anomians openly declared that the Son had a different *ousia* (essence) from the Father and that the Spirit was a third essence again. Basil of Ancyra attempted a compromise formula, stressing that the likeness of Father and Son had to be a likeness of essence, and offered *homoiousios* as a formula.[41] When a compromise of homoians and homoiousians was reached, Athanasius, exiled in the Egyptian desert, wrote a series of treatises defending the original Nicene position, defending himself to Constantius and extending the terminology of *homoousios* to the Holy Spirit. Yet, at the same time, he continued to describe his now very diverse opponents as "Arians" or "Eusebians."

Given these complications, does it make any sense to speak of "Arianism" at all? I believe it still does. In this book, the diversity of anti-Nicene theologies will not play a major role. My object is to examine Athanasius's views of Scripture and metaphysics, and my aim is more to distill Athanasius's positive theology from the polemics than to examine the rhetoric or accuracy of those polemics. For this reason, I will generally use "Arian" in the way that Athanasius uses the term, to describe a collection of views that are not necessarily derived from Arius himself nor held by all who are labeled "Arians." For the sake of simplicity, I will in subsequent sections drop the scare quotes that Rowan Williams thought should surround the term. This procedure is legitimate, not only because it reflects Athanasius's own usage, but also because, despite the diversity, there were common themes among the various anti-Nicene parties. They were, at the very least, all anti-Nicene, and thus it makes sense to ask what the overall agenda of "Arianism" or "anti-Nicene theology" was.[42]

Motivations of Arian Theology

What was Arius after? What drove the Arians to take the positions that they did? In recent research, Arius has had his defenders, and even the critics have attempted to assess his teaching sympathetically. Maurice Wiles has noted that in Arius's own summaries of his teaching he draws on biblical terminology at least as often as he does on philosophical terminology. Though he is using extrabiblical terminology when he says that God is "ingenerate," he also quotes directly from Paul's letters, which describe God as "alone immortal, alone eternal, only wise" (Rom. 16:27; 1 Tim. 1:17).[43]

Rowan Williams has characterized the divergent theologies of the fourth century as a contest between "Academic" and "Catholic" theologies. Arius continued the Alexandrian tradition of speculative theology, while Alexander and Athanasius were pastoral and Catholic theologians. Prior to Constantine's conversion, when the church did not have to bear a burden of social and political authority, academic theologians like Arius could get on "tolerably well." After Constantine, not so well.[44]

Robert Gregg and Dennis Groh argue that Arius is soteriologically motivated. Arius and early Arians offer a Christ who is warmer, freer, more human in his changeability and struggles than the orthodox Christ. The orthodox Christ keeps his distance, wrapped in the mantle of his flesh, safely resisting temptation with his irresistible divine power. The Arian Jesus is more like us, and his risky story of suffering and ascent provides a model for us to emulate and so be saved.[45]

According to R. P. C. Hanson, the debate was about the cross of Jesus. The Arians confessed a suffering savior and knew that a human sufferer was not sufficient. To be a saving death, Jesus's death on the cross must be the death of God; to deliver humanity, we need a God who suffers. Since they shared with Athanasius the view that God is in himself impassible, however, they made allowance for the suffering of Jesus by arguing that he is not equal to the Father. Jesus is God dying on a cross, just not the supreme Ungenerate God.[46]

Others have supported Hanson's account. Drawing on Asterius's *Homilies on the Psalms*, Maurice Wiles and Robert Gregg have made the intriguing argument that, far from being motivated by cosmological or philosophical concerns, some within the Arian camp sidestepped such questions. In his homilies, Asterius ignores the issues that became the preoccupations of the debate. "No stress is laid," Wiles and Gregg conclude, "on the transcendence of the Father, and nothing is said about the created status of the Son." Instead, Asterius's concern is wholly with the cross. Salvation demanded that God go to the cross; only God could overcome death by death and overcome demons through the cross. How exactly the God on the cross related to the eternal God is left unexplained. The Father-Son relation becomes central not because it was central to the preaching of the Arian party; rather, these issues become crucial "because the relation of the Son to the Father was the thing about which the Arians were least inclined to speak."[47] The Arian controversy arose because those sympathetic to Arius left themselves vulnerable on one flank.

Prior to the revisionist scholarship of the past several decades, it was commonly said that Arius's theology was driven by prior commitments to some form of Hellenistic theology or metaphysics. Arius believed that an absolute God had to be wholly other, wholly transcendent, wholly beyond the "limit" of a necessary relation to something outside himself. The high God, further, is far too exalted to have much to do with the mess and muck and mayhem of the creation, and so he must act through a created mediator in creating and redeeming the world, a mediator who cannot be equal to the high God. Arius, it was said, was among the "hellenizers" of Christian faith.

Hellenization, like Arianism, must today learn to live within scare quotes, but it has played a large role in efforts to understand the early history of Christianity. In his monumental *History of Dogma*, Adolf von Harnack traced the infiltration of Hellenism into Christianity during the first three centuries AD. Among the early apologists, one finds a "positive" form of hellenization, the identification of the Greek *Logos* with Jesus Christ. According to Harnack, the "most important step that was ever taken in the domain of Christian doctrine" occurred when "the Christian apologists of the second century drew the equation." The epoch-making character of this equation was not so much in the specific claim being made but in the larger stance that the church adopted by this equation. By equating the Greek *Logos* with Jesus, the church came to view itself as a philosophical school; *Logos* speculation is the spirit of Greek philosophy transferred into the church. The danger is that the church becomes attached to a message that does not depend on the gospel. Harnack writes,

> The message of religion appears here clothed in a knowledge of the world and of the ground of the world which had already been obtained without any reference to it, and therefore religion itself has here become a doctrine which has, indeed, its certainty in the Gospel, but only in part derives its contents from it, and which can only be appropriated by such as are neither poor in spirit nor weary and heavy laden. . . . The characteristic of this dogma is that it represents itself in no sense as foolishness, but as wisdom, and at the same time desires to be regarded as the contents of revelation itself. Dogma in its conception and development is a work of the Greek spirit on the soil of the Gospel.[48]

Dogmatic, or hellenized, Christianity had its benefits, Harnack recognizes, since it enabled the church to defeat paganism in the short run. In the long run, though, the triumph of hellenization in the Catholic Church was simply the half-victory of "acute Hellenism," that is, gnosticism. "Historical inquiry," he remarks, "sees in Gnosticism a series of undertakings, which in a certain way is analogous to the Catholic embodiment of Christianity, in doctrine, morals, and worship. The great distinction here consists essentially in the fact that the gnostic systems represent the acute secularizing or hellenizing of Christianity, with the rejection of the Old Testament; while the Catholic system, on the other hand, represents a gradual process of the same kind with the conservation of the Old Testament."[49]

Even while struggling with gnosticism, the church was being co-opted by it, since the battle "compelled the church to puts its teaching, its worship, and its discipline into fixed forms and ordinances, and to exclude everyone who would not yield them obedience." Defining "Catholic" as "the church of doctrine and of law," Harnack concludes that "the Catholic church had its origin in the struggle with Gnosticism." Though it "kept Dualism and the acute phase of Hellenism at bay," it became "a community with a fully worked out scheme of doctrine, and a definite form of public worship," and these liturgical forms were "analogous to those which it combated in the Gnostics."[50] Binding dogma, intellectualism, institutionalization, and the decline of evangelistic zeal resulted.

Harnack excepts Athanasius from this trend, viewing him as a great exemplar of an earlier, simpler, more biblical Christianity. More recently, some theologians have claimed that Athanasius's theology, as well as the Nicene theology that he defended and elaborated, is also a hellenized faith. Catherine Mowry LaCugna argues that after the Council of Nicaea in 325, the focus of Christian theology changed decisively from the *oikonomia* of redemption to the *theologia* of God's inner life. According to LaCugna, the pressing issue of the fourth-century debate concerned the suffering of God. One option, taken by Arius and those who later were labeled "Arians," was to acknowledge that God suffers but to argue that the God who suffers is not the high God who begets the Son; rather, the God who suffers is the Son, a secondary and subordinate being.

Athanasius pursued the other, "orthodox" option, which, in LaCugna's view, involved the claim that the "sufferings of Christ were feigned, or belonged to the flesh but not to the soul." All "signs of weakness or limitation were also denied to the Logos," as "Athanasius went to great exegetical lengths to explain how the biblical texts that show human defects do not mean what they say they mean." In the process, she argues, the meaning of *oikonomia* changes from "the plan of salvation hidden in God from the beginning but made manifest in Christ" to the "more narrow meaning of 'the work of salvation by Christ *qua homo*.'"[51] LaCugna hedges on whether to call these shifts "hellenization," but she argues that the Nicene use of the term *homoousios*, and the strict opposition to subordination of the Son to the Father, unmoored *theologia* from its connection to *oikonomia*, with fateful results for the later history of theology.

Harnack's hellenization thesis has been subjected to searching criticism, and an alternative account of the interaction of Christianity with Greco-Roman civilization has been offered. Writing not as a historian of dogma but as one of Harnack's dreaded "dogmaticians," Robert Jenson describes the relation of the gospel to philosophy during the first four centuries as an "evangelization of metaphysics." Far from being conformed to Hellenistic categories and forms, the church in the persons of her theologians employed Greek concepts and terms to express something that Greek philosophy could never have envisioned. For Jenson, the central issue concerns time. Greek metaphysics and religion, he argues, were an elaborate effort to escape the corrosive effects of time.

> It was the great single dogma of late Mediterranean antiquity's religion and irreligion, that no story can be "really" true of God, that deity equals "impassibility." It is not merely that the gospel tells a story about the object of worship; every religion of antiquity did that. The gospel identifies God as "He who brought Israel from Egypt and our Lord Jesus from the dead." Therefore the gospel cannot rescind from its story at any depth whatsoever of experience, mystical penetration or *theologia*. Developed trinitarian liturgy and theology appeared as the church maintained the gospel's identification of God in the very teeth of what everybody knew to be of course and obviously true of God, and in every nook of practice or theory where uncircumcised theological self-evidency lurked.[52]

To Jenson, Arianism is of a piece with this standard Greek metaphysics. According to the Arian perspective, there must be something or someone that escapes time and change. Otherwise, we are all unmoored, adrift in a shifting sea of time-bound being. God is the anchor because he is outside time. Since God is that timelessness, temporal reality has to be transcended in order to get to God. From a premise of the incompatibility of God and time, one arrives at a wholly apophatic theology.

Soteriological concerns were also central to Arianism, and here again Jenson finds worries lurking about God and time. Salvation involves an ascension out of temporality, so if we are to be saved, there must be something that utterly transcends time. Any being involved with time, such as Jesus the Son manifestly is, cannot be the ultimate Savior. Unless he transcends time, he cannot enable us to transcend time. Against all the pressures of Greek philosophy, the church in the fourth century began to fulfill what Jenson describes as the calling of trinitarian theology, namely, "to maintain against all compunctions that the biblical story about God and us is true of and for God Himself."[53]

From the perspective of the chief participant, Athanasius, Jenson's account draws the battle lines more clearly than Harnack's. On the one hand, as noted above, Athanasius regularly charges that the Arians are "Jews." There is certainly an element of Jew-baiting in the label, and in this Athanasius adopts the standard Christian rhetoric of his day. Athanasius's vitriol is mild by comparison with comments from Constantine and other early fourth-century Christians, but it is still indefensible.[54] The rhetorical excess should not, however, blind us to the fundamental and wholly legitimate theological issue that Athanasius raises. He recognizes a common thread between the Jewish affirmation of a "strict" (i.e., nontrinitarian) monotheism and the

Arian denial that the Son is eternal God. In a discussion of the christological hymn of Philippians 2, Athanasius insists that the Son both humbled himself and was exalted. He challenges the Arians to explain what the Son was before the incarnation. If he was not Son before, what was he? Did he exist at all? Is Jesus simply a man? If the Arians draw that conclusion, they are no better than the first-century Jews who failed to recognize the deity of Jesus (*Discourses* 1.38). Arians look "at what is done divinely by the Word" and then "deny the body, or looking at what is proper to the body, deny the Word's presence in the flesh, or from what is human entertain low thoughts concerning the Word." Arius, "as a Jewish vintner, mixing water with the wine, shall account the Cross an offense, or as a Gentile, will deem the preaching folly" (*Discourses* 3.35).

On the other hand, Athanasius also makes clear that he regards the Arians, and not the orthodox, as the ones who have sold out to Hellenism. Especially in his apologetic *Against the Pagans*, Athanasius makes it clear that he recognizes a fundamental antithesis between Greek and Christian religion. Similarly, in the *Discourses*, he contrasts the local and changeable gods of Greece to the eternal and faithful God of Scripture: "Now the so-called gods of the Greeks, unworthy the name, are faithful neither in their essence nor in their promises; for the same are not everywhere, nay, the local deities come to naught in course of time, and undergo a natural dissolution" (*Discourses* 2.10). All heretics, not just the Arians, are in the same genealogy. All are like the gentiles, who are atheists because they do not know the true God.

> There are many other heresies too, which use the words only, but not in a right sense, as I have said, nor with sound faith, and in consequence the water which they administer is unprofitable, as deficient in piety, so that he who is sprinkled by them is rather polluted by irreligion than redeemed. So Gentiles also, though the name of God is on their lips, incur the charge of Atheism, because they know not the real and very God, the Father of our Lord Jesus Christ. So Manichees and Phrygians, and the disciples of the Samosatene, though using the Names, nevertheless are heretics, and the Arians follow in the same course, though they read the words of Scripture, and use the Names, yet they too mock those who receive the rite from them, being more irreligious than the other heresies, and advancing beyond them, and making them seem innocent by their own reck-lessness of speech. For these other heresies lie against the truth in some certain respect, either erring concerning the Lord's Body, as if He did not take flesh of Mary, or as if He has not died at all, nor become man, but only appeared, and was not truly, and seemed to have a body when He had not, and seemed to have the shape of man, as visions in a dream; but the Arians are without disguise irreligious against the Father Himself. For hearing from the Scriptures that His Godhead is represented in the Son as in an image, they blaspheme, saying, that it is a creature, and everywhere concerning that Image, they carry about with them the phrase, "He was not," as mud in a wallet, and spit it forth as serpents their venom. (*Discourses* 2.43)

To Athanasius, the substance of Arianism is Hellenistic. They are Greek in claiming that the wisdom to create can be learned and passed on from one being to another (*Discourses* 2.28). Like the Greeks, the Arians believe in an original monad that comes to a triad by a process of addition.

> It belongs to Greeks, to introduce an originated Triad, and to level It with things originate; for these do admit of deficiencies and additions; but the faith of Christians acknowledges the blessed Triad as unalterable and perfect and ever what It was, neither adding to It what is more, nor imputing to It any loss (for both ideas are irreligious), and therefore it dissociates It from all things generated, and it guards as indivisible and worships the unity of the Godhead Itself; and shuns the Arian blasphemies, and confesses and acknowledges that the Son was ever; for He is eternal, as is the Father, of whom He is the Eternal Word,— to which subject let us now return again. (*Discourses* 1.18)

Like all Hellenists, the Arians are ultimately idolaters, worshiping the creature rather than the Creator. Arius and Eusebius, Athanasius argues, attempt to use human categories to explain God and thus come under Paul's charge against pagans who "change God's glory into an image made like to corruptible man" (*Discourses* 1.22). Arians say that the Son is originate, but this amounts to the equalizing of the originate and Unoriginate, which means an equalizing of the creature and the Creator. Arians want to measure God by the same standard they apply to creatures (*ex isou*): "If they will have it that the one is like the other, so that he who sees the one beholds the other, they are like to say that the Unoriginate is the image of creatures; the end of which is a confusion of the whole subject, an equaling of things originated with the Unoriginate, and a denial of the Unoriginate by measuring Him with the works; and all to reduce the Son into their number" (*Discourses* 1.31).

Arians are even worse than Greeks. Greeks worship a single Unoriginate being and many originate beings, but the Arians attribute diverse natures to God himself:

> For their subtle saying which they are accustomed to urge, "We say not two Unoriginates," they plainly say to deceive the simple; for in their very professing "We say not two Unoriginates," they imply two Gods, and these with different natures, one originate and one Unoriginate. And though the Greeks worship one Unoriginate and many originate, but these one Unoriginate and one originate, this is no difference from them; for the God whom they call originate is one out of many, and again the many gods of the Greeks have the same nature with this one, for both he and they are creatures. (*Discourses* 3.16)

He follows up by linking the Hellenistic Arians once again with the Jews: "They have fallen from the truth, and are greater traitors than the Jews in denying the Christ, and they wallow with the Gentiles, hateful as they are to God, worshipping the creature and many deities" (*Discourses* 3.16).

At several points, Athanasius argues that Arianism reduces to pantheism or polytheism. If the Son participates in the Unoriginate, just like everything else, and yet the Son is called "God," then what difference is there between the nature of the Son and the nature of all other originated things? "The Ario-maniacs with reason incur the charge of polytheism or else of atheism," he writes, "because they idly talk of the Son as external and a creature, and again the Spirit as from nothing. For either they will say that the Word is not God; or saying that He is God, because it is so written, but not proper to the Father's Essence, they will introduce many because of their difference of kind (unless forsooth they shall dare to say that by participation only, He, as all things else, is called God; though, if this be their sentiment, their irreligion is the same, since they consider the Word as one among all things" (*Discourses* 3.15). If the Son is a creature we call God, can we call *all* creatures God? For Athanasius, the Arian theology of "total otherness" collapses into a pantheistic monism.

Elsewhere, Athanasius worries that the Arians will end up claiming that the creation account of Genesis 1 is describing the formation of the Son, thus drawing God himself into the "all" of the creation. He hedges the argument and formulates it as a "fear" for the direction of Arianism, but the import is clear. "From hearing, 'In the beginning God made the heaven and the earth,' and 'He made the sun and the moon,' and 'He made the sea,'" Athanasius argues, the Arians "should come in time to call the Word the heaven, and the Light which took place on the first day, and the earth, and each particular thing that has been made, so as to end in resembling the Stoics, as they are called, the one drawing out their God into all things, the other ranking God's Word with each work in particular; which they have well near done already, saying that He is one of His works" (*Discourses* 2.11).

Similarly, Arianism collapses back into Greek polytheism. If the Son is not eternal God, he is either a creature or a second God. If the latter, then the Arians are starting down a slippery slope, because if there is a second God, why not a third, fourth, tenth, millionth?

> If it be not so, but the Word is a creature and a work out of nothing, either He is not True God because He is Himself one of the creatures, or if they name Him God from regard for the Scriptures, they must of necessity say that there are two Gods, one Creator, the other creature, and must serve two Lords, one Unoriginate, and the other originate and a creature; and must have two faiths, one in the True God, and the other in one who is made and fashioned by themselves and called God. And it follows of necessity in so great blindness, that, when they worship the Unoriginate, they renounce the originate, and when they come to the creature, they turn from the Creator. For they cannot see the One in the Other, because their natures and operations are foreign and distinct. And

with such sentiments, they will certainly be going on to more gods, for this will be the essay of those who revolt from the One God. (*Discourses* 3.16)

Conclusion

What would Athanasius say about "Scripture and metaphysics"? He would charge that the Arians have been co-opted by an alien metaphysical scheme and that their Hellenism has led them into idolatry and polytheism. Despite their professed adherence to Scripture, their real convictions come from elsewhere. For himself, Athanasius would claim that all his "metaphysical" convictions arise from the gospel, from meditation on Scripture. Though we have not quite begun to examine the intersection of Scripture and metaphysics in Athanasius's theology, we have begun to see how he might make good on that claim. Athanasius reads his life, and the history that surrounds him, through biblical lenses. What justifies that procedure? Is this anything more than hubris, a bishop thinking of himself more highly than he ought? I suspect that his answer would be that he was doing just what Paul does in 2 Corinthians, that is, describing his own ministry as a ministry conformed to the pattern of Christ's sufferings. Scripture illuminates Athanasius's life because Scripture is about Christ, and Christ has impressed his image on Athanasius so that Athanasius's life is remade in the image of his suffering, the image of his cross.

2

Types, Terms, and Paradigms

Theological Interpretation: Villains and Heroes

Theological interpretation of Scripture is all the rage today.[1] Everyone is doing it, but what is it that everyone is doing?

The enemies are obvious: theological interpretation opposes modern critical approaches to Scripture, which, putatively, dissect the biblical text to get to the real historical events behind it, or to get to the convictions of the community in which the text was written. R. R. Reno, editor of the Brazos Theological Commentary on the Bible, cites Benjamin Jowett's insistence that interpreters can rightly approach biblical texts only after being purified "from the refinements or distinctions of later times," having cleared "away the remains of dogmas, systems, controversies" that have barnacled Scripture over the centuries. By this process, interpreters are capable of recovering "the original spirit and intention of the authors." For Jowett, Reno says, tradition and doctrine form a "moldering scrim of antique prejudice obscuring the Bible."[2]

If the bad guys are obvious, so are the good guys. Precritical interpreters considered doctrine not an obstacle to understanding but rather "a clarifying agent, an enduring tradition of theological judgments that amplifies the living voice of Scripture." Such a "pedagogy" of "a doctrinally ruled reading of Scripture characterizes the broad sweep of the Christian tradition from Gregory the Great through Bernard and Bonaventure, continuing across Reformation differences in both John Calvin and Cornelius Lapide, Patrick Henry and Bishop Bossuet, and on to more recent figures such as Karl Barth and Hans Urs von Balthasar." In particular, the "Nicene tradition, in all its diversity and controversy, provides the proper basis for the interpretation of the Bible as Christian Scripture." Commitment to Nicene Christianity does not prejudge

methods or determine all outcomes. Instead, it highlights the fact that faith
in the God who created and redeemed the world through Son and Spirit, and
in his "vocation of love for the world is the lens through which to view the
heterogeneity and particularity of the biblical texts."[3]

In his introduction to *The Dictionary for Theological Interpretation of
the Bible*, Kevin Vanhoozer also takes aim at modern critical scholarship.
He acknowledges the usefulness of modern and postmodern techniques and
methods, so long as they aim to expound the text rather than to get "behind"
or "before" it. But he attacks biblical scholarship's capitulation to Lessing's
ugly ditch between faith and reason, which has translated in theology into a
gap between the "theology-free zone" of strictly textual and historical investigation of the biblical texts, on the one side, and the dogma and preaching of
the church on the other. Positively, theological interpretation recognizes that
one's view of God shapes interpretation, and that interpretation of Scripture
shapes theology in turn. Theological interpretation is critical, but not in the
way modern interpretation is critical. Rather than focusing critical energy
on the text or the author, theological interpretation is "critical of readers."
Theological interpretation assists the formation and edification of the church
by enabling the Christian community "to hear God's work and to know God
better."[4] Theological interpretation is a kind of "quality control" exercised on
the church's preaching and teaching. As Barth emphasized, such theological
interpretation is the heart of dogmatics, whose purpose is to test the variegated
proclamation of the church by the standard of the Bible.

Theological interpretation of Scripture thus involves respect for premodern
interpretation, attention to the doctrinal tradition of the church, recognition
that Bible scholarship takes place within the church and exists for the edification of the church, and acknowledgment that interpretation is not a clinical
scientific enterprise but a form of piety and properly preceded and followed
by prayer, praise, and worship. Athanasius is among the precritical interpreters of Scripture whom contemporary theological readers of Scripture seek to
emulate. Lessing's ditch was unknown to him, as was Benjamin Jowett. Of
course, so too was the Nicene tradition to which Reno appeals. Athanasius
does appeal to the authority of the "fathers" at Nicaea, but he is one of the
key formulators of the Nicene tradition, rather than an heir of it. His biblical
interpretation is therefore of peculiar importance, since by following his lead we
can discover some of the paths by which he moved from Scripture's narrative,
law, gospel, and epistle to the metaphysical claims inherent in Nicene theology.

Typology

Much of Athanasius's work interpreting biblical texts occurs in polemical
treatises. He refutes Arian interpretations of particular texts, rubs Arian noses

in texts that Arian theology had difficulty explaining, and draws theological conclusions from Scripture concerning the nature of the Son, the Triad within the Godhead, and the character of redemption. The anti-Arian treatises are the works of Athanasius most relevant to a discussion of Athanasius's views on Scripture and metaphysics, and much of this chapter will focus on what Athanasius draws from Scripture concerning these theological and quasi-philosophical issues, and what tools he uses to draw such conclusions. In these works, Athanasius focuses on specific words, gathers proof texts from various places in Scripture, and applies some of his characteristic hermeneutical ideas to unscramble a confused Arian interpretation. His approach is largely "deductive."[5]

Yet we cannot focus wholly on polemical treatises without distortion. Athanasius was a bishop, and though he spent a large segment of his episcopacy away from Alexandria writing polemics and apologetical works, much of his biblical exposition took place not in theological dispute against heresy but in preaching and teaching within the church. What Athanasius said to his congregation on a Sunday morning is largely irrecoverable—largely, but fortunately not completely. In addition to his anti-Arian treatises, Athanasius left behind a body of pastoral and personal letters and a handful of sermons, in which we gain a glimpse of the bishop's general approach to biblical teaching and exposition.[6] In them we see the heart of Athanasius's biblical interpretation. He reads Scripture christocentrically, that is, typologically.[7] The Bible is about the Word of the Father made flesh. Once we have seen that, we will be in a position to evaluate more accurately what is going on even in the "deductive" readings of his polemical treatises.

Typological readings appear in many of Athanasius's *Festal Letters*, annual public encyclicals circulated to exhort his congregation to prepare for the celebration of Easter.[8] According to Athanasius, the Christian celebration of Easter was rooted in the history of ancient Israel. The ancient Pascha was the redemption of Israel, and thus it typified in an especially dramatic way the redemption of the world through Jesus, the Passover Lamb who goes to the cross and rises again at Pascha. Athanasius repeats the typological truism that all the old rites and institutions are but shadows dispelled now that the reality of Christ has appeared, but he gives this particular concreteness by emphasizing the fall of Jerusalem. While Judea and Jerusalem stood, "there were a type, and a lamb, and a shadow, since the law thus commanded," but now that the city "since the coming of our Savior, has had an end, and all the land of the Jews has been laid waste," then "there must of necessity be an end of the shadow" (*Festal Letter* 1.7–8).

In place of the shadows, Christians enjoy the reality, a new exodus, a new Moses, a new feast. Following this Moses and "rejoicing in afflictions, we break through the furnace of iron and darkness, and pass, unharmed, over that terrible Red Sea" so that we can sing "with Moses" the "great song of praise" (*Festal Letter* 3.5). As Israel was delivered by blood, so God "made the world free by the blood of the Savior"; as Pharaoh was conquered, so "He has caused the grave to be trodden down by the Savior's death, and furnished a way to the heavenly gates free from obstacles to those who are going up." Citing Romans 5, Athanasius declares that "death reigned from Adam to Moses," but the word of the new order is, "Today you shall be with me in paradise" (*Festal Letter* 5.3).

Jesus, in short, is "everything at once to us": shepherd, high priest, way, door, feast, holiday, and Passover sacrifice.[9] Everything hidden behind the veil of the temple is now summed up and openly manifest in the incarnate Son:

> He it was who was expected, He caused a light to shine at the prayer of the Psalmist, who said, "My Joy, deliver me from those who surround me"; this being indeed true rejoicing, this being a true feast, even deliverance from wickedness, whereto a man attains by thoroughly adopting an upright conversation, and being approved in his mind of godly submission towards God. For thus the saints all their lives long were like men rejoicing at a feast. One found rest in prayer to God, as blessed David, who rose in the night, not once but seven times. Another gave glory in songs of praise, as great Moses, who sang a song of praise for the victory over Pharaoh, and those task-masters (Exod. 15). Others performed worship with unceasing diligence, like great Samuel and blessed Elijah; who have ceased from their course, and now keep the feast in heaven, and rejoice in what they formerly learned through shadows, and from the types recognize the truth. (*Festal Letter* 14.1)

Though the *Festal Letters* are rich christological meditations, the bishop cannot keep himself from exhortation. Typology is not only about the transition from the Old to the New, from shadows to the Eternal Light that has come in Jesus, but also about the way the faithful must respond to the Light. Christ imprinted himself on the events and institutions of Israel, and now that he has fulfilled those types he is impressing his character on the church. By hearing, believing, and doing the feast, Christians are made over into the image of the Lord. In terms of the later medieval fourfold method, or "quadriga," allegorical typology immediately entails hortatory tropology.

Athanasius emphasizes this by repeatedly drawing attention to the requirements for the "true feast" of Christians. "What else is the feast," he asks, "but the service of the soul? And what is that service, but prolonged prayer to God, and unceasing thanksgiving?" (*Festal Letter* 3.2). Like Judith and Esther, who gained victory after devoting themselves to fasting and prayer, Christians overcome "the devil, that tyrant against the whole world," not through fleshly feasts but through "an eternal and heavenly one" (*Festal Letter* 4.2–3). To prepare for this feast, "we should approach such a feast, not with filthy raiment, but having clothed our minds with pure garments." That means that "we need in this to put on our Lord Jesus, that we may be able to celebrate the feast with Him." Clothing ourselves with Christ means loving virtue, hating wickedness, pursuing temperance, and avoiding lust; it involves open-doored hospitality and open-handed generosity, as humility dispels pride (*Festal Letter* 4.3). The Christian feast "does not consist in pleasant intercourse at meals, nor splendor of clothing, nor days of leisure, but in the acknowledgment of God and the offering of thanksgiving and praise." Such feasting is possible only to the saints, those "who live in Christ" (*Festal Letter* 7.3), the Christ who is the true feast, the giver of the Spirit who binds and harmonizes the festive assembly (*Festal Letter* 10.2).

Because the feast is the Christ who is continuously available by the Spirit, and because the true feast is a feast of virtue and charity, there is no time limit. The feast is not confined to specific days. So great is the Father's kindness that he not only brings us back from the dead but also "makes His grace illustrious through the Spirit." Athanasius sees in the parable of the prodigal (Luke 15:11–32) a type of God's kindness to sinners: "Instead of corruption, He clothes him with an incorruptible garment; instead of hunger, He kills the fatted calf; instead of far journeys, the Father watched for his return, providing shoes for his feet; and what is most wonderful, placed a divine signet-ring upon his hand; while by all these things He begat him afresh in the image of the glory of Christ" (*Festal Letter* 7.9). Thus clothed and thus fed, "if at all times we cleave to our Savior, and if we are pure, not only in these six days of Easter," then we may "consider the whole course of our life as a feast, and continue near and . . . not go far off" (*Festal Letter* 7.9). Moses was allowed to draw near to the Lord on Sinai, but through the gift of the Spirit, we are continuously in his presence, continuously filled with the fruits of festal joy and love and peace (*Festal Letter* 3.4).

Athanasius looks to Israel's festival calendar for specific guidance regarding the nature of Christian feasting and, since the feast is continuous, the pattern of Christian living. Because Israel "was then but a child," the Lord summoned the Israelites to feasts with trumpets. Three times a year, the men of Israel were to respond to the sounding trumpets and draw near to the Lord in his sanctuary. The same trumpets summoned Israel both "to fasting and to war." Through the use of trumpets, Yahweh made it clear that the proclamation of a feast was not "merely human" but "superhuman," so that the men of Israel would gather in proper reverence (*Festal Letter* 1.2–3). With his own priestly trumpet, apparently in the proclamation of the gospel, Jesus now calls the church to a new form of life. Jesus too blasts the call to war, the battle against principalities and powers and rulers of darkness in heavenly places. Jesus's trumpet calls the faithful "to virginity, and self-denial, and conjugal harmony" and sometimes to fasting (*Festal Letter* 1.3–4). What Israel did in a shadowy way, Christians now do openly and fully. Christian worship and Christian living are a new covenant form of Israel's life and worship. The pattern of Christ, which shaped the old order, now shapes the new, partly through hearing, studying, and obeying the Scriptures of Israel.

While typological excursions are comparatively rare in the polemical/"dogmatic" works, they are not absent. In one passage of the *Discourses*, Athanasius teases out the quite exact correspondence between Aaron's ordination as priest and the incarnation, by which the Son is "made" a priest for us:

> Aaron was not born a high-priest, but a man; and in process of time, when God willed, he became a high-priest; yet became so, not simply, nor as betokened by his ordinary garments, but putting over them the ephod, the breastplate (Exod. 29:5), the robe, which the women wrought at God's command, and going in them into the holy place, he offered the sacrifice for the people; and in them, as it were, mediated between the vision of God and the sacrifices of men. Thus then the Lord also, "In the beginning was the Word, and the Word was with God, and the Word was God"; but when the Father willed that ransoms should be paid for all and to all, grace should be given, then truly the Word, as Aaron his robe, so did He take earthly flesh, having Mary for the Mother of His Body as if virgin earth, that, as a High Priest, having He as others an offering, He might offer Himself to the Father, and cleanse us all from sins in His own blood, and might rise from the dead. (*Discourses* 2.7)[10]

There is discontinuity as well, since the old was only a "shadow" of the new (*Discourses* 2.8). While Aaron had successors, Jesus as high priest is unique, "without transition and without succession" (*Discourses* 2.9).

The exodus also provides a shadow of incarnation. Just as Israel groaned under slavery until the Lord came to defend and deliver, so all mankind groaned under slavery to the Pharaoh-like idols, until the Lord came near in the incarnation (*Discourses* 2.14). For Athanasius, drawing on New Testament texts like John 2:21, the temple provides a particularly fitting model of incarnation. He innovatively takes the reference to the "founding" of Wisdom (Prov. 8:23) as a prophecy of the incarnation, and the image of "founding" leads him to expound the incarnation as a construction project:

> Therefore according to His manhood He is founded, that we, as precious stones, may admit of building upon Him, and may become a temple of the Holy Ghost who dwells in us. And as He is a foundation, and we stones built upon Him, so again He is a Vine and we knit to Him as branches—not according to the Essence of the Godhead; for this surely is impossible; but according to His manhood, for the branches must be like the vine, since we are like Him according to the flesh. Moreover, since the heretics have such human notions, we may suitably confute them with human resemblances contained in the very matter they urge. . . . Now what is founded is founded for the sake of the stones which are raised upon it; it is not a random process, but a stone is first transported from the mountain and set down in the depth of the earth. And while a stone is in the mountain, it is not yet founded; but when need demands, and it is transported, and laid in the depth of the earth, then immediately if the stone could speak, it would say, "He now founded me, who brought me hither from

the mountain." Therefore the Lord also did not when founded take a beginning of existence; for He was the Word before that; but when He put on our body, which He severed and took from Mary, then He says "He has founded me"; as much as to say, "Me, being the Word, He has enveloped in a body of earth." For so He is founded for our sakes, taking on Him what is ours, that we, as incorporated and compacted and bound together in Him through the likeness of the flesh, may attain unto a perfect man, and abide immortal and incorruptible. (*Discourses* 2.74)[11]

Two foundings are in view here, and they are integrally related. In founding his Wisdom through the incarnation, the Father is also founding the temple of the Spirit that is the church. The temple of Israel thus serves as a double type, both of the body of the Son and of the body of the church.

Criteria of Interpretation

For Athanasius, conformity to Scripture is the touchstone of all theological truth. The Arians agree, and as a result the battle over Arianism is largely an exegetical battle—not a battle for the Bible, but a battle over the Bible. Scripture communicates the knowledge of God, the true God, and Athanasius is self-conscious in his belief that human language is capable of communicating such knowledge. Discussing the nature of religious language, he argues that we must follow Scripture because otherwise God is unknown. Arians demand an explanation of the eternal generation of the Son. Athanasius charges that the question is impertinent: one cannot demand that "a thing ineffable and proper to God's nature, and known to Him alone and to the Son" should be "explained in words." One cannot determine "where God is, and how God is, and of what nature the Father is"; such questions are "irreligious" and betoken "an ignorance of God." When we are perplexed by the mysteries of God, it is preferable to remain perplexed in silence and simply believe, rather than "disbelieve on account of the perplexity." A perplexed man may receive some mercy, but when someone in perplexity proudly seeks to penetrate the mysteries of God he will ultimately be frustrated. Still, God has not left himself without a witness: "In such perplexities divine Scripture is able to afford him some relief, so as to take rightly what is written." In this case, it is useful to dwell on human language "as an illustration." Scripture calls him the Word, hinting that "as it is proper to us and is from us, and not a work external to us, so also God's Word is proper to Him and from Him, and is not a work; and yet is not like the word of man, or else we must suppose God to be man" (*Discourses* 2.36). Ultimately the Arians get the problem of religious language backward, Athanasius says. They claim that the Logos takes its name from creation. He is called Logos because of created *logika*. No, says Athanasius: creation takes its name from the Creator (*Discourses* 2.38).

On Athanasius's view, Arianism does not pass the scriptural test. This is not because Arius or his followers avoid scriptural language.[12] In fact, they present themselves as biblicists and condemn the Nicene council for introducing extrabiblical language into the church. For Athanasius, however, this is just a smoke screen. He gleefully points out that the Arians themselves employ extrabiblical terms when it suits them. Arians "proceeded to borrow of the Greeks the term Unoriginate, that, under shelter of it, they might reckon among the things originated and the creatures, that Word of God, by whom these very things came to be" (*Defense of the Nicene Definition* 7.28). And the Arians don't even know what the term means. Philosophers know that the word can be used in all sorts of different senses. At times, it means "what has not yet, but may, come to be," but in other contexts it can mean "what neither exists, nor can come into being." To apply either of these uses to God is absurd, so the relevant usage in the Arian debate is the third: the ungenerate is "what exists indeed but was neither originated nor had origin of being, but is everlasting and indestructible." Even here, there is a distinction to be made, for the word can refer either to "what has no origin of being" or to a being that has no source of origin at all. In the first of these senses, the word applies to both Father and Son, while in the second sense only to the Father. The import of the Arian usage is clear, however: "If the Son be of things originate, it follows, that He too came to be from nothing; and if He has an origin of being, then He was not before His generation; and if He is not eternal there was once when He was not" (*Defense of the Nicene Definition* 7.28).

Worse than the hypocrisy of using extrabiblical terms, the Arians are guilty of distorting the Scriptures. And at the outset and repeatedly through the *Discourses*, Athanasius claims that Arians are like the devil, who employs scriptural language but does not accept the truth of Scripture. Athanasius teaches that the Arian heresy is the most thorough of all heresies and as such is a "harbinger of the Antichrist." What makes Arianism worse than all that has gone before it is the "craft and cunning" of the Arians who attempt to "array" themselves in Scripture language. Just like the devil, the Arians are forcing their way "back into the Church's paradise," all the while pretending to be Christians. Athanasius is provoked to respond because "she [the Arian heresy] has already seduced certain of the foolish, not only to corrupt their ears, but even to take and eat with Eve" (*Discourses* 1.1). The devil can speak Scripture even while denying it. What matters is not the use of scriptural language but actual conformity to scriptural truth. But that raises the question of how anyone is able to judge what counts as a legitimate reading of Scripture. Instead of cloaking falsehood with scriptural language, as the Arians satanically do, the Scriptures ought to be put on a lamp stand: "We take divine Scripture, and thence discourse with freedom of the religious Faith, and set it up as a light upon its candlestick" (*Discourses* 1.9).

But how are differences of interpretation resolved? Who adjudicates between Arius and Athanasius, and how? What makes an interpretation of Scripture genuine rather than a deceptive disguise? What's the difference between a cloak and a lamp stand?

In answering that question, Athanasius sometimes appeals to tradition, to the "fathers," from whom he claims the Arians have deviated. In *Defense of the Nicene Definition* (6.25–27), Athanasius includes a long list of writers who affirm the Nicene position on the nature of the Son, and he is at pains to defend Dionysius, former bishop of Alexandria, against the charge of being Arian (*On the Opinion of Dionysius*). Once the council made its decision, Athanasius took it as the voice of God, virtually equating the creed with the Scriptures themselves. He charges that the Arians are guilty of giving a private sense to Scripture, a sense that does not reflect the mind of the church but is "according to their own mind" (*kata ton idion noun*; *Discourses* 1.37).

Tradition plays a role in interpretation through liturgical practice. An interpretation of Scripture that is discordant with the sacramental and liturgical life of the church must be wrong. We are baptized in the name of the Father, not of the "Unoriginate," so the name "Father" must be preferable to the Arian term (*Discourses* 1.34). Baptism is in the name of the Father *and* the Son. Arianism makes nonsense of this formula, since it implies that we are baptized in the name of both the Creator and a creature. The baptismal formula supports the orthodox view that the Father's works are the works of the Son, and vice versa, for when the Father baptizes so also does the Son (*Discourses* 2.41). Arians, in fact, rob baptism of its efficacy, since they imply that baptism is done in the name of a creature:

> And these too hazard the fullness of the mystery, I mean Baptism; for if the consecration is given to us into the Name of Father and Son, and they do not confess a true Father, because they deny what is from Him and like His Essence, and deny also the true Son, and name another of their own framing as created out of nothing, is not the rite administered by them altogether empty and unprofitable, making a show, but in reality being no help towards religion? For the Arians do not baptize into Father and Son, but into Creator and creature, and into Maker and work. And as a creature is other than the Son, so the Baptism, which is supposed to be given by them, is other than the truth, though they pretend to name the Name of the Father and the Son, because of the words of Scripture. For not he who simply says, "O Lord," gives Baptism; but he who with the Name has also the right faith. On this account therefore our Savior also did not simply command to baptize, he first says, "Teach"; then thus: "Baptize into the Name of Father, and Son, and Holy Ghost"; that the right faith might follow upon learning, and together with faith might come the consecration of Baptism. (*Discourses* 2.42)

A Christology that shakes a believer's confidence in his baptism is not only mistaken but spiritually dangerous.[13]

Yet, in rebutting Arians, Athanasius returns again and again to the question of whether Arian theology conforms to Scripture, and the bulk of the *Discourses* is taken up with polemics about particular passages of Scripture. Scripture is God's self-communication, necessary because of the frailty of man, to which he has added the evils of sin. For Athanasius, any defense of an interpretation of one passage of Scripture must be internal to the Scriptures themselves. But if there is no external adjudication, that simply intensifies the question: What is the difference between a cloak and a lamp stand? And how can we tell?

For Athanasius, one test is conformity to the overall pattern of biblical usage. He examines syntax, the range of meaning in particular words and phrases, the Bible's habitual turns of thought and phrase. He observes the distinction between statements about the Son's eternal nature, which are unqualified, and statements about the Son's being "made," which are always qualified by a purpose clause. When Scripture "signifies the fleshly origination of the Son, it adds also the cause for which He became man; but when He speaks or His servants declare anything of His Godhead, all is said in simple diction, and with an absolute sense, and without reason being added." In himself, the Son "is the Father's Radiance; and as the Father is, but not for any reason, neither must we seek the reason of that Radiance." But when the Son takes flesh, he assumes something that is not his according to his essential nature as God, and thus a causal clause is attached. John 1 provides a stark example of this biblical habit of speech. "In the beginning was the Word and the Word was with God, and the Word was God" (John 1:1) contains no statement of purpose, but in verse 14, when John announces that the "Word became flesh," he adds the reason: "and dwelt among us." Similarly, Philippians 2 states absolutely that the Son was "in the form of God," but when he is said to take the form of a servant, Paul adds that "He humbled Himself unto death, even the death of the cross" (*Discourses* 2.53).[14] From this grammatical difference, Athanasius draws a theological conclusion: the begetting is absolute while the creation or being-made is always qualified and relative. Moreover, all passages concerning the "making" of the Son are about the incarnation (*Discourses* 2.60).

Right interpretation, though, is not simply a matter of repeating the terms of Scripture. Sticking with the specific terms and language of the Bible does not guarantee right interpretation. Athanasius admits at times that the language of "created" can be applied to the eternal Son, but that does not make the Son a creature. Arians get hung up on terminology (*lexeis*), which is secondary (*Discourses* 2.45). What matters is capturing the *sense* of Scripture. For Athanasius, this is a principle of right reading for every text. In rejecting the Nicene settlement, the Arians complained about the use of extrabiblical terms, especially the suspect *homoousios*. Athanasius urges them to "consider the sense in which the Council so wrote," and to "anathematize what the Council anathematized." If they accept the sense of the council's decision, they will also accept the terms in which it is stated, and the fact that they haggle over words is a sign of their bad faith and impiety. "Even if the expressions are not in so many words in the Scripture, yet, as was said before, they contain the sense of the Scriptures, and expressing it, they convey it to those who have their hearing unimpaired for religious doctrine" (*Defense of the Nicene Definition* 5.21).

Athanasius does not believe that terms are indifferent. As noted earlier, he attacks the Arian use of "Unoriginate" as the name of the Father. In addition to mocking the Arians for their imprecision in using the term, he argues that the terminology shapes their theology in a particular, dangerous direction. Given its negative prefix, "Unoriginate" is an inherently contrastive term, and it is used in contrast to "things originated." Biblical terms like "Almighty" and "Lord of the Powers" are similar, for these teach that "the Father has power and mastery over all things by the Word, and the Son rules the Father's kingdom, and has the power of all, as His Word, and as the Image of the Father." To name God "Unoriginate" is thus to name him "not by contrast to the Son, but to the things which through the Son come to be." This is perfectly legitimate in itself: it is true that "God is not as things originated, but is their Creator and Framer through the Son," and "he who names God Maker and Framer and Unoriginate, regards and apprehends things created and made." The word can thus be used "religiously" (*Discourses* 1.33).

But the Arians' intention, and thus their usage, is impious. They "bring it forth for the dishonor of the Son," since the term "Unoriginate" is used in contrast to the "originate" Son: "In calling God unoriginate, they are, as I said before, calling Him from His works, and as Maker only and Framer, supposing that hence they may signify that the Word is a work after their own pleasure. But that he who calls God Father, signifies Him from the Son being well aware that if there be a Son, of necessity through that Son all things originate were created" (*Discourses* 1.33). Thus it is more pious and accurate (*eusebesteron kai alēthes*) to call him "Father," as the Bible does. Scriptural language is superior to extrascriptural language. Extrabiblical terms are ambiguous, while the biblical terms are "simple" and "accurate" (*Discourses* 1.34). By naming the Creator from his works, rather than from the Son, the Arians implicitly make God dependent upon his creation. "Father" is much preferable, since naming God "Father" is to name him in relation to one who is fully God with him.

Because the goal is to capture the sense of Scripture, however, it is legitimate to use language and terms that are not found in Scripture itself. Athanasius regularly defends the Nicene use of the technical term *homoousios* because it captures the sense of Scripture. Of course, part of his rationale for the term is that it distinguishes between the orthodox and the Arian interpretation of the phrase "from God" (*ek theou*). Arians were only too happy to affirm this vague claim, noting that since everything is from God, then surely the Son is from God as well. To emphasize the difference between orthodox and Arian understanding, the phrase had to be extrapolated with extrabiblical terminology, either as "from the essence of God" or as "the same essence." Scripture's language is more "exact" and profound than that of the Greeks, but it had become necessary to borrow from Greek philosophy to overcome the Arians (*Defense of the Nicene Definition* 7.32). Confession is more important than specific terminology (*Discourses* 2.3). Scripture's terminology for the Son ought not trouble anyone, so long as we apply what Athanasius describes as the "double" canon of interpretation. Some biblical descriptions name the Son in his "genuine and natural" essence, while others speak of him as incarnate, using terms proper to a work of the Father (*Discourses* 2.4).

This line of argument creates some difficulties for Athanasius. On the one hand, Scripture's terminology is preferable, because it is more accurate and more straightforward. On the other hand, the specific terminology of Scripture is not as important as the sense of Scripture. When these twin principles work him into a corner, Athanasius can respond with special pleading. On the one hand, Athanasius admits that the Son is described in terms that imply he is a creature, but he insists that these are "improper" uses. "When the essence is a work of creature," he writes, "then the words 'He made,' and 'He became,' and 'He created,' are used of it properly, and designate the work." On the other hand, "when the Essence is an Offspring and Son, then 'He made,' and 'He became,' and 'He created,' no longer properly belong to it, nor designate a work; but 'He made' we use without question for 'He begot.'" Athanasius observes this shift in human experience: "Fathers often call the sons born of them their servants, yet without denying the genuineness of their nature; and often they affectionately call their own servants children, yet without putting out of sight their purchase of them originally" (*Discourses* 2.3).[15] If that is the case, though, it does not seem possible to rest much weight on the way Scripture speaks about the Son. How does one distinguish a proper from an improper use? Again, how can we distinguish a cloak from a lamp stand?

Athanasius at times responds to Arian interpretations by applying rules and methods that resemble the "hermeneutical" rules and procedures of modern scholarship. In defending Dionysius against the charge of Arianism, for instance, he argues that Dionysius must be understood in the light of his times. Dionysius was occupied with modalism, not with Arianism, and that context explains the particular phrases he uses. Athanasius also examines specific statements in light of Dionysius's whole corpus of writings. Athanasius argues that "Dionysius not only wrote other letters also, but composed a defense of himself upon the suspicious points, and came out clearly as of right opinions." The apparent inconsistency can be resolved by attending to the different audiences and context of Dionysius's writings: "When he had written his letter to Ammonius, and fallen under suspicion, he made his defense so as to better what he had previously said, but did so without changing, it must be evident that he wrote the suspected passages in a qualified sense. But what is written or done in such a sense men have no business to construe maliciously, or wrest each one to a meaning of his own." A physician "applies to the wounds he has to deal with, remedies which to some seem unsuitable with a view to nothing but health." So too a wise teacher such as Dionysius: "In like manner it is the practice of a wise teacher to arrange and deliver his lessons with reference to the characters of his pupils, until he has brought them over to the way of perfection" (*Opinion of Dionysius* 6).

Athanasius immediately adds that similar attention must be paid to the context of apostolic writings and preaching. After quoting several sermons from Acts (2:22; 4:10; 13:23; 17:31) that emphasize the humanity of Jesus, he asks if we should conclude that the apostles saw "Christ as only a man and nothing more." *Mē genoito*! he cries. The emphasis on Christ's humanity was part of an apologetic strategy aimed at Jewish hearers. Jews of the first century "thought that the Christ was coming as a mere man of the seed of David, after the likeness of the rest of the children of David's descent, and would neither believe that He was God nor that the Word was made flesh." Thus "the blessed Apostles began by proclaiming to the Jews the human characteristics of the Savior, in order that by fully persuading them from visible facts, and from miracles which were done, that the Christ had come, they might go on to lead them up to faith in His Godhead, by showing that the works He had done were not those of a man but of God" (*Opinion of Dionysius* 8).

In other passages, Athanasius points to genre as a way of defining the interpretive context. When defending his reading of Proverbs 8, a popular passage with the Arians because it speaks of a "created" Wisdom, Athanasius notes the character of proverbial speech. Proverbs and other texts "expressed in the way of proverbs" must not be understood "nakedly in their first sense." Proverbs state things not "plainly" but "latently"; therefore, in reading Proverbs "we must inquire into the person, and thus religiously put the sense on it." In such cases, "it is necessary to unfold the sense of what is said" (*Discourses* 2.44).

None of these procedures and convictions, though, get to the heart of Athanasius's "hermeneutics." Even more basic in Athanasius than these maneuvers, which often appear *ad hoc*, are the following three criteria: first, the appeal to the *skopos* and the "tripartite rule"; second, the use of biblical images (*paradeigmata*); and finally, the biblical use of terminological markers that distinguish between Creator and creature. We will examine each of these in turn, and we will find that, in his "deductive" interpretations as much as in his "typological" ones, his reading is christologically formed.[16] Scripture is all about Christ, not only in content but in "method." For Athanasius, Christ is the substance of Scripture and the criterion of correct interpretation.

The Scope and Rule

Athanasius's arguments from the *skopos* or *kanōn* of Scripture seem, at times, to be appeals to the faith of Christians as expressed in creeds, and have sometimes been taken as such.[17] Arian interpretations are "unsound," a fact evident from their failure to consider the scope or canon of Scripture (*Discourses* 3.28). More usually, the *skopos* is not a tradition or creed per se, but the overall thrust of the biblical story, with its focus on the incarnation. To appeal to the scope of Scripture is to appeal to the "double [*diplēn*] account of the Savior," as both "ever God" and "the Father's Word and Radiance and Wisdom," and also as the one who took the flesh of Mary and was made man (*Discourses* 3.29).

In short, Christ himself—understood in the Athanasian sense as the eternal Word made flesh—is the criterion of appropriate reading. There is a hermeneutical circularity here that Athanasius never openly acknowledges or defends. A right reading must be consistent with true faith in Jesus, and that true faith is predefined in anti-Arian terms. The question is, "Which of the two theologies sets forth our Lord Jesus Christ as God and Son of the Father?" (*Discourses* 1.10). Yet the *skopos* is not Christ simply in his "person" as Word made flesh, but in his entire history and work. It is not just that interpretations must give due attention to whether the text speaks of the Word in his divine nature or the Word having become flesh. That is necessary, but attention to Word and flesh is not the same as attention to the full *skopos* of Scripture. Rather, the standard of right reading is the ground motif of Scripture as a whole, the history of creation, fall, incarnation, glory. As Frances Young puts it, "Athanasius is not neglectful of the details of the text," but more basically his reading is guided by a "sense of the overarching plot" that he has inherited as the fundamental narrative of salvation. Thus "the 'Canon of Truth' or 'Rule of Faith' expresses the mind of scripture, and an exegesis that damages the coherence of that plot, that *hypothesis*, that coherence, that *skopos*, cannot be right."[18] Arian readings fail because they create dissonance in what should be a harmonious story—for instance, they deny that the Creator and Savior are one character.

This principle guides his interpretation of various disputed passages, such as Proverbs 8, a classic Arian passage because it speaks of the "creation" of Wisdom. But Athanasius has already established that the Son is eternal. Therefore, the biblical marker "created" cannot apply to the nature of the Son. It must describe him in some other aspect. It must describe the Son insofar as he enters creation and participates in it as created Son, the Son of God "created" as Son of Man. Athanasius's interpretation of the passage is questionable, but he comes to a brilliant theological conclusion, namely, that in the incarnation the uncreated Son is created as man.

Athanasius also employs what has come to be called the "tripartite rule" of attending to person, time, and circumstance.[19] Most often, he brings this "rule" into play in responding to Arian misrepresentations of various texts. Arians employed Hebrews 5:8 ("He learned obedience from the things which he suffered") to show that the Son could not be unchangeably equal to the Father. In rebuttal, Athanasius points to the context of the chapter, which in

his mind makes it clear that Paul is writing about the incarnation, not about
the eternal nature of the Son.

> But further, since the drift also of the context is orthodox, showing the time and
> the relation to which this expression points, I ought to show from it also how
> the heretics lack reason; viz. by considering, as we have done above, the occasion
> when it was used and for what purpose. Now the Apostle is not discussing things
> before the creation when he thus speaks, but when "the Word became flesh;" for
> thus it is written, "Wherefore, holy brethren, partakers of the heavenly calling,
> consider the Apostle and High Priest of our profession Jesus, who was faithful
> to Him that made Him." Now when became He "Apostle," but when He put
> on our flesh? And when became He "High Priest of our profession," but when,
> after offering Himself for us, He raised His Body from the dead, and, as now,
> Himself brings near and offers to the Father those who in faith approach Him,
> redeeming all, and for all propitiating God? (*Discourses* 2.7)

Similarly, the immediate context of Proverbs 8 indicates that it is about the
incarnation (*Discourses* 2.44).[20]

Superficially, both Athanasius's terminology and his use of this "rule" appear to bring him close to modern hermeneutical procedures. Such a conclusion,
though, misses the real center of Athanasius's approach. When Athanasius
appeals, for instance, to the "time" of a text, he is not attempting "to determine
the 'original' literary or historical meaning, but to disclose the true sense of
Scripture, speaking of or in the 'person' of Christ, as revealed when the 'time'
is fulfilled by Christ himself." For Athanasius, the time spoken of in Proverbs
8:22 is not the time of Solomon, its author, but is the time of the incarnation.
Similarly, the question of *prosōpon* (person) is the question of "*how* Christ
is spoken of, that is, in which 'character'—whether as God, which he always
is, or whether as human, which he becomes for the specific purpose of the
Passion."[21] Once again, interpreting Scripture is not about applying a general
theory of language. Even when he turns from "typological" pastoral letters to
"deductive" polemical interpretations, it is all about Christ.

Paradigms

Athanasius's interpretation of specific passages is governed not by a philosophical framework so much as by privileged biblical images that he describes
as *paradeigmata*.[22] Behind this usage is an analogical vision of reality. As noted
above, Athanasius believes that the human language of Scripture accurately
and precisely reveals God. God remains incomprehensible, but we do know
truth about God when we understand Scripture. That is possible because the
world images God, because it is stamped with the *typos* of the creating Word.
Against what he claims is the Arian view that divine names are drawn from
creation, Athanasius insists that creation imitates God, not vice versa.

At the same time, analogy includes difference. We cannot reason from the fact that an architect needs materials to the conclusion that God too needs materials. The fact that humans are always located in a place does not mean that God must be in a place too. Similarly, Arians cannot reason directly from human generation to divine generation, from the fact that human fathers exist before becoming fathers to the conclusion that "there was when He was not." Thoughts about making and generation must be purified in the apophatic fires of the Creator-creature distinction: God is an architect, perhaps, but God is not an architect like a human architect or a father like a human father. "The bare idea of God transcends such thoughts," and since "He is in being, not as we are, and yet in being as God, and creates not as man creates, but yet creates as God, it is plain that He begets also not as men beget, but begets as God." Quoting Ephesians 3:15, Athanasius summarizes the point by insisting that the Father is truly and solely (*kyriōs kai monon alēthōs*) Father and that all other fathers are named by mimesis of the divine Father: "God does not make man His pattern; but rather we men, since God is properly, and alone truly, Father of His Son, are also called fathers of our own children" (*Discourses* 1.23).

In a universe such as this, creation as a whole manifests the beauty, glory, and rationality of God and is imprinted with the character of the Creator. Scripture exploits this reality by drawing on images that reveal the nature of God. We cannot comprehend the nature of God in itself, but we can gain some "poor and dim" idea of that nature through Scripture paradigms (*Discourses* 2.32). "It is a custom with divine Scripture," Athanasius notes, "to take the things of nature as images and illustrations for mankind; and this it does, that from these physical objects the moral impulses of man may be explained; and thus their conduct shown to be either bad or righteous." Paradigms work within a specific realm, and the reality that is revealed in the paradigm remains within that realm. Thus Scripture uses natural phenomena to describe a moral transformation. When the psalmist urges us not to be like "horse and mule which have no understanding" (32:9) or Jeremiah warns against becoming like "wanton horses" (5:8) or Jesus describes Herod as "that fox" (Luke 13:32) and urges his disciples to be "wise as serpents and harmless as doves" (Matt. 10:16), they are speaking metaphorically. The psalmist is worried not about humans being transformed into the nature of beasts of burden but about stubborn behavior. Jesus warns so that "we might eschew the irrational motions of the one, and being aware of the wisdom of that other animal, might not be deceived by it, and might take on us the meekness of the dove" (*Discourses* 3.18).

Paradigms may have both ontological and ethical significance (*Discourses* 3.20), and in some cases, Athanasius combines the ethical and ontological quite closely. Commenting on Paul's exhortation to the Corinthians to follow his example (1 Cor. 4:6), he notes that "as Paul to the Corinthians, so is the oneness of the Son and the Father a pattern and lesson to all, by which they may learn, looking to that natural unity of the Father and the Son, how they themselves ought to be one in spirit towards each other." The "as" in Paul's exhortation signifies not identity, but shows that Paul is an image and example (*Discourses* 3.21). The Son is a "paradigm" of the Father, and thus the uncreated eternal relation between the Son and the Father is manifested in the creation's relation to God. Because the Son patterned after the pattern of the Father, he is also a pattern for us, and insofar as the Son's pattern has been imprinted on the apostle, so the apostle also becomes a pattern for the church.

For Athanasius, this analogical vision of reality is of a piece with typological interpretation. Created patterns and paradigms derive from the creative activity of the Father through his Word, and in time one event among created events becomes a pattern for other, later created events. For Athanasius, therefore, typology was not merely a method of reading but the key to metaphysics. Creation bears the impress (*typos*) of God's own wisdom, which is the Word, and for that reason there is an impression on earlier events that foreshadow later events, especially the incarnation. It is not startling if "the Son should be speaking of the impress that is within us as if it were Himself," since, "when Saul was persecuting the Church, in which was His impress and image, He said, as if He were Himself under persecution, 'Saul, why do you persecute Me?' [Acts 9:4]." In this passage, Athanasius is disputing about the phrase from Proverbs 8, "The Lord created me for the works." He denies that this passage teaches that God's Wisdom is a creature of God. On the contrary, Wisdom "is Creative and Framer," and as a result "its impress is created in the works, as the copy of the image." When Solomon says that "before the world He founded me [Prov. 8:23]," it is as much as to say that Wisdom's "impress [on] the works remain settled and eternal" (*Discourses* 2.80).

The metaphysical and hermeneutical dimensions of typology come together in a dramatic fashion in Athanasius's discussion of the typology of the "sign of Jonah." In context, Athanasius is discussing the force of the comparative "as" in Jesus's statement about the unity of disciples being "as" the unity of Father and Son (John 17). To explicate the nature of this comparative, he appeals to Jesus's prediction of the "sign of Jonah," in which Jesus says that he will be in the earth three days and nights "as" Jonah was in the sea.

> For Jonah was not as the Savior, nor did Jonah go down to hades; nor was the whale hades; nor did Jonah, when swallowed up, bring up those who had before been swallowed by the whale, but he alone came forth, when the whale was bidden. Therefore there is no identity nor equality signified in the term "as," but one thing and another; and it shows a certain kind of parallel in the case of Jonah, on account of the three days. In like manner then we too, when the Lord says "as," neither become as the Son in the Father, nor as the Father is in the Son. For we become one as the Father and the Son in mind and agreement of spirit, and the Savior will be as Jonah in the earth; but as the Savior is not Jonah, nor, as he was swallowed up, so did the Savior descend into hades, but it

is but a parallel, in like manner, if we too become one, as the Son in the Father, we shall not be as the Son, nor equal to Him; for He and we are but parallel. (*Discourses* 3.23)

To say that Jonah is a type of Jesus is to say that there is a certain parallel and likeness (*homoioteta . . . pos deiknysi*), not that there is identity (*tautotes, isotes*). And the relation of type and antitype, described with "as," is analogous to the relation between the unity within the Trinity and the unity of the disciples in Christ. The ultimate origin of this pattern is in the Godhead. Father and Son are identical in deity, but the Son is the "image" of the Father, so closely resembling the Father that the comparative "as" fails. At the same time, the Father and the Son are not simply two names for the same reality, and thus there is a qualified sense in which the Father is the archetype of which the Son is the image. In the "as" of the Father and the Son is the uncreated root of the "as" of natural revelation and the "as" of typology.

RADIANCE OF THE GLORY

What are the primary paradigms or images that Athanasius finds in Scripture? There are four. The first is taken from Hebrews 1:3, where the Son is described as the "radiance of His glory" and the "exact representation of His nature."[23] The word "radiance" is *apaugasma*, used only in Hebrews 1:3, a passage that also describes the Son as the precise character or expression (*charakter*) of the Father. The point of the radiance image is to emphasize that the Son is necessary to the Father's existence, as necessary as the rays of light are to the light source, and therefore the Son is just as eternal as the Father. Just as there is no light that does not radiate, so the Father is not without the radiance of his glory. When one reads of the Son as the "radiance" of the Father's glory, "who has so little sense as to doubt of the eternity of the Son? For when did man see light without the brightness of its radiance, that he may say of the Son, 'There was once, when He was not,' or 'Before His generation He was not'?" (*Discourses* 1.12).

Later in the first *Discourse*, Athanasius links the radiance of light with "image" (*eikon*). Arianism "impairs" the "perfection and plenitude of the Father's essence" by denying that he has an eternal Son. Just as "unseemly" is the Arian conception of the Son. Scripture describes the Son as "Image and Radiance of the Father, and Expression and Truth," and this shows that the Son and the Father are inseparably and eternally God: "For if, when Light exists, there be withal its Image, viz. Radiance, and, a Subsistence existing, there be of it the entire Expression, and, a Father existing, there be His Truth (viz. the Son); let them consider what depths of irreligion they fall into, who make time the measure of the Image and Form of the Godhead" (*Discourses* 1.20). The radiance of the light source is an image of the light itself. Athanasius returns to this theme repeatedly throughout the *Discourses* (cf. 2.33).

The light-radiance imagery not only proves the co-eternity of the Father and the Son but also shows, in Athanasius's view, that the Arian position is nonsensical. "Denying the Logos," he notes, they cannot help but be "illogical" (*alogoi*). What could be more absurd than a division of the sun and its radiance? Anyone seeing the sun and then imagining that the light coming from the sun was "external" to it would be judged mad. Just so, "to speculate concerning the Son and the Father and thus to inquire, is far greater madness, for it is to conceive of the Word of the Father as external to Him, and to idly call the natural offspring a work" (*Discourses* 1.25). This marks a revolution in metaphysics: the ultimate, the absolute, is a *related* absolute. The source is inseparably supplemented by something that is begotten by the source.

The image of light also indicates that God is not barren. If the Father is a light without radiance, he is fruitless; but for the orthodox, the essence of God is "fruitful in itself" (*Discourses* 2.2). Since the Father is fruitful in himself, he also is fruitful in creating. Without the Word, "things originate could not . . . be brought to be." As a Son proper to the Father's essence, he is the one through whom creatures come, without whom creation could not be at all. The relation of the Father's radiance to creation is not merely willed; it does not just happen that the Father created through the Son. The Father *cannot* create without his Son, any more than a light can illuminate without its radiance. As Athanasius puts it, "As the light enlightens all things by its radiance, and without its radiance nothing would be illuminated, so also the Father, as by a hand, in the Word wrought all things, and without Him makes nothing" (*Discourses* 2.31). In contrast to the Arians, who imply that the Father is barren and fruitless in himself, the orthodox teach that the Father has a "generative nature" (*gennētikēs physeōs*), since he is always with his generated Word, Wisdom, and image that is proper to his substance (*Discourses* 2.2). Without the Son, there could be no creation. Light lightens by radiance, and if the Father's light did not eternally radiate, it could not form the bright world of creation.

The paradigm of light and radiance qualifies other scriptural descriptions of the Son. As the Arians recognize, the fact that the Son is begotten might imply some sort of "interval" between the Father and the Son, as well as implying that the Father's begetting is passionate like human begetting. Athanasius addresses the problem by highlighting a different aspect of the parallel between divine and human begetting. Instead of defining father-son relations in terms of priority and subordination, he emphasizes the community of essence between source and offspring: "Who hears of a son but conceives of that which is proper to the father's essence? Who heard, in his first catechizing, that God has a Son and has made all things by His proper Word, but understood it in that sense in which we now mean it?" (*Discourses* 2.34). When the imagery of begetting and sonship is joined with the imagery of light and radiance, we come to a proper idea of sonship. If in "originate and irrational things" we find examples where "offsprings are found which are not parts of the essences from which they are, nor subsist with passion, nor impair the essences of their originals," then we can more readily imagine a passionless eternal begetting of an eternal Son (*Discourses* 2.34). The image of light and radiance thus assists in the apophatic purgation of our thoughts about God as Father and Son. One paradigm cleanses another.

The light-radiance connection provides a way of expounding the reality of grace, and particularly of the perichoretic union of the grace of the Father and the grace of the Son. The grace of the Father is not different from the grace of the Son; rather, the one indwells the other, as light indwells its radiance. Jesus promised that he and the Father would come and "make Our abode in him" so that as the Father and Son are one, so the disciples "may be One in us." This unity of the disciples in the Father and the Son depends on the fact that the "grace given is one, given from the Father in the Son." Paul confirms this reality with the greeting of every epistle: "Grace to you, and peace from God our Father and the Lord Jesus Christ." The grace of the Father must be in the Son, since "the light must be with the ray, and the radiance must be contemplated together with its own light" (*Discourses* 2.42). Elsewhere, Athanasius lines up grace, light, and the Father-Son relation in an illuminating fashion (*Discourses* 3.13):

Grace	from Father	through Son
Light	from Sun	through Radiance
Face	of Father	in Son

Grace thus follows the structure of triune life. As the Father is seen in the Son, so the grace of the Father comes through the Son, and this is expounded with the image of light and its radiance.

Athanasius uses the paradigm of light and radiance to explain the baptismal formula. It might seem that a baptism in the name of the Father and the Son implies that the Father is insufficient in himself. That is not true, and Athanasius sees instead that the baptismal formula shows how the Father works through the Son, inseparably "dependent" on him in the same way that light is inseparably dependent on the radiances that necessarily come from it. The Son is named in the baptismal formula because "He is God's Word and own Wisdom, and being His Radiance, is ever with the Father." Since the Son is inseparably with the Father, "it is impossible, if the Father bestows grace, that He should not give it in the Son, for the Son is in the Father as the radiance in the light." Baptism is a new creation, and the pattern of divine action in recreation follows the pattern of the original creation. The Father founded the earth "in His own Wisdom" and "made all things in the Word which is from Him." In the same way, the "Son confirms the Holy Laver." Since the

Son does only what he sees the Father doing, "when baptism is given, whom the Father baptizes, him the Son baptizes; and whom the Son baptizes, he is consecrated in the Holy Ghost." It is just like the sun and its beams: "And again as when the sun shines, one might say that the radiance illuminates, for the light is one and indivisible, nor can be detached, so where the Father is or is named, there plainly is the Son also; and is the Father named in Baptism? Then must the Son be named with Him" (*Discourses* 2.41).

FOUNTAIN AND STREAM

The second image is that of the fountain and the stream, which Athanasius finds in various Scripture passages. Jeremiah rebukes Israel for forsaking "the Fountain of living waters" (2:13), and Baruch calls Yahweh the "Fountain of wisdom" (3:12; *Discourses* 1.19). At one level, the import is the same as the image of light and radiance: just as there is no fountain without a flow from that fountain, so there is no paternal "origin" without the Son who is from him. Just as a fountain is no fountain without a stream flowing from it, so the Father is no Father without a Son.

This image leads to further insight into the character of the Son and his relation to the Father. "Living water" means life, and just so the Son is the "life and wisdom" that is not "foreign to the essence of the Fountain, but proper to it." This inference is confirmed by the words of Jesus ("I am the Life"; John 14:6) and Proverbs ("I Wisdom dwell with prudence"; 8:12). Even more than the light-radiance image, the fountain image underscores the fruitfulness of the Father's essence. To say "once the Son was not" is to say "once the Fountain was dry, destitute of Life and Wisdom." That is impossible, since "a fountain it would then cease to be; for what begets not from itself, is not a fountain." It is not only logically impossible, but it runs contrary to the promise of Isaiah 58:11: "And the Lord shall satisfy your soul in drought, and make your bones fat; and you shall be like a watered garden, and like a spring of water, whose waters fail not." How can the Lord keep this promise if he is himself barren and dry? (*Discourses* 1.19).

With these two images, the key point is not logical consistency so much as whether Arian theology honors God. If, as Arius argues, there was when the Son was not, then there was when the fountain was without a flow from it. If the Son is not eternal, then God would not be a fountain but "barren and dry" and this is an insult to the Father. The same is true of the image of light and radiance (*Discourses* 1.13): "The Son did not come out of nothing, nor is in the number of originated things at all, but is the Father's image and Word eternal, never having not been, but being ever, as the eternal Radiance of a Light which is eternal. Why imagine then times before the Son? Or why blaspheme the Word as after times, by whom even the ages were made?" "Blasphemy" is for Athanasius not a term of opprobrium. It is a precise description of the dishonor to the Father implied by Arian theology.

ETERNAL SON

The leading image is the third: the Son. The nature of sonship controls what Athanasius says about the ontological relation of the Father to the Son, but controls it in a specific fashion. Initially, he characterizes the difference between Father-Son and Creator-creature by distinguishing between participation and whole participation, or participation and generation from essence. Everything exists by virtue of participation in the Word through the Spirit. With regard to created things, "other beings, to whom He said, 'I said you are Gods,' had this grace from the Father, only by participation of the Word, through the Spirit" (*Discourses* 1.9). Elsewhere, Athanasius argues that "all other things partake of the Spirit" (*Discourses* 1.15), while the Son gives the Spirit and does not exist by participation in him.

But the Scripture speaks in very different ways about the Son (*Discourses* 1.15). The Son is not a partaker of the Spirit, but rather the Spirit comes from the Son. That difference marks the Son as ontologically different from all created things. Instead of participating in the Spirit as the source of life, the Logos is proper to the Father, from the essence of the Father. Athanasius sometimes describes this as "whole participation" and sometimes as "generation" or "begetting." Whatever is of the essence of the Father and proper (*idios*) to him is "entirely the Son," for "it is all one to say that God is wholly participated, and that He begets." The Son is not son by the participation of the Spirit, but on the contrary the Spirit who gives life to all creation comes from him. This shows that the Son does not partake of anything, but "what is partaken from the Father, *is* the Son." How else would we partake in God by partaking of the Son, if the Son were not himself that which partakes wholly of, or is begotten by, the Father? And Scripture teaches that we partake of divine nature by sharing in Jesus (2 Pet. 1:4) and thus are made into temples of the living God.

At the same time, divine begetting is not the same as human begetting. Human begetting involves a division of essence, the breaking free of one bit of human essence from another. This is impossible with God, since his essence is indivisibly one. Human generation also occurs through passion, and this too differs from divine generation, which is impassible. Since the Son is an offspring of this kind, essence from the essence of the Father, proper to the Father so that we are to define the Godhead as the Father begetting the Son, then "it is not fitting, rather it is full of peril, to say, that He is a work out of nothing, or that He was not before His generation. For he who thus speaks of that which is proper to the Father's essence, already blasphemes the Father Himself; since he really thinks of Him what he falsely imagines of His offspring" (*Discourses* 1.16). The nature of sonship also helps Athanasius to distinguish between the Son and the "works" of the Father. Again, he is thinking analogically: a work is not from the essence of the craftsman, but an external thing, not "proper" (*idios*) to the maker. But a son is from the essence of the father, the same nature as the father. So when the Bible calls Jesus the Son, it implies that he is not a work, since sons are not works.

Again, the sonship image is about the honor of God. Would it be honoring to God to say that he was incomplete (*atelēs*)? No. A father who has no son is not a father at all. Therefore, it is an insult to the Father to say that the Son is anything less than eternal.

> If He is called the eternal offspring of the Father, He is rightly so called. For never was the essence of the Father imperfect, that what is proper to it should be added afterwards; nor, as man from man, has the Son been begotten, so as to be later than His Father's existence, but He is God's offspring, and as being proper Son of God, who is ever, He exists eternally. For, whereas it is proper to men to beget in time, from the imperfection of their nature, God's offspring is eternal, for His nature is ever perfect. (*Discourses* 1.14)

A son is the perfection of a father's nature. Humanity is perfected in time, through a succession of generations. God is perfected eternally. If the Son is not eternal, then the Father is without his perfection, which is his creative power. Athanasius wants to insist that God is never without creativity, though he has not eternally created. But if the Arians are right, then the power to create is "extrinsic" to the Father's being. The Father is too weak to create on his own, or he is too proud to create us without the help of a mediating power.

WORD AND WISDOM

The scriptural language of Word, Wisdom, and power functions similarly. If the Son is not eternal to the Father, "proper" to his essence, then the Father at one time was powerless, wisdomless, and wordless. But that cannot be. How dare we slander God by saying that he was ever *alogos* (*Discourses* 1.14)? Some Arians would respond that the Wisdom that the Father has is eternal, but that is not the Wisdom that creates, the demiurgical wisdom. There is a more basic wisdom that belongs to the Father and is not hypostatized into a son until the generation of the Son. But Athanasius will not have this. First Corinthians 1:24 says that Christ is the Wisdom and power of God, and Athanasius takes that statement quite literally. He denies that the Father is the eternal power of God; the eternal power of God is his Son. And this eternal power that is the Son is evident in the creation. Athanasius interprets 1 Corinthians 1:24 in the light of Paul's description of the revelation of God in creation (Rom. 1:18–20):

> While silencing the Greeks, he has said, "The visible things of Him from the creation of the world are clearly seen, being understood by the things that are made, even His eternal Power and Godhead"; and what the Power of God is, he teaches us elsewhere himself, "Christ the Power of God and the Wisdom of God." Surely in these words he does not designate the Father, as you often whisper one to another, affirming that the Father is "His eternal power." This

is not so; for he says not, "God Himself is the power," but "His is the power."
(*Discourses* 1.11)

For Athanasius, all these images qualify one another. Son and begetting
seem to imply temporality and passion, so Word and Wisdom are added. Word
and Wisdom might imply that the Son is not a distinct person but merely an
attribute of the Father, so the biblical image of the Son is needed. As Athanasius
says, "The divine generation must not be compared to the nature of men, nor
the Son considered to be part of God, nor the generation to imply any passion whatever; God is not as man; for men beget passibly, having a transitive
nature, which waits for periods by reason of its weakness. But with God this
cannot be; for He is not composed of parts, but being impassible and simple,
He is impassibly and indivisibly Father of the Son." How does he know this?
He appeals to Scripture: "The Word of God is His Son, and the Son is the
Father's Word and Wisdom; and Word and Wisdom is neither creature nor
part of Him whose Word He is, nor an offspring passibly begotten. . . . What
affection then, or what part of the Father is the Word and the Wisdom and the
Radiance?" Those who inquire into sonship might examine the phenomenology of words, "and they will find that the word which they put forth is neither
an affection of them nor a part of their mind." If human beings, "who are
passible and partitive," produce words without passion and without division,
"why speculate they about passions and parts in the instance of the immaterial and indivisible God, that under pretense of reverence they may deny the
true and natural generation of the Son?" In short, "the offspring from God
is not an affection; and now it has been shown in particular that the Word is
not begotten according to affection. The same may be said of Wisdom; God
is not as man; nor must they here think humanly of Him" (*Discourses* 1.28).

Words Worthy of God

The problem, of course, is that the Arians also use images. In fact, one
could say that the whole Arian position rests on an analogy between human
and divine begetting. Begetting implies a process and something produced that
is a different individual from the producer. Before a son is begotten, he isn't;
after he's begotten, he is. Arians also point to the paradigm of human and
divine language. Human beings utter words, but these words are not eternally
uttered, and they pass away as soon as they are spoken. Human words are not
of the essence of the speaker, but contingent and voluntary. Wisdom, of course,
is an attribute of some human beings; God is eternally wise, but that does
not require that he beget wisdom. His wisdom is eternally internal to God.

When Athanasius encounters an argument like this, he answers it by saying
that God is God and man is man: "God does not make man His pattern; but
rather we men, for that God is properly, and alone truly, Father of His Son,

are also called fathers of our own children; for of Him 'is every fatherhood in heaven and earth named'" (Eph. 3:15; *Discourses* 1.23). Seeing an angel and seeing God in the flesh are not the same, since "greatly, or rather wholly, do things by nature originate differ from God the Creator" (*Discourses* 3.14). In sum, "the divine generation must not be compared to the nature of men" (*Discourses* 1.28).

Athanasius's interpretation of Scripture is thus qualified by an assumed theology proper. Athanasius presumes that God's nature is unchanging and atemporal, and this is the key to the right use of the biblical paradigms. "If they were disputing concerning any man," he writes, "then let them exercise reason in this human way, both concerning His Word and His Son." Arians forget they are talking about God. If they want to speak rightly of him, "no longer let them entertain human thoughts, but others which are above human nature" (*Discourses* 2.35).

Fundamentally, distinguishing God from creation means distinguishing the timeless from the time bound and, implied in that distinction, the indivisible from the divisible, and the impassible from the passible. "Man, begotten in time, in time also himself begets the child," and human words partake in the same temporality as man himself: "Whereas from nothing he came to be, therefore his word also is over and continues not." Yet "God is not as man." Since he is "existing and is ever," so also "His Word is existing and is everlastingly with the Father, as radiance of light." Human language is composite and divisible, constructed from letters and syllables; it is temporary, going forth and going by, never again to appear, not existing at all until spoken. This is not the character of God's Word: "God's Word is not merely pronounced, as one may say, nor a sound of accents, nor by His Son is meant His command; but as radiance of light, so is He perfect offspring from perfect. Hence He is God also, as being God's Image; for 'the Word was God'" (*Discourses* 2.35).

Once the Arians implicitly introduce temporality into the Father-Son relation, they implicitly introduce temporality into the existence of the Father himself. If there is an interval between Father and Son, and yet the Son is somehow "God," then God is subject to becoming (*Discourses* 1.17). If the Triad emerges, then true religion is not fixed; piety is trying to hit a moving target (*Discourses* 1.18). For the Arians, God becomes Father only after begetting the Son (*Discourses* 1.24). The Arians imply in various ways that God is subject to time, that he is a God-in-process.

The point of the paradigm of sonship thus cannot be to highlight a temporal interval between Father and Son. To be sure, there is such an interval in human life, but since God is beyond time, there can be no interval. This is precisely the point of discontinuity, Athanasius thinks, between divine and human generation, since it is one of the central points of discontinuity between God and creatures. The point of similarity must rather be something consistent with the timeless nature of God, and Athanasius argues that this analogy is found in the fact that the divine Son shares the same nature as the divine Father, just as children share nature with their parents.

The Arians are inconsistent, he charges: "If then they assume from human examples that generation implies time, why not from the same infer that it implies the Natural and the Proper, instead of extracting serpent-like from the earth only what turns to poison?" The temporal interval between parent and child in human life displays the time-restrained condition of human existence as such: "Though the parent be distinct in time, as being man, who himself has come to be in time, yet he too would have had his child ever coexistent with him, but that his nature was a restraint and made it impossible" (*Discourses* 1.26).

Of course, Athanasius is equally inconsistent, and his argument begs the Arian rejoinder: "If you assume from human examples that generation implies common nature, why not infer time?" Athanasius never addresses this potential objection, but it is fairly clear what his answer would have been: God is by definition eternal, therefore above time; therefore temporality is always the point of difference between Creator and creature.

Passibility is bound up with temporality.[24] A changeable, time-bound creature is necessarily also passible, and, conversely, a changeless eternal God is for Athanasius necessarily impassible. The paradigms of Scripture need to pass this test as well: as we reason by way of eminence from the created things that Scripture likens to God, that reasoning has to be purified by a passage through the "impassibility partition." Just as begetting and sonship must be understood in a way consistent with the timeless divine nature, so must it be thought of consistently with God's impassibility. It is a mistake to consider the Son "to be part of God," and an equal mistake to believe that the generation implies "any passion whatever," since "God is not as man." Of course, "men beget passibly, having a transitive nature, which waits for periods by reason of its weakness. But with God this cannot be; for He is not composed of parts, but being impassible and simple, He is impassibly and indivisibly Father of the Son." By "uniting then the two titles, Scripture speaks of 'Son,' in order to herald the natural and true offspring of His essence; and, on the other hand, that none may think of the Offspring humanly, while signifying His essence, it also calls Him Word, Wisdom, and Radiance; to teach us that the generation was impassible, and eternal, and worthy of God." He concludes, "What affection then, or what part of the Father is the Word and the Wisdom and the Radiance?" (*Discourses* 1.28).

If the Son is going to be the image of the Father, of the Father's essence in particular, he must be as changeless, indivisible, impassible, and eternal as the Father. Nature follows origin for Athanasius; if the Son originated from nothing, if his beginning was a transition from non-existence to existence, then he must be a changeable creature. And "if the Word be alterable and changing, where will He stay, and what will be the end of His development?

How shall the alterable possibly be like the Unalterable? How should he who has seen the alterable, be considered to have seen the Unalterable?" Not only is a changeable Son incapable of imaging a changeless Father, but a changeable Son is a moving target, another God-in-process. If that is the case, do we have to wait for him to evolve to a condition where we are able to behold the Father in him?

The godness of God also helps Athanasius to avert some pesky Arian interpretations. If the Son is the image of the Father, then he should also have a Son. How else could he manifest Fatherhood? Athanasius of course acknowledges that human sons often eventually become fathers themselves, but to project this succession onto the divine nature is again to measure God by human standards. God is not in time and thus does not need a succession of generations to reach his fulfillment. He is completely fulfilled in the generation of a single, eternal Son. To put the same point another way, the Father is essentially Father (*kyriōs patēr*) and the Son is essentially Son (*kyriōs huios*). To think otherwise is to think of Father and Son as "mixed" persons and thus to threaten the simplicity of the persons (*Discourses* 1.21).

Athanasius never defends this assumed theology nor even acknowledges how it is operative in his reading of Scripture. Pressed, he would no doubt have assembled passages of Scripture to support his presumption that God is not time bound or subject to passions. That he failed to do this is hardly surprising, for the theological assumptions that guide interpretation of particular texts are assumptions shared by Athanasius and his opponents.

Athanasius's biblical work is, throughout, a theological hermeneutics. Christ is both the substance of Scripture and the criterion of right interpretation. Anything that damages the story of redemption through the Word incarnate is erroneous and wicked, and any interpretation that projects human limitations onto God is heresy. There is a circularity, as we have seen, but for Athanasius this is the inevitable circularity of biblical interpretation. We study Scripture to know God; as we come to know him, Scripture is illumined, so that we might study it further to know God yet more deeply.

Conclusion

One final crucial element of Athanasian hermeneutics: it is situated, always, in the church, and that means that it is always embattled. All his biblical interpretation was directed toward edification of the people he oversaw as bishop or to win his battles with the Arians and other threats to the gospel. Athanasius considered his biblical work to be a part of a spiritual warfare, not just against the Arians but against the spiritual forces that, in his mind, inspired their heresies. The devil impersonates the name of God now, just as he did in Eden.

Our adversary the devil, envying us the possession of such great blessings, goes about seeking to snatch away the seed of the word which is sown within us. Wherefore as if by His prophetic warnings He would seal up His instructions in our hearts as His own peculiar treasure, the Lord said, "Take heed that no man deceive you: for many shall come in My name, saying, I am he; and the time draws near; and they shall deceive many: go ye not therefore after them" (Luke 21:8). This is a great gift which the Word has bestowed upon us, that we should not be deceived by appearances, but that, howsoever these things are concealed, we should all the more distinguish them by the grace of the Spirit. For whereas the inventor of wickedness and great spirit of evil, the devil, is utterly hateful, and as soon as he shows himself is rejected of all men—as a serpent, as a dragon, as a lion seeking whom he may seize upon and devour—therefore he conceals and covers what he really is, and craftily personates that Name which all men desire, so that deceiving by a false appearance, he may thenceforth fix fast in his own chains those whom he has led astray. And as if one that desired to kidnap the children of others during the absence of their parents, should personate their appearance, and so putting a cheat on the affections of the offspring, should carry them far away and destroy them; in like manner this evil and wily spirit the devil, having no confidence in himself, and knowing the love which men bear to the truth, personates its appearance, and so spreads his own poison among those that follow after him. (*Bishops of Egypt* 1.1)

This demonology is only half of the Athanasian hermeneutics of spiritual warfare. As we have already seen, for Athanasius, the overarching aim of understanding and teaching Scripture is to honor God. Any interpretation that insults God, as the Arian interpretations of Scripture do, cannot be true. Arian blasphemies are often implicit. To claim that the Triad is not eternal insults the Son and thus insults the Father as well (*Discourses* 1.18). It is likewise an insult—and not, importantly, merely illogical—to call the Father a fountain but then to deny that he flows with eternal wisdom; that insults him as "barren and void of His proper Wisdom" (*Discourses* 1.19). The Arians assume God is weak. He needs the Son, and the Son is not proper to him. The question is "whether He who was needed was one who was not for the framing of the universe, or one who was? You said that He made for Himself His Son out of nothing, as an instrument whereby to make the universe. Which then is superior, that which needs or that which supplies the need? Or does not each supply the deficiency of the other? You rather prove the weakness of the Maker, if He had not power of Himself to make the universe" (*Discourses* 1.26). How dare the Arians speak of the Father, the light, the fountain, the beginning of all, as weak? How dare they?

Once again, it is all about Christ, but not merely about contemplating Christ as the hero of the biblical narrative or appealing to Christ as the standard of correct interpretation. The interpreter does not view Christ from a distance but participates in him and his work. Through the cross, Jesus triumphed over demons, and through his Spirit, he gives his deified "brothers" a share in that triumph. Death and fear of death are trampled down by his one death, and we are made new by his resurrection. As Athanasius studied Scripture, expounded its truth against the falsehoods of heretics, and refuted what he saw as devilish distortions of Scripture, he believed he was sharing in that triumph.

3
The One God

Rahner and His Rule

Since Karl Rahner's little treatise on the Trinity, Catholic and Protestant theology have both witnessed a resurgence of trinitarian reflection.[1] Theologians have been busy attempting to redress the flaw in theology proper that Rahner identifies in medieval and modern trinitarian theology, the separation of the "philosophical" treatise on the one God from the "theological" treatise on the Trinity, a separation that Rahner claims became standard in theology sometime between Peter Lombard's *Sentences* and Thomas Aquinas's *Summa Theologiae*. Rahner's famous axiom that "the 'economic' Trinity is the 'immanent' Trinity and the 'immanent' Trinity is the 'economic' Trinity" has, however, given this trinitarian resurgence a particular shape.[2] Guided by "Rahner's rule," theologians have eschewed the "abstractions" of scholastic trinitarian theology and given attention to the historical particularities of the gospel story.[3] The trinitarian revival has been a fundamentally *evangelical*, that is, a gospel-centered, revival.

Though widely accepted, Rahner's axiom has proved ambiguous and controversial. It is, as David Bentley Hart has argued, subject to two opposite temptations. One is the danger of forsaking "the economic for the immanent Trinity, by allowing some far too thoroughly developed speculative account of the Trinity to determine what in the story of Christ's relation to the Father and the Spirit is or is not genuinely revelation, genuinely Trinitarian." Taken correctly, Hart argues, Rahner's rule means that "nothing can be assumed to be *merely* economic,"[4] and this implies that there can be no final closure in our doctrine of God that would encompass and simplify the story of Jesus.

More commonly in recent theology, Rahner's rule serves as the basis for a collapse of the immanent or ontological Trinity into the economic, producing a theological Hegelianism that obliterates any distinction of history and theology, any distinction between who God is and what God has done. God becomes locked into interdependence with creation, and if this is so, Hart argues, Christian faith becomes another story of necessity.[5] Christianity confesses, however, that God has no need of his creation and need not be our God, because "all we are, all we can ever become, is already infinitely and fully present in the inexhaustible beauty, liveliness, and 'virtue' of the Logos." God loved and knew us before we were; he loved and knew us, as he now loves and knows us, in the Son. This "freedom of God from ontic determination" is not a piece of hellenizing, but the basis for creation's goodness and beauty: "Precisely because creation is needless, an object of delight that shares God's love without contributing anything that God does not already possess in infinite eminence, creation reflects the divine life, which is one of delight and fellowship." In short, "in being the object of God's love without any cause but the generosity of that love, creation reflects in its beauty that eternal delight that is the divine perichoresis and that obeys no necessity but divine love itself." Hart points out that the misreading of Rahner's rule also damages the infinity of God, and specifically suggests that, on this erroneous understanding of Rahner, God's will is viewed as being other than his being, as is the case with the wills of finite beings. Since God is infinite, will and being are one, and thus his will to create manifests his being, his beauty. To make God dependent on the creation undermines the Christian doctrine of God; but, equally, to make God dependent on the creation damages the Christian doctrine of creation. Hart notes that in some cases the desire for a suffering God is a desire to escape God as judge by making him co-sufferer.[6] We may be sinners, sure, but God does after all sympathize, and he affirms that we too have a valid perspective, one that God should and does acknowledge.

Hegelianized theology presents itself as an effort to weed Hellenistic metaphysics out of the biblical idea of a narrated God who reveals himself in history, including the history of the cross. Hart argues, though, that the Christian narrative arises precisely from the double affirmation of divine *apatheia* and the story of the cross; if the cross is some necessary stage in God's self-realization, it is not an act of utter and bottomless grace.[7] Further, contrary to intentions, a God who suffers with us becomes "the metaphysical ground of Auschwitz."[8] For if God realizes his identity by identification with our suffering, suffering itself becomes necessary. The problems of collapsing the ontological into the economic are, finally, moral as much as they are metaphysical.[9]

Rahner's work has also been one of the inspirations behind the effort to develop a de-hellenized trinitarianism,[10] often elaborated in a "social trinitarian" direction. According to social trinitarians, "Christians should not imagine God on the model of some individual person or thing which has three sides, aspects, dimensions, or modes of being; God is instead to be thought of as a collective, a group, or a society, bound together by mutual love, accord and self-giving of its members."[11] Social trinitarians are typically quite happy to employ the word "person" to describe the Father, Son, and Spirit, and though acknowledging that the word is not used univocally of God and human beings, they typically find significant continuity between the theological and the anthropological uses. The problem with the modern idea of "person" is its individualism, which social trinitarians are eager to challenge. Once shorn of its modernist individualism, the term "person," applied to God or humans, is legitimate, and in both cases refers to a distinct center of self-consciousness and a being that is inherently relational. Because God is exhaustively person, his life is exhaustively communal. For God, being is communal.

The challenge for social trinitarians is to demonstrate that their theology is in fact a form of monotheism. How can God be one God if Father, Son, and Spirit are all "distinct centers of consciousness"? Some social trinitarians flirt with tritheism, and some go so far as to tumble happily into bed with tritheists. Most attempt to protect against tritheism by an emphasis on perichoresis, the unity of the three persons arising from their exhaustive mutual relationality.[12]

Rahner himself never comes close to flirting with social trinitarianism. Like Karl Barth, he suspects that the modern concept of "person" is so corrupted that it is beyond recovery for trinitarian theology. Also similar to Barth, he prefers to use the phrase "distinct ways of subsisting," and he makes clear that in the Trinity there are not "several spiritual centers of activity" or "several subjectivities and liberties." This is so because "there is only *one* essence, hence *one* absolute self-presence," and also because there is "only *one* self-utterance of the Father, the Logos":

> The Logos is not the one who utters, but the one who is uttered. And there is properly no mutual love between Father and Son, for this would presuppose two acts. But there is loving self-acceptance of the Father (and of the Son, because of the *taxis* of knowledge and love), and this self-acceptance gives rise to the distinction. Of course, that which we call "three persons in God" exists in God with self-awareness. . . . But there are not three consciousnesses; rather, the one consciousness subsists in a threefold way. There is only one real consciousness in God, which is shared by Father, Son, and Spirit, by each in his own proper way.[13]

Whatever Rahner means by stressing the identity of the immanent and economic, he does not mean that we can simply "read off" the immanent relations from the economic, for in the economy the love of the Father and Son is evidently mutual, reciprocal, responsive.

What Rahner does want to emphasize is the incarnation. His general axiom, he claims, could be justified by reference to a "defined doctrine of the faith," namely, in the fact that "the second divine person, God's Logos, is man, and only he is man." In the incarnation "something occurs 'outside' the intra-divine life in the world itself, something which is not a mere effect of the efficient causality of the triune God acting as one in the world, but something which belongs to the Logos alone, which is the history of one divine person, in contrast to other divine persons." To be sure, the union of the Logos and flesh is "causally effected by the whole Trinity,"[14] the Father sending and the Spirit as the agent of the Son's human conception, yet it still belongs alone to the Son to be incarnate. To put it in dogmatic/systematic categories, Rahner is attempting to unite theology proper with Christology, to ensure that Christology is not an added extra to the doctrine of God but rather at its center.

Patristic Trinitarian Theology

"Reunite" would be more accurate, for in pushing Christology and theology proper together, Rahner is pushing theology back toward the patristic mode of trinitarian reflection. John Behr has recently argued that Nicene theology is not "trinitarian theology" in the sense that later theology understands it. In its later "textbook form," trinitarian theology begins with "what can be known and said of this God; that he is one, the uncreated origin of all creation, love, goodness and so on; and then proceeds to analyze how this same God is three—how the persons of the Trinity are related, their different characteristics and relationships." Once the "immanent Trinity" is in place, "the next step is to relate this Trinity to the activity of revelation, the economy of salvation recorded in Scripture, the 'economic' dimension of Trinitarian theology." Trinity is thus made into a "realm unto itself," supplemented by reflection on the person and work of Christ, with the result that Christian faith is understood as fundamentally "trinitarian" and "incarnational."[15]

This has the unfortunate effect of detaching Nicene theology from its roots in biblical exegesis, of separating the interests of the apostles from those of the fathers, of encouraging the myth of hellenization, and of making it difficult to see how the Trinity is found in Scripture, "except by a forced exegesis." Behr affirms that "the Christian faith is intrinsically Trinitarian" but suggests that this is only evident when the gospel is put at the heart of theological reflection: "The basic proclamation of Christianity, that Jesus is Lord, the one of whom the Spirit spoke through the prophets, makes necessary a confession of faith in the Trinity." The apostles

> were concerned to explain, through the medium of Scripture, how the Lord Jesus relates to the one God, his Father, in the Spirit. This basic scriptural grammar of Trinitarian theology—that the one God, the God of Abraham, Isaac, and Jacob, is the Father of the Lord Jesus Christ, the Son of God, made known in and through the Spirit—is preserved in the most abstract discussions of the fourth century, in the creeds of Nicaea and Constantinople, and in liturgical language.[16]

What Behr claims about patristic trinitarian reflection is particularly true of Athanasius. Athanasius does not run afoul of Rahner's complaint about the division of the doctrine of God into a treatise on "the One God" and a treatise "on the Trinity." For Athanasius, to speak of God is to speak of the Triad. He knows no other God and cannot conceive of another way of speaking about God.

He is surely no social trinitarian. Throughout his writings, Athanasius sees this elaboration as simply an elaboration of monotheism. God is one as Trinity. He insists that "God is One and Only and First," and yet insists at the same time that this is not said to the denigration of the Son. The Son too is "in that One, and First and Only, as being of that One and Only and First the Only Word and Wisdom and Radiance. And He too is the First, as the Fullness of the Godhead of the First and Only [*plērōma tēs tou prōtou kai monou theotētos*], being whole and full God. This then is not said on His account, but to deny that there is other such as the Father and His Word" (*Discourses* 3.6). When Scripture affirms that God is one, it is not a denial of the Triad within God but rather a statement about the true God and a condemnation of all false gods. Since the Son is himself the truth, the Son is not excluded along with idols. When the Scripture records the Lord's "I only," it includes the Son (*en tō monō kai ho tou monou semainetai logos*; *Discourses* 3.9). Jesus's claim that "I and the Father are One" (John 17) asserts that the Son is "proper and like the Father's essence"; the Son is not "foreign" to the essence but of the same essence with the Father (*Discourses* 3.17).

In much of the later tradition, especially post-Reformation, the doctrine of the Trinity was defended by establishing the deity of each person individually. If Scripture teaches that the Father is God, and the Son is God, and the Spirit is God, then there are three subsistences or persons in the one God. As Behr indicates, Athanasius goes about things quite differently. He does not formulate a general "immanent trinitarian theology" that is then "applied" to the economy. His reflections on the intimate relations of the immanent Trinity all arise from the confession that Jesus is the eternal Word of the Father. It is possible to isolate a "patrology" or a "Christology" within Athanasius's writings, and that is what I have done in the following pages. But that is something of a distortion of Athanasius's own approach, just as it is a distortion to separate Athanasius's teaching on God from his teaching about God's works in creating and, especially, in redeeming humanity. For Athanasius, meditating on the Father, on Christ, on incarnation, on deification (discussed in more detail in chapter 6) is meditation on one reality.

The density of Athanasius's treatment of these themes is nicely captured by his paraphrase of Jesus's prayer in John 17. Jesus asks his Father, in effect, "Whence is this their perfecting, but that I, Your Word, having borne their body, and become man, have perfected the work, which You gave Me, O Father?" and answers that "the work is perfected, because men, redeemed from sin, no longer remain dead; but being deified, have in each other, by looking at Me, the bond of charity" (*Discourses* 3.23). According to Athanasius, Jesus speaks his work of perfecting, *telos*-ing, humanity so that humanity reaches its destined end. He "completes" the work and in so doing "completes" his disciples. This perfection is linked with redemption from sin and death, but also to deification. Man, made in the image of God, was created to become more godlike, and the contingency of sin and death does not cause God to deviate from that purpose. Deification is closely connected with resurrection, overcoming death. God cannot die, by nature, and, in part, our deification is a participation by grace in the immortality he has by nature.

This perfecting of the human race, though, depends on the incarnation. It is because the Word has borne the body and become man that he can perfect men. He became incarnate to die in the flesh, to overcome death, to grant human beings a share in his own power and wisdom and knowledge and deathless joy. Through the Son, especially in the Son's unity with the Father, believers have a paradigm of charity. And not merely a paradigm: it is axiomatic for Athanasius that the contemplative gaze is a transforming gaze. When Jesus says that his disciples will live "by looking at Me," he is not speaking of examining a model, to which one then strives to conform. Conformity comes through the transforming impact of the gaze itself. By looking at Jesus, contemplating his unity with the Father, disciples are bound in charity with one another. When we gaze at the archetype, the archetype impresses himself on us.

And this, finally, as always, takes us back to the Arians. This entire passage is embedded within an anti-Arian polemic, and the whole point is that the Son is eternal Son, equal to the Father. Arians do not contemplate the Son in unity with the Father but profess a false Son who is alien to the Father. Their christological heresy thus cannot be anything but schismatic, since they cannot be transformed and bound in proper charity by contemplation of the Son who is proper to the Father's essence. Their christological heresy must also fail eschatologically: since the end of humanity is deification, and the Arians lack any "mechanism" for deification, their God cannot bestow this perfecting gift.

That is how Athanasius writes: Father-Son, incarnate Son, common communal perfection and deification in the church, transformation into the image of the Son through contemplation of the Son, and all this packed into a brief bit of anti-Arian polemic. Athanasius cannot speak of the Father without immediately speaking of the Son, nor of the Son without the Father. He cannot speak of the Son without also noting that the Son is the one who became incarnate and the one through whom we are knit into the life of the Trinity. Given the density and interconnectedness of these themes, the best option might be to offer a series of commentaries on entire treatises of Athanasius.[17] I have chosen instead to lay out Athanasius's theology of God, creation, the incarnation, and redemption in separate chapters, in the hope that this more "systematic" arrangement will simplify and clarify his thought somewhat. Throughout, however, I have tried to make it plain that these cannot really be separated, or even neatly distinguished.[18]

Always Father

Arianism is a heresy about the Son, but Athanasius recognizes that it is equally about the Father. He takes Jesus's words quite literally: "He who does not honor the Son does not honor the Father who sent Him" (John 5:23). In dishonoring the Son, the Arians also do injustice to the Father. As Peter Widdicombe points out, "The denial of the eternal fatherhood of God is the first of the heretical doctrines with which Athanasius charges his Arian opponents." They believe, by Athanasius's account, that "God was not eternally Father," and that "God was not always Father, but became so later," and they say both "not eternal Father" and "not eternal Son." Because the Son did not always exist, "God was not always Father" (*ouk aei ho theos patēr ēn*).[19]

According to Athanasius, God is eternally and essentially Father because the Father eternally has the Son, but this is not because the Father lacks anything. The Father is fullness and perfect (*plērēs* and *teleios*) in himself. Refuting Arian distortions of Jesus's statement, "I in the Father and the Father in me" (John 14:10), Athanasius argues that if Arians knew God "they would not dishonor and ridicule the Lord of glory, nor interpreting things immaterial after a material manner, pervert good words." Piety demands that "on hearing only words which are the Lord's, at once to believe, since the faith of simplicity is better than an elaborate process of persuasion." Jesus's statement does not imply that Father and Son are "discharged into Each Other, filling the One from the Other, as in the case of empty vessels, so that the Son fills the emptiness of the Father and the Father that of the Son." That too is an insult to both. On Arian premises, "each of Them by Himself is not complete and perfect (for this is proper to bodies, and therefore the mere assertion of it is full of irreligion), for the Father is full and perfect, and the Son is the Fullness of Godhead" (*Discourses* 3.1).

This is a central anti-Arian argument. If the Arians deny the eternity of the Son, then they should likewise deny that the Father is eternally Father. Athanasius draws an ontological conclusion from the terminology of Scripture concerning Father and Son:

> For the Son is such as the Father is, because He has all that is the Father's. Wherefore also is He implied together with the Father. For, a son not being, one cannot say father; whereas when we call God a Maker, we do not of necessity intimate the things which have come to be; for a maker is before his works. But when we call God Father, at once with the Father we signify the Son's existence. Therefore he who believes in the Son, believes also in the Father: for he believes

in what is proper to the Father's Essence; and thus the faith is one in one God. (*Discourses* 3.6)

What was God before becoming the Father of the Son? As we have noted, for the Arians, God is most basically not Father but "Unoriginate." Athanasius objects to the term "Unoriginate" as a name for the Father because it links the Father's eternal being to the creation. "Unoriginate" names the Father by contrast with the originated things of creation, rather than with the Son, who is his eternal essence. God's fundamental name, then, on Arian premises, is dependent on the creation. That too is an insult to the Father, who is not in need of the creation nor defined by it. "If," Athanasius argues, "this term is not used in contrast with the Son . . . but with things originated," then the same can be said of terms like "Almighty" and "Lord of the Powers." But Scripture teaches that "the Father has power and mastery over all things by the Word, and the Son rules the Father's kingdom, and has the power of all, as His Word, and as the Image of the Father," and so "it is quite plain that neither here is the Son reckoned among that all, nor is God called Almighty and Lord with reference to Him, but to those things which through the Son come to be, and over which He exercises power and mastery through the Word." Thus "the Unoriginate is specified not by contrast to the Son, but to the things which through the Son come to be" (*Discourses* 1.33).

The name "Father," though, implies a different contrasting pole. It is a relational term, but a term that names God in relation to the Son and not to creation: "As the word 'Unoriginate' is specified relatively to things originated, so the word 'Father' is indicative of the Son," so that "he who names God Maker and Framer and Unoriginate, regards and apprehends things created and made; and he who calls God Father, thereby conceives and contemplates the Son." Again, the Arians are guilty of insulting the Father. Athanasius repeats Jesus's claim that those who dishonor the Son also dishonor the Father (John 5:23), and he adds, "If they had any concern at all for reverent speaking and the honor due to the Father, it became them rather, and this were better and higher, to acknowledge and call God Father, than to give Him this name." Since they name God from his works and not from his eternal Son, they are in no better position than the "Greeks," who know God only from the creation. They are stuck with the limited revelation of God in creation, a revelation that can only condemn. If they want to know the Father as Father, they must know him as Father of the Son: "They, when they call Him Unoriginate, name Him only from His works, and know not the Son any more than the Greeks; but he who calls God Father, names Him from the Word; and knowing the Word, he acknowledges Him to be Framer of all, and understands that through Him all things have been made" (*Discourses* 1.33). Though the Father is in fact "Unoriginate," the biblical name "Father" is "more pious and more accurate," since it names the Father by reference to his Word.

The debate over the use of "Unoriginate" is more intricate than the English translations would make it appear. In Greek, the terms "Unbegotten" and "Unoriginate" differ in only one letter. Unbegotten is *agennētos* and Unoriginate is *agenētos*. For earlier theologians like Eusebius of Caesarea, the two terms are for all practical purposes synonymous. Thus, to say that God is "Unoriginate" is also to say that he is "Unbegotten." Athanasius, however, distinguishes the two, applying "Unoriginate" in somewhat different senses to both the Father and the Son, but applying the term "Unbegotten" only to the Father. The result is that, for Athanasius, it is possible for there to be a "Begotten God."[20] Edward Gibbon claimed that in the fourth century Christians went to war over the "iota" that divided *homoousios* from *homoiousios*.[21] But that is only part of the story: they were debating about a "double nu" as well.

All that is said of the Father may be said of the Son, and vice versa, except that the Son is Son and the Father is Father. Because the Godhead (*theotēs*) of the two is a single Godhead, God is one: "The Godhead of the Son is the Father's; whence also it is indivisible; and thus there is one God and none other but He. And so, since they are one, and the Godhead itself one, the same things are said of the Son, which are said of the Father, except His being said to be Father" (*Discourses* 3.4).

Athanasius considers it an insult to the Father to say that he is without his Son. Denying the Son involves denial of the Father because it involves denying the Father's fatherhood. Athanasius finds further problems in the Arian account of how the Son created the world. Some Arians suggest that the Son might have learned to be *dēmiourgos*, or framer, of the world from the Father. The Father has this power of framing the world in himself and does not need anything, certainly not an assistant. When the Father determines to create, however, then he also wills to beget the Son as his *dēmiourgos*. To Athanasius, this leaves the Arians in a dilemma. If the power to create can be learned, it might be unlearned, and if the Son can learn and unlearn this skill in creating, might the Father not also lose the power to create? Did the Father too learn wisdom? (*Discourses* 2.28).

The Arian position also insults the Father by implying that he is selfish with his gifts. If the power to create can be taught to creatures, why did the Father not bestow this power on all his creatures? Why limit it to the Son? If the Arians take the latter course, they imply that the Father is jealous of his own abilities and refuses to share them broadly. He keeps his gifts close to himself. If creative power can be taught, then the Arians "are ascribing jealousy and weakness to God—jealousy, in that He has not taught many how to frame, so that there may be around Him, as Archangels and Angels many, so framers many." On the other hand, the Arian position might imply that the Father is weak, "in that He could not make by Himself, but needed a fellow-worker, or under-worker." God is neither jealous nor deficient: "Perish the thought! For He has said Himself, 'I am full'" (*Discourses* 2.29).

Eternal Son

If most of Athanasius's "patrology" is simultaneously a Christology, the same, *mutatis mutandis*, goes for the Christology. The Word must be eternal Word, or else the Father is "speechless"; the Wisdom must be eternal, or else the Father is a fool who becomes wise; the Son must be eternal and proper to the Father's essence, or else the Father is incomplete.

Athanasius builds up to these conclusions by offering a metaphysical distinction between the manner of the Son's relation to the Father and the manner of creation's relation to the Father. Created things participate (*metechein*, *metochē*) in God, or they would not exist at all, but created things are still external (*exōthen*) to the Father. But what does participation mean for Athanasius?[22]

Participation in general means receiving a share in something and originally referred to the common share that two similar things have in the eternal Platonic form of those things. Two similar couches share in the eternal form of the couch, and thus the two couches are said to "participate" in the form. If Alexander and Athanasius are both wise, they are wise because they both participate in, to a greater or lesser degree, the eternal form of Wisdom. Participant things have a real but derived and partial "possession" of what they participate in. Participation can take several different forms or exist in several different modes. Participation can be linked with being, as two human beings share in the same human nature. It can also be a participation by will, as when two rational beings share in a common purpose, or a participation by grace.

For Athanasius, participation has a number of additional implications. Participation always involves a share in something external. Participation and externality go together; the participated (original) and the participant (i.e., the derived) are divided from each other and are usually divided ontologically. That which participates and that which is participated are not just different beings but different sorts of beings. Athanasius does little with the Platonic doctrine of ideas and makes little use of the technicalities of the modified Platonisms with which he was glancingly familiar. But he uses the concept from Plato and plugs it into a biblical worldview, that is, a worldview that distinguishes Creator and creature. In place of participated forms, then, Athanasius has a Creator. Creatures exist by participation in God because creation is not part of God's existence nor internal to him.

For Athanasius, too, participation implies dependence. Creation is by participation because it is dependent for its life, stability, and existence on power and energy that is not inherent in the creation itself. It exists only by a continuous gift of life and stability from the Triune God. For Athanasius, to speak of participation is to speak of creaturehood, contingency, and dependence, but also of grace, the gracious provision of existence out of nothing. To speak of participation is, in Athanasius's sense, to give a philosophical term to the reality that Paul (citing Greek thinkers) affirms: "In Him we live and move and exist" (Acts 17:28).

That is not how the Son relates to the Father. The Son does not participate in the Father in the way that creatures do, externally and dependently. What then is the Son's relation to the Father? Athanasius has two ways of answering. On the one hand, he frequently speaks of the Son as "proper" (*idios*) to the Father's essence, while on the other hand he makes the same claim by using the notion of "whole participation."[23] In both formulations, the Son is viewed as being internal and inherent to the Father's essence, rather than external to it. Even when the Son is said to be a "partaker" of the Father, participating in him, this is not participation in the same sense that creatures participate. The Son is "wholly participant" in the Father:

> It is the Father that He partakes; for this only remains to say. But this, which is participated, what is it or whence? If it be something external provided by the Father, He will not now be partaker of the Father, but of what is external to Him; and no longer will He be even second after the Father, since He has before Him this other; nor can He be called Son of the Father, but of that, as partaking which He has been called Son and God. And if this be unseemly and irreligious, when the Father says, "This is My Beloved Son" (Matt. 3:17), and when the Son says that God is His own Father, it follows that what is partaken is not external, but from the essence of the Father. And as to this again, if it be other than the essence of the Son, an equal extravagance will meet us; there being in that case something between this that is from the Father and the essence of the Son, whatever that be. (*Discourses* 1.15)

Further, "such thoughts then being evidently unseemly and untrue, we are driven to say that what is from the essence of the Father, and proper to Him, is entirely the Son; for it is all one to say that God is wholly participated, and that He begets; and what does begetting signify but a Son?" (*Discourses* 1.16).

In this, Athanasius makes the somewhat stronger claim that the Son is not only wholly participant in the Father, but that he *is* what is participant in the Father. That which participates in the Father simply *is* the Son: "The Son Himself partakes of nothing, but what is partaken from the Father, is the Son; for, as partaking of the Son Himself, we are said to partake of God; and this is what Peter said 'that you may be partakers in a divine nature'" (*Discourses* 1.16). Only in this way can the Father see himself in his Son, and only in this way can the Son reveal the Father to us: "If the Son be not all this, but, as the Arians consider, originate, and not eternal, this is not a true Image of the Father, unless indeed they give up shame, and go on to say, that the title of Image, given to the Son, is not a token of a similar essence, but His name only" (*Discourses* 1.21).

His more characteristic way of describing the relation is with the term *idios*, "proper," which, as we shall see, is crucial to Athanasius's theology. It functions as a descriptor not only of the relation of Father and Son but also of the relation of the Son to his appropriated (*idiopoieisthai*) body. The concept also plays a role in his account of deification. The force of the term is evident when Athanasius uses it with reference to God's "attributes." God is "properly"—in himself and not by participation or derivation—one, simple, good, love. Created beings too have their "properties" proper to them: we are instable, corruptible, bodily. When Athanasius uses the term "proper" to describe the relation of the Father to his Son and Spirit, he is stressing "that the Son and Spirit are as closely related to the Father as characteristics are to their natural subjects, as radiance to light, and streams to fountains." Son and Spirit are *not* characteristics but are the Father's Word and Spirit. Yet they are as essential to the being of God, to the being of the *Father*, as any of the Father's divine attributes.[24]

The biblical description of the Son being "in" the Father is a pointer to the fact that the Son is "proper" (*idios*) to the Father's essence. Arians do not believe that the Son is a "genuine Son from the Father," and thus "they belie Him who is such, whom alone it befits to say, 'I in the Father and the Father in Me.'" That "in" points to the inseparability of the Father and the Son. The fact that the Son is in the Father means that "the whole Being of the Son is proper to the Father's essence, as radiance from light, and stream from fountain; so that whoso sees the Son, sees what is proper to the Father, and knows that the Son's Being, because from the Father, is therefore in the Father" (*Discourses* 3.3).

It is true that believers are also "in" the Father through the Son, but Athanasius argues that our manner of dwelling-in differs from the manner of the Son's indwelling of the Father. John 17:21, which draws the analogy between the way we are "in" the Father and the way the Son is, also distinguishes the two. Jesus says simply that he is in the Father, but when he speaks of believers, he says that they are "in us." In saying this, "He has pointed out the distance and difference; that He indeed is alone in the Father alone, as Only Word and Wisdom; but we in the Son, and through Him in the Father." Jesus was saying that "by Our unity may they also be so one with each other, as We are one in nature and truth; for otherwise they could not be one, except by learning unity in Us" (*Discourses* 3.21).

While the Son and the saints are both "in" the Father, the Creator-creature distinction runs between the two. This means, in Athanasius's terminology, the distinction of grace and nature runs between the two (see chapter 4, below). Believers are in the Father by grace, while the Son is Son by nature. "Since the Word is in the Father, and the Spirit is given from the Word," he argues, "He wills that we should receive the Spirit, that, when we receive It, thus having the Spirit of the Word which is in the Father, we too may be found on account of the Spirit to become One in the Word, and through Him in the Father." There is a comparative "as" involved. The disciples are to be united "as" the Father and the Son are united; the disciples are to be one "as" Father and Son are one. But this is "only a request that such grace of the Spirit as is given to the disciples may be without failure or revocation." Athanasius explains: "What the Word has by nature . . . in the Father, . . . He wishes to be given to us through the Spirit irrevocably." The permanence of this grace is dependent on the work of the Spirit and is not rooted in anything in ourselves: "It is the Spirit then which is in God, and not we viewed in our own selves; and as we are sons and gods because of the Word in us, so we shall be in the Son and in the Father, and we shall be accounted to have become one in Son and in Father, because that Spirit is in us, which is in the Word which is in the Father" (*Discourses* 3.25). The distance between the Son and his people is overcome by the grace of the Spirit: "Because of the grace of the Spirit which has been given to us, in him we come to be, and he in us; and since it is the Spirit of God, therefore through his becoming in us, reasonably are we, as having the Spirit, considered to be in God, and thus is God in us" (*Discourses* 3.24).

Some Arians respond to this argument by positing a Word and a Wisdom that *is* inherent in the Father, "proper" to his essence and yet not identical to the Son. There is a Word and Wisdom that is the Father's own and, given the simplicity of God, in no way different from the Father himself. This is the Wisdom and Word by which the Son is generated. Athanasius finds this doubling of Wisdom and Word incoherent. This reduces the Son, the Word of the Father, to one among many (*Discourses* 3.2). This pluralization of the Son is inherent in the Arian claim that the Son is a creature. Participant beings are multiple; a begotten Son inherent in the Father's nature is a single Son, the unique and utterly final Word of the Father. Creatures become "sons," not *the* Son. They are "gods" (Ps. 82:6), not God as the Father is God. When human beings become one as the Father and the Son are one, "we shall be such, not as the Father is by nature in the Son and the Son in the Father, but according to our own nature, and as it is possible for us thence to be molded and to learn how we ought to be one, just as we learned also to be merciful." Everything from flesh shares a natural likeness, since "like things are naturally one with like," but the Son and Word of the Father is of a different character, "unlike us and like the Father." Though "He is in nature and truth one with His own Father, we, as being of one kind with each other (for from one were all made, and one is the nature of all men), become one with each other in good disposition, having as our copy the Son's natural unity with the Father" (*Discourses* 3.20). God's Word is one, single, final. Our words are fragmentary, partial, temporary, and therefore multiple. We can never say the final word. Because God is beyond this temporal fragmentation, his Word is stable, single, final (*Discourses* 2.36).

In other contexts, Athanasius makes the same point by distinguishing between begetting and making. In part, his arguments demonstrate how the Arian position ends in contradiction, both of itself and of Scripture. If the Son is a work, then the Son must come under judgment, since all works come under judgment (Eccles. 12:14). But the Son is the judge, and how can the judge be judged (*Discourses* 2.3)? If the Son is a creature, then there is an interval between the Father and the Son, an interval that must be temporal. But the nature of the interval does not really matter. The Arian position implies space and distance between Father and Son, but Scripture says that the Son is the one who made "the world [*aiōnas*, ages]" (Heb. 1:1–3). He is the Lord of intervals, the measure of all temporal and spatial distance. How, then, can an interval exist before he exists (*Discourses* 2.58)? He is the measure of all things, the standard by which all ratios are measured: how can there be something measurable before he is?

The Arian claim that he is a "creature but not as one of the creatures" is simply a smoke screen and an evasion. All creatures differ from other creatures, so "difference" is no mark of the Son's uniqueness. Quite the opposite: since all creatures differ, the fact that a created Son differs from other creatures is a mark of his sameness with other creatures (*Discourses* 2.19). If the Son is a creature, then the Arians should have the courage of their convictions and admit that the Son is in the same condition (*tēn autēn homologeisthō taxin echein*) as every other creature (*Discourses* 2.20).

Reasoning from the paradigm of sonship, Athanasius argues that sons are born of the nature and essence of their fathers, not made from external material. So too with divine sonship. As we saw in chapter 2, Arians emphasize the temporal priority of parents over children, but Athanasius stresses the community of essence. "Those who ask of parents, and say, 'Had you a son before you begot him?' should add, 'And if you had a son, did you purchase him from without as a house or any other possession?' And then you would be answered, 'He is not from without, but from myself.'" There is a difference between possessions and children. "Things which are from without are possessions, and pass from one to another; but my son is from me, proper and similar to my essence, not become mine from another, but begotten of me." Human sonship is a perichoretic reality and a paradigm of divine life. A human father can say, "I too am wholly in him, while I remain myself what I am," and the same applies to the Father with his Son. Thus, "though the parent be distinct in time, as being man, who himself has come to be in time, yet he too would have had his child ever coexistent with him, but that his nature was a restraint and made it impossible" (*Discourses* 1.26). There certainly are discontinuities between divine and human begetting, but there is also analogy: "Granting the parent had not a son before his begetting, still, after having him, he had him, not as external or as foreign, but as from himself, and proper to his essence and his exact image, so that the former is beheld in the latter, and the latter is contemplated in the former" (*Discourses* 1.26).

In other words, the Son is Son by nature and not by will (*Discourses* 3.59–60).[25] The Son cannot be made by will because he himself *is* the good pleasure and will of the Father. "If," Athanasius argues, "in whom He makes, in Him also is the will, and in Christ is the pleasure of the Father, how can He, as others, come into being by will and pleasure?" Again the Arian position implies temporality and change in God. If the Son was not before he was begotten, and if, as Athanasius argues, this can only be understood as a temporal statement, then God willed and determined to beget and to create before the Son was. That is nonsense, since the Son is the Word, and how can God deliberate about anything when he is yet wordless? As Athanasius puts it, planning

> goes before things which once were not, as in the case of all creatures. But if the Word is the Framer of the creatures, and he coexists with the Father, how can his counsel precede the Everlasting as if he were not? For if counsel precedes, how through him are all things? For rather he too, as one among others is by will begotten to be a Son, as we too were made sons by the Word of Truth; and it rests, as was said, to seek another Word, through whom he too has come to be, and was begotten together with all things, which were according to God's pleasure. (*Discourses* 3.61)

Since everything is done by the counsel of the Father with his will, there can be no counsel except the Son. The Son is the "living counsel" of the Father, as well as "power, and Framer of the things which seemed good to the Father." The Son is the "good pleasure of the Father" (*Discourses* 3.63) and the "living will" (*zōsa boulē*) of the Father (*Discourses* 2.2). The Son is not made by the good pleasure of God but is the "object of the Father's pleasure," just as surely as the Father is the "object of the Son's love, pleasure, and honor" (*Discourses* 3.66). Athanasius defends this conclusion by appeal to some of his standard texts: Proverbs 8:24; 1 Corinthians 1:24; Isaiah 9:6.

In saying that the Son is not Son by will, Athanasius is not arguing that the Father involuntarily begets the Son. The Father does not beget the Son *against* his will, since the Son is the Son of his good pleasure. Athanasius's point is that will is not the same in God as it is in human existence. Or, to put it differently, will and being are identical in God. God wills to be what he is, and he is what he wills. As Rowan Williams points out, Athanasius is insisting that the whole "anthropomorphic model of 'deliberation'" fails when considering God's existence and will. We ought not think that God, after due consideration, determines to be Trinity today and might determine to be something else another day, nor even that he determines, after deliberation, that he will be Trinity from ages to ages. "What sense does it make to say that God 'decides' to be what he is? Yet it is part of the definition of God that no other reality *makes* him what he is, no necessity is imposed on him. The human antitheses between purposeless and purposive (deliberative) action and between my choice and what is imposed on me from outside cannot apply to God. He does not *decide* to be good; yet he is consciously and purposively good, and no external force compels him to be so."[26] The Word is the will of the Father and thus cannot be the product of will, unless we are willing to multiply wills.

Athanasius also frequently reasons from the biblical names of the Second Person as "Word" and "Wisdom." As we noted in the previous chapter, Athanasius uses the different titles of the Second Person to highlight different aspects of his relation to the Father. The paradigms are mutually qualifying. Since the claim that the Second Person is eternal "Son" might imply possibility or temporality, the Scriptures also designate the Second Person as "Word," since words are generated without passion. The Word is the Son, and the Son is Word and Wisdom. Since God is eternally himself, "Word and Wisdom is neither creature nor part of Him whose Word He is." Nor, though he is a Son, is he "an offspring passibly begotten." Scripture delivers us from materialist and anthropomorphic conceptions of God's fatherhood and sonship by "uniting then the two titles." Scripture calls him Son to highlight the fact that he is of the essence of the Father, the Father's "natural and true offspring of His essence," while it designates him as Word and Wisdom so that "none may think of the Offspring humanly." Scripture "calls Him Word, Wisdom, and Radiance; to teach us that the generation was impassible, and eternal, and worthy of God. What affection then, or what part of the Father is the Word and the Wisdom and the Radiance?" (*Discourses* 1.28). These titles too imply that the Son is eternal, for the Father has never been speechless, unreasonable (*alogos*), or a fool. He demands to know whether God was "ever without Reason" or, being light, if he was ever "ray-less." "Who indeed can bear to hear them say that God was ever without Reason?" (*Discourses* 1.24).

Athanasius argues that unless the Word is eternal and proper to the Father's essence, the Father cannot even be the Creator that Arians want him to be. Scripture makes it clear that the Father creates through his Word. If God is to be inherently and properly a maker (*poiētēs*), he must have his framing Word (*dēmiourgikos logos*), not as an external assistant or instrument (*organon*), but as a word proper to him (*Discourses* 2.2). The Father does not use the Son the way a carpenter or shipwright might use "adze and saw" (*Discourses* 1.25). By implying that the Father needs some external assistance to create, the Arians again insult the Father, suggesting that he is weak unless he takes in hand an external Word.

In several places, Athanasius argues that the Arian position makes creation impossible. The Arians claim that the creation cannot endure the direct touch of God, and therefore creation has to be mediated through a created Son. But if the creation cannot handle God's direct touch, how can the Son? An infinite regression threatens:

> For it follows either that, if He could endure it, all could endure it, or, it being endurable by none, it was not endurable by the Word, for you say that He is one of originate things. And again, if because originate nature could not endure to be God's own handiwork, there arose need of a mediator, it must follow, that, the Word being originate and a creature, there is need of medium in His framing

also, since He too is of that originate nature which endures not to be made of God, but needs a medium. But if some being as a medium be found for Him, then again a fresh mediator is needed for that second, and thus tracing back and following out, we shall invent a vast crowd of accumulating mediators. (*Discourses* 2.26)

If the Father has to create through a creature, how does that first, creating creature get created? Does there not have to be a prior mediating creature? "If the Son be a creature," Athanasius asks, "by what word then and by what wisdom was He made Himself?" Scripture teaches that "all the works were made through the Word and the Wisdom," and "if it be He who is the Word and the Wisdom, by which all things come to be, it follows that He is not in the number of works, nor in short of things originate, but the Offspring of the Father" (*Discourses* 2.5).

If the Son is generated or made in order to enable the Father to create, then the Son exists for us rather than we for the Son. This makes God look niggardly: if God is capable of making a hardy Word that can endure his direct creation, why should he make so few such creatures and so many of the fragile beings who cannot endure his presence and power? For Athanasius, the Arian position also implies a flawed arrangement within the divine counsel. If the Son alone could endure the direct creating hand of God, then it seems that God would give priority in his counsel to the Word. Though the Word is *made* first, yet in the counsel of God, other creatures are prior, since the Son is created for us: "He creates Him first, yet counsels first about us; and He wills us before the Mediator; and when He wills to create us, and counsels about us, He calls us creatures; but Him, whom He frames for us, He calls Son and proper Heir. But we, for whose sake He made Him, ought rather to be called sons; or certainly He, who is His Son, is rather the object of His previous thoughts and of His will, for whom He makes all us" (*Discourses* 2.30). This implies a priority to the "weak" (us); God's favor is to the weak more than to the strong (*Discourses* 2.30), and for Athanasius this is unworthy of God. On Arian premises, in the "decrees" of God, *we* are considered first, and the Son is merely an instrument for our creation.

The unity of the Father and the Son, Athanasius insists, cannot be a unity of will. That kind of unity again pluralizes the Word and Wisdom of God that must be single. Many beings are one in will with the Father but are not for that reason equal to the Word and Wisdom of God. "Since what the Father wills, the Son wills also, and is not contrary either in what he thinks or in what he judges," he argues, "but is in all respects concordant with him, declaring doctrines which are the same, and a word consistent and united with the Father's teaching," it follows that "He and the Father are One." If this is the nature of the unity of Father and Son, then "the Angels too, and the other beings above us, Powers and Authorities, and Thrones and Dominions, and what we see, Sun and Moon, and the Stars, should be sons also, as the Son; and that it should be said of them too, that they and the Father are one, and that each is God's Image and Word" (*Discourses* 3.10). The likeness and unity that the Son bears to the Father must be ontological, not voluntary. Otherwise, there is nothing to distinguish the Word of the Father from created words, the Son from creatures (*Discourses* 3.11).

When Jesus says that he and the Father are one, therefore, he is speaking of an identity of Godhead (*tautotēs tēs theotētos*) and the single nature (*physis*) that he shares with the Father.[27] Father and Son "are one, not as one thing divided into two parts, and these nothing but one, nor as one thing twice named, so that the Same becomes at one time Father, at another His own Son, for this Sabellius holding was judged a heretic." On the contrary, "they are two, because the Father is Father and is not also Son, and the Son is Son and not also Father" while "the nature is one . . . and all that is the Father's, is the Son's." It is not accurate to say that the Son is "another God," since that would imply that the Son was "procured from without" and the Son would be a "godhead procured foreign from the Father's." Rather, though "the Son be other, as an Offspring," yet "He is the Same as God; and He and the Father are one in propriety and peculiarity of nature, and in the identity of the one Godhead" (*Discourses* 3.4). Succinctly, the "Godhead of the Son is the Father's" (*Discourses* 3.4). The Word has an identity of nature with the Father (*tēn ontōs kai alēthōs tautotēta tēs physeōs tō patri echei*).

This can be taken to mean that there is a something—"Godhead"—that the Father and the Son both share. That is not Athanasius's meaning. That would imply that the Father and the Son exist by participation in something else and would also suggest that the Father and the Son are "brothers," since they both derive from something prior, the true "father" of the divine persons. In saying that the Godhead of the Son is the Father's Godhead, Athanasius is saying that the Son is the form of the Father's divinity. What makes the Father God is the Son. Athanasius states it this way: "There is but one form of Godhead, which is also in the Word; and one God, the Father, existing by Himself according as He is above all, and appearing in the Son according as He pervades all things, and in the Spirit according as in Him He acts in all things through the Word" (*Discourses* 3.15).

The fact that the Son receives from the Father is no impairment of his identity as the form of the Father's Godhead, as the one whose nature is identical with that of the Father. Athanasius sometimes hedges on passages like John 5, which claim that the Son has received all he has from the Father. He applies such statements of receptivity to the incarnation: it is as incarnate Son, as flesh, that the Son receives (see *Discourses* 3.38). At other times, and more properly, he recognizes that the doctrine of the Trinity implies receptivity within the life of God. To say that the Son receives all he has from the Father is not to say that the Son lacked something at one time. He has always had what he received from the Father. The point is to underline that "whereas the Son has eternally what He has, yet He has them from the Father" (*Discourses* 3.35). Such passages do not prove the Arian position but the opposite, for if the Son received "all things" from the Father, he is not among the "all" but superior to them (*Discourses* 3.36).

Athanasius defends the Nicene term *homoousios*, particularly in his various defenses of the Nicene settlement (*Defense of the Nicene Definition*; *On the Synods*). Sanctified by the council's approval, it is a standard of orthodoxy. Yet Athanasius appeals to and uses the term infrequently in his anti-Arian treatises. He uses various equivalent phrases (e.g., *ek tēs ousias tou patros*) but does not appeal to the slogan. He gravitates more commonly to other terms: to participation, to the fact that the Son is "proper" to the Father.

The Wisdom of God

Throughout this discussion, Athanasius relies heavily on Paul's statement in 1 Corinthians 1:24 that Christ is the "Wisdom" and "Power" of God. He takes that statement quite straightforwardly. The Father *does* have "His own" Wisdom and Word and Power, but "His own" Wisdom and Power *is* the Son himself, a hypostatic Word and Wisdom, the Word and Wisdom that is the Father's image.[28] Not every theologian has been so bold with Paul's claim. Augustine spends two books of *On the Trinity* trying to figure out what Paul means, and he comes to a position quite different from that of Athanasius.[29]

In book 6, Augustine tries out the notion that the Father's power and wisdom is simply the power and wisdom that he begets as Son, so that the Father is wise only by virtue of the begotten wisdom, powerful by virtue of begotten power, great by virtue of begotten greatness, and so on. In general, he explores the idea that all terms we use to describe God's attributes are relational, all attributes encircled by the Father's begetting of the Son. In book 7, however, he rejects this solution. Being God and being great are not different for God; he is simple. If the Father is great by virtue of the greatness that he begets, then he is God by virtue of the Son, but that would mean that the Father begets his own godness. Since his being God and his being are the same for God, then, on the theory Augustine explores in book 6, the Father would *be* by virtue of begetting the Son. The Father not only begets his own godness but begets his own being. That, Augustine argues, is irrational. How, he demands, could the Father do this without having deity, power, wisdom, being in himself, first? He must *have* it to give it to the Son. Finding the strong reading of 1 Corinthians 1:24 absurd, Augustine insists that the Father must have power, wisdom, and all other attributes in himself rather than simply in the Son.

These are powerful objections, but there appear to be conundrums in every direction. Augustine says that "the Father is powerful" is a statement about the *esse* of the Father, rather than a statement *ad Filium relative*. But in making that distinction, Augustine seems to threaten God's simplicity, which he is trying to protect, from another direction. To protect simplicity, he insists that being-God is not separable from being-powerful, being-great, being-good. But then he distinguishes the Father's being from the Father's being-Father: in *himself*, he is great, wise, powerful. Those are descriptions of his being per se, rather than descriptions of him as Father. And speaking of the Father's being-wise, powerful, great is not the same as speaking of the Father's being-Father. Apparently in defiance of simplicity, Augustine implies that "being-Father" is not identical to the Father's being-God, not identical to his being.

Everything, he concludes, that is something in relation to another must also be something additional to that relation (*omnis essentia quae relative dicitur est etiam aliquid excepto relativo*). Augustine uses created examples to illustrate and concludes that "if the Father is not also something with reference to himself, there is absolutely nothing there to be talked of with reference to something else." That solves one problem only to raise another. How can the *Father* be something other than what he is in relation to the Son? Father, as Augustine has said, is a relative term, and it would seem that we cannot even rationally ask, who is the Father *aside from* the relation to the Son? In that direction lies an abyss, for we cannot help but ask who or what the Father might be when he is not Father, and the answer will be that we simply do not have any idea.

Augustine would probably answer these queries by appealing again to his distinction between relational and substantive terms. The Father is, because he is the First Person of the Godhead, good, just, loving, holy; he is also inherently Father, since, though "Father" is a relational term, he always has a Son. But the way Augustine finally interprets 1 Corinthians 1:24 suggests that the Father has attributes that are more proper than the Son, more intrinsic to the being of the Father than his being Father. Perhaps this is where the criticisms leveled against Augustine hit home, particularly the criticism that he privileges the one essence over the persons. Saying that the Father has "his own" wisdom is not exactly "privileging" unity over plurality, but Augustine leaves open the possibility that the Father has some surplus godness left over that is not exhaustively poured out in the Son, that is not wholly expressed in his being Father. We can see how the pressure of this argument led Thomas and others to conclude that the persons simply are their relations, top-to-bottom: the Father is Father all the way down, the Son is simply and sheerly Son.

Athanasius points, I think, in another direction, a path toward cognitive rest, if not "resolution." He insists that the Father's wisdom simply *is* the Son, as is his power. This might be taken in two ways. On one view, the Father truly is nothing without the Son. Of course, since the Son is begotten of the Father, the Son is nothing without the Father either. Of course, too, the Father never has been without the Son, who is his own Word, "proper" to his essence, so the Father has never been without his power, wisdom, goodness, being. Yet the Father's attributes are utterly dependent on the existence of the Son and are realized in the Son, just as much as the sun is realized and is light because of the radiance that supplements it. On this interpretation, God is radically dependent internally. I am before I am a father; I *am* apart from at least some of my human relations; I am more than my fatherhood. The heavenly Father *is not* before or apart from being Father; the person Paul calls "God" is not God except as he is Father of the Son. On another interpretation, Athanasius is saying that the Father has "his own" wisdom, but that wisdom is paternal wisdom, which means wisdom that exists in the Father (*ad se*) only as it is the wisdom poured out for and manifest in the Son. The Son too has "his own" wisdom, but has that wisdom only as receptive wisdom, received eternally from the Father. Each of the persons shares all the same attributes, and these attributes are their "own," but these attributes are "inflected" relationally, "held" by each person distinctly as a person. All the Father's attributes are inflected paternally, the Son's filially, the Spirit's spiritually.

I suspect that the first of these readings more accurately captures Athanasius's thought. By linking 1 Corinthians 1:24 with Romans 1:18–20, Athanasius says that the power and Godhead that is seen in the creation is the Son (*Discourses* 1.12: *idios autou dynamis kai theiotēs, hina ton huion sēmainē*), and also that the Son simply is the Father's Wisdom and power. But since the Son is *idios* to the Father, he is as "proper" to the Father as any of his "attributes." Augustine would agree that there is not the slightest sliver of space between the Father and the Son, just as he would not allow the slightest sliver of space between the Father and his attributes. But for Athanasius, those two statements are identical: there is not the slightest sliver of space between the Father and his attributes because he has all that he has *in the Son*, who is proper to his essence. Augustine believes as strongly as Athanasius in an eternal radiance from the light of the Father. Yet Augustine is still capable of *conceiving* an unsupplemented origin: the Father "in himself" having attributes "in himself," the light without radiance, the fountain without the stream. Augustine seems to leave a small crack open for thinking that the Father has something that is "his own," something that appears more intimate and intrinsic to his being than the Son. Athanasius will have none of this, and so he is more radically trinitarian, because he does not envision any glimmer of life for the Father that is not realized in the Son. In slight but significant contrast to Augustine, he sees that the Scriptures entail the conclusion that "*the Son is the Father's All*; and nothing was in the Father before the Word" (*Discourses* 3.67, emphasis added). For the Father, too, it is all about the Son, all about the eternal Word that became flesh.

Image of the Son

Given the circumstances of his life and work, Athanasius has less to say about the Spirit than about the Son. Yet he does write about the Spirit, notably in *Letters to Serapion concerning the Holy Spirit*.[30] His approach to the question of the Spirit is similar to his approach to the question of the Son. In both cases, he emphasizes the simple and accurate biblical terminology. While it might appear that the Spirit should be considered a second Son, and brother of the Son, there is a simple refutation of this. The Spirit is never "called Son in the Scriptures, so as to be considered as a brother, nor is it called the son of a Son, lest the Father be conceived as a grandfather" (*To Serapion* 1.16). Behind this is the basic distinction of God and human beings. "God is not like a human being," and specifically so in the fact that he is not made up of components or divisible into parts. This means that the Father is begetter, and only begetter, and the Son begotten and only begotten. The Father is begotten of none, and the Son begets none. Unlike human beings, who have composite and complex identities, the identities of the divine persons are simple: "Just as the Father will never cease to be uniquely Father, so also the Son will never cease to be uniquely Son" (*To Serapion* 1.16).

The Spirit too is utterly unique within the Godhead, and he is no more a creature than a Son. God is not a Monad coming to completion as a Triad. He is eternally complete as Triad (*To Serapion* 1.16–17). Scripture again is the key. Creatures come from nothing, but Scripture says nothing like this of the Spirit, who is "said to be from God" in 1 Corinthians 2:11–12. Since, according to the same passage (v. 10), he searches God, he must be in God in the same way, as Paul says, that "the spirit of a human being" is intrinsic to the human being. Like the Son, the Spirit is known to be God by what he does. What he does manifests who he is. The Spirit is the Spirit of holiness and of new birth (Rom. 1:4; 1 Cor. 6:11; Titus 3:4–7). Creatures do not sanctify and renew, but are sanctified and renewed by God. So the Spirit must be God (*To Serapion* 1.22). The "direction" of participation confirms this. The Spirit does not participate but instead communicates life and holiness to those who participate in him, and thus, again, he is God. Were he not God, then it would not be the case that those who participate in the Spirit participate in God. But Scripture says that we remain (*menein*) in God by the gift of the Spirit (*To Serapion* 1.23–24). All this shows that the Spirit is just as proper (*idios*) to the Father and the Son as the Son is to the Father.

One of the more striking turns in the letter is Athanasius's description of the Spirit as the "image" of the Son. Appealing to the biblical *paradeigmata* light and fountain (*To Serapion* 1.19), he draws connections, as he does elsewhere, between "image" and radiance, expression, and river. Since the fountain is in the river, and the light source in the radiance, and the expression in the subsistence, so "the Son is in the Spirit as in his own image," just as the Father is in the Son. As the Father is to the Son, so the Son is to the Spirit, and Athanasius expounds in some detail on the Spirit's imaging of the Son. The Son is "one," and therefore the Spirit who is "his living energy and gift which sanctifies and illumines" must also be "one, full, perfect." The Son is sent by the Father, but the Spirit is sent by the Son, and so, in the Son's sending of the Spirit, we have an analogy to the incarnation. So too the Son's glorification of the Father (John 17:4) is imaged in the Spirit's glorification of the Son (John 16:14). The Son came "in the name of the Father," but he says the Father will send the Spirit "in my name" (John 14:26; *To Serapion* 1.20).

This does not, Athanasius insists, make the Spirit a son of the Son, or a grandson of the Father. That would violate the pattern of scriptural language. But there is still an analogy, and that analogy bolsters Athanasius's interweaving of Trinity, incarnation, and redemption. As we shall see in chapter 6, the Spirit is the one through whom the Son deifies the faithful. But that does not mean that the work of deification is done at a distance from the Son. The Spirit is the Son's image, and when the Spirit deifies and spiritualizes the believer, he is necessarily making the believer over into the image of the Son. The Son bears the imprint of his Father, that imprint is in the Spirit, and the Spirit comes to us to form us according to the heavenly pattern.

Elsewhere in his writings, Athanasius frequently appeals to the Son's gift of the Spirit as a way of highlighting the Son's divinity. If the Son received the Spirit, then the Arians might have a point; then the Son would be on the same level as we are, as recipients of the Spirit. But the Son gives the Spirit and therefore must be divine (*Discourses* 3.24). To be sure, the Scriptures speak of the Son also receiving the Spirit, but, for Athanasius, these statements are spoken "humanly," of the Son's life as creature, as man. Athanasius affirms the full divinity of the Spirit, and does so in connection with the indwelling presence of the Spirit in believers. Because the Spirit is in us, we are "knit" to God, because we are in God and God is in us. Citing 1 John 4:13 ("by this we know that we abide in Him and He is us, because He has given us of His Spirit"), Athanasius notes that "because of the grace of the Spirit which has been given to us, in him we come to be, and he in us." Given that the Spirit is the Spirit of God, it follows that "through His becoming in us, reasonably are we, as having the Spirit, considered to be in God, and thus is God in us." Without the Spirit, we "are strange and distant from God," but "by the participation of the Spirit we are knit into the Godhead; so that our being in the Father is not ours, but is the Spirit's which is in us and abides in us." Again citing 1 John (4:15), he concludes that we maintain the indwelling Spirit "by the true confession" (*Discourses* 3.24). In short, Jesus's prayer that "they might be in us" is a prayer for the Spirit, since the Spirit is the person who joins us to the Son. Jesus is praying not that we would come to have "identity with Him" but that "the Spirit should be vouchsafed through Him to those who believe, through whom we are found to be in God, and in this respect to be conjoined in Him" (*Discourses* 3.25).

More specifically, Jesus is praying for the *irrevocable* gift of the Spirit. Citing the example of King Saul, who received the Spirit, sinned, and was abandoned by the Spirit, Athanasius concludes that it is possible to fall from the Spirit. If anyone "falls from the Spirit for wickedness," grace will remain in him if he is "willing." But "otherwise, he who has fallen is no longer in God (because that Holy Spirit and Paraclete which is in God has deserted him)" (*Discourses* 3.25). Hence Jesus prays that the Spirit would remain in the disciples. The Word is from the Father, and the Spirit from the Word, and thus Jesus "wills that we should receive the Spirit, that, when we receive It, thus having the Spirit of the Word which is in the Father, we too may be found on account of the Spirit to become One in the Word, and through Him in the Father." The prayer that the disciples will become one "as we are One" is also "a request that such grace of the Spirit as is given to the disciples may be without failure or revocation. For what the Word has by nature, as I said, in the Father, that He wishes to be given to us through the Spirit irrevocably." Paul teaches that the Father answered this prayer, assuring believers that nothing can separate us from the love of Christ and that the gifts and graces of God's call are "without repentance" (*Discourses* 3.25).

God Indwelling God

The triune life, Athanasius says, is, to use the later patristic term, perichoretic life.[31] The Father and the Son dwell in each other in inexhaustible mutuality and intimacy. While it is true that all creatures also "live and move and have being" in the Father, the Son's being-in the Father is unique: "He as being from the Fount of the Father is the Life, in which all things are both quickened and consist; for the Life does not live in life, else it would not be Life, but rather He gives life to all things" (*Discourses* 3.1). The language of indwelling does not mean that the Father is emptied out into the Son or that the Son is emptied into the Father. Athanasius does not leave room for internal triune kenosis. On the contrary, he sees such an idea as blasphemous, since it implies that the Father and the Son are empty and need filling, or that they become empty. Rather than a self-emptying, Athanasius sees Father and Son each as supremely full and perfect, filled with all the fullness of God (*Discourses* 3.1).

Perichoresis provides Athanasius with answers to a number of Arian objections. The "one God" of which Scripture speaks is not the Father alone, since the Son is in the Father; therefore the "one God" includes the Son (*Discourses* 3.9). The Son is different from the Father, but the Son is not a second God alongside the Father. This is clear from their perichoretic union. The Arians "cannot see the One in the Other, because their natures and operations are foreign and distinct. And with such sentiments, they will certainly be going on to more gods, for this will be the essay of those who revolt from the One God" (*Discourses* 3.16). He appeals to the perichoresis of Father and Son to solve an apparent contradiction in Scripture. On the one hand, the Son is said to sit at the Father's right hand, yet, at the same time, other Scriptures suggest that the Father is at the right hand of the Son. How can both be true?

Athanasius believes that perichoresis solves the dilemma. Though the Son sits on the right, "yet He does not place His Father on the left." On the contrary, "the Son, though sitting on the right, also sees the Father on the right," though in human terms he says, "'I saw the Lord always before My face, for He is on My right hand, therefore I shall not fall.'" This is possible because "the Son is in the Father and the Father in the Son," so that "the Father being on the right, the Son is on the right; and while the Son sits on the right of the Father, the Father is in the Son" (*Discourses* 1.61).

Athanasius expounds the image of light and radiance perichoretically, arguing that the source is always in the radiance, the spring always in the stream that flows from the spring (*Discourses* 3.3). Because of the union of Father, Son, and Spirit, the works of God are all works of the three persons together. The Father always acts and works in the Son and through the Spirit: "There is but one form of Godhead, which is also in the Word; and one God, the Father, existing by Himself according as He is above all, and appearing in the Son according as He pervades all things, and in the Spirit according as in Him He acts in all things through the Word." In this way, Christians "confess God to be one through the Triad, and we say that it is much more religious than the godhead of the heretics with its many kinds, and many parts, to entertain a belief of the One Godhead in a Triad" (*Discourses* 3.15).

Behold Your God

For Athanasius, triunity is not some odd datum about God, a peculiar accident of his personality, like having a mole or flaming red hair. To say God is triune is not simply to say that he is plural, but to say what is most fundamental about his character and actions. Saying that God is triune, the Father with the Son and the Spirit proper to him, means that there is mutual love, glory, and no rivalry between Father and Son. Biblical statements about the one unique God would disprove the existence of the Son if there were rivalry (*hamilla*) between them. But there is none:

> If there then is rivalry of the Son towards the Father, then be such words uttered against Him; and if according to what is said to David concerning Adonijah and Absalom, so also the Father looks upon the Son, then let Him utter and urge such words against Himself, lest He the Son, calling Himself God, make any to revolt from the Father. But if he who knows the Son, on the contrary, knows the Father, the Son Himself revealing Him to him, and in the Word he shall rather see the Father, as has been said, and if the Son on coming, glorified not Himself but the Father, saying to one who came to Him, "Why do you call Me good?" (*Discourses* 3.7)

Unlike David, the Father does not have to worry about the Son's usurpation. Unlike Kronos, the father of Zeus, the Father does not have to keep watching his back in case his Son attacks, wielding a sharp sickle. To say that the God-head is plural, yet without rivalry, is to toss every ancient theogony safely into the dustbin of history.

God is the truth, but he is the truth as Triune God and not otherwise: "If the Son was not before His generation, Truth was not always in God, which it were a sin to say; for, since the Father was, there was ever in Him the Truth, which is the Son, who says, 'I am the Truth'" (*Discourses* 1.20). To say that the Son might not have been is to suggest that the Father might not have been good, since the Son is the Father's goodness (*Discourses* 3.66).

Unless God is eternally triune, further, he is not eternally complete but comes to completion. The Arian view implies that God was first a "Monad" and only afterward "by addition became a Triad." On Arian premises, then, "what we know concerning God grew and took shape." And this means that God's being as Triad is a formation *ex nihilo*: "If the Son is not proper offspring of the Father's essence, but of nothing has come to be, then of nothing the Triad consists, and once there was not a Triad, but a Monad." A Triad that comes from nothing can return to nothing, and so the Arian position threatens the eternal character of God. It will not do to begin with a defective Triad that is later completed with the begetting of the Son, since that would imply that "a thing originated is reckoned with the Creator, and what once was not has divine worship and glory with Him who was ever" (*Discourses* 1.17). Without the Son, the Father would not possess plenitude and perfection (*Discourses* 1.20). It is a good thing for the Father to be Father, and if he was not always Father, then, at one time, he lacked some good. Athanasius insists that the Father must have an eternal Son, because the Father's essence could never have been imperfect: "If He is called the eternal offspring of the Father, He is rightly so called. For never was the essence of the Father imperfect [*atelēs*], that what is proper to it should be added afterwards" (*Discourses* 1.14).

Athanasius implies that the begetting of a son is the perfection of nature, a perfection that human beings reach in the course of time. God has never fallen short of this perfection, this completion of his nature, because he has eternally had a Son. The Father's goodness is not, for Athanasius, something that he has in himself as an isolated divine person, because he is not an isolated divine person. If the Father is *kyriōs* Father, Father in the full and proper sense of the word, then it is impossible for the Father to be what he is unless he has a Son, and if he is not what he is, he is certainly not good. Thus, again, it is not quite correct to say, as the later tradition often did, that each person has all the perfections of the divine nature, as if each person could contain those perfections without the others. Each person exhibits all perfections precisely by being a member of the triune communion.

Athanasius introduces the pregnant language of *telos*, "perfection" or "end," here. This might be taken in the more or less "static," Apollonian sense that God has always been in a motionless condition of harmony and balance.

Telos, though, more typically carries a temporal connotation.[32] Having a Son thus perfects, completes, brings to its fulfillment the Father's essence. The Father does have a *telos*, and that *telos* is reached in begetting a Son. Since it would be unworthy of God to suggest that he ever fell short of that fulfillment, the Son must be eternal. This implies that the Father is not complete "in Himself" (contrary to what one finds in Augustine). Athanasius also implies that it is necessary for the Father to be completed in another. Of course, since the Son is eternal, the Father has always already reached his complete end, but the Father's being is such that it is not completed without the Son. He is Light, and Light, to be complete, requires radiance. The Father is origin, but, Athanasius implies, cannot be origin without the eternal supplement of the Son. And this, in turn, implies a kind of eternally realized eschaton in the life of the Trinity. The Father has always already reached the consummation; he is always already the God of the future, the God whose future is wholly realized in the Son, the God who is always waiting to greet us down the road.

That God is a Trinity also implies that there is eternal difference in God. Some of Jesus's statements about his relation to the Father are given in order to establish just this point. Jesus says that he has "received" from the Father and that things have been "delivered" to him "only to show that He is not the Father, but the Father's Word, and the Eternal Son, who because of His likeness to the Father, has eternally what He has from Him, and because He is the Son, has from the Father what He has eternally" (*Discourses* 3.36).

Because God is Triune, the life of God is a life of eternal gift-exchange. The Son receives from the Father for us. Adam received gifts and quickly lost them, but if the Son receives gifts from his Father, he will retain them:

> When then the Savior uses the words which they allege in their defense, "Power is given to Me," and, "Glorify Your Son," and Peter says, "Power is given unto Him," we understand all these passages in the same sense, that humanly because of the body He says all this. For though He had no need, nevertheless He is said to have received what He received humanly, that on the other hand, inasmuch as the Lord has received, and the grant is lodged with Him, the grace may remain sure. For while mere man receives, he is liable to lose again (as was shown in the case of Adam, for he received and he lost), but that the grace may be irrevocable, and may be kept sure by men, therefore He Himself appropriates the gift. (*Discourses* 3.38)

This is stated in the context of the economy. The Son receives and is glorified "humanly." Yet what makes the reception and glory permanent is the fact that they are received by the Son in human flesh and retained by him for us (*Discourses* 3.38).

Only a Triune God can be a creating God. If the Father did not always have his "framing Word" (*dēmiourgikos logos*), he could not always have been a maker. If the Word and Wisdom of the Father once was not, then "it is the same as saying, that God is not Maker, if He had not His proper framing Word which is from Him, but that that by which He frames, accrues to Him from without, and is alien from Him, and unlike in essence" (*Discourses* 1.17). If the Son is not an eternal framing word, then the Father must have relied on something external to himself to create, and that would imply weakness in the Father, or lack of completeness.

If God is always maker, always accompanied by his "Framing Word," why did that Word not always frame? Why is the creation not eternal? Why did God not always make? Athanasius answers in part by rebuking speculation: "'Who has known the mind of the Lord, or who has been His Counselor?' or how 'shall the thing formed say to' the potter, 'why did you make me thus?'" More intriguingly, he answers by claiming that created things could not be eternal because temporality, being-from-nothing, is part of the definition of a created thing: "Although God always had the power to make, yet the things originated had not the power of being eternal. For they are out of nothing, and therefore were not before their origination; but things which were not before their origination, how could these coexist with the ever-existing God?" God created when it was best for creatures to be created: "God, looking to what was good for them, then made them all when He saw that, when originated, they were able to abide" (*Discourses* 1.29).

Yet the Father was always capable of making the world, since the Son was always at his side, the Son who was his creative Wisdom and Word. He creates by will but can create only if he has a creative capacity "proper" to himself. He does not have to receive that power from without. How can God's essence be fruitful in itself if he did not possess an eternal "framing energy"? Can God be a "light that lightens not" or a "dry fountain"? The Arians answer that God brought forth his framing energy by will, but Athanasius dismisses this as an embarrassment: "If He frames things that are external to Him and before were not, by willing them to be, and becomes their Maker, much more will He first be Father of an Offspring from His proper Essence." This is true because the will depends on something that is "above the will": "It is a something that surpasses will, that He should be by nature, and should be Father of His proper Word. If then that which comes first, which is according to nature, did not exist, as they would have it in their folly, how could that which is second come to be, which is according to will?" (*Discourses* 2.2). In short, the Father's "generative nature" is evident in the eternal production of the Word (*Discourses* 2.2), and it is this generative nature that makes it possible for the Father to make a world other than himself.

This line of argument puts the lie to the common charge that Athanasius and other "classical trinitarians" depict God as a static, immobile being. Quite the contrary, classical orthodoxy insists that God is by nature generative, productive, fruitful, and fecund. The Father is eternally Father, having begotten the eternal Son in an eternal begetting. Arians, by contrast, must conclude that the Father has something less than a "generative nature." Generation for them is necessarily by will. But that simply raises the question of how a nongenerative God can will himself to become generative. Be that as it may, it is orthodox theology that presents a God of life and not a barren god of death.

Most dramatically, the Trinity, and the associated doctrine of the incarnation, implies that God honors and glorifies his creatures, rather than using creatures for his own promotion. If the Arians are correct, and the Son was not exalted in glory until after his death and resurrection, then the flesh of the Son is a means for self-promotion (*Discourses* 3.29). Orthodoxy, by contrast, insists that the Son advances the flesh rather than being advanced by it:

> If then He is an ordinary man as the rest, then let Him, as a man, advance; this however is the sentiment of the Samosatene, which virtually indeed you entertain also, though in name you deny it because of men. But if He be God bearing flesh, as He truly is, and "the Word became flesh," and being God descended upon earth, what advance had He who existed equal to God? Or how had the Son increase, being ever in the Father? For if He who was ever in the Father, advanced, what, I ask, is there beyond the Father from which His advance might be made? Next it is suitable here to repeat what was said upon the point of His receiving and being glorified. If He advanced when He became man, it is plain that, before He became man, He was imperfect; and rather the flesh became to Him a cause of perfection, than He to the flesh. And again, if, as being the Word, He advances, what has He more to become than Word and Wisdom and Son and God's Power? (*Discourses* 3.51)

The Son became incarnate, and bore our flesh and its passions and pains, for us, to lighten our sufferings (*Discourses* 3.56). As Khaled Anatolios says, a key difference between Arian and Nicene theologies, as Athanasius saw it, was a difference between a "self-humbling" and a "self-promoting" God.[33] The world, Athanasius thought, had seen plenty of the latter, but the one living and true God is the former, the God who shows himself in the cross.

Conclusion

Critics are wrong to suggest that "classical trinitarianism" announces a static, motionless, inert God to whom it would be nonsense to pray, before whom no one would dance or sing. They are wrong if they are criticizing Athanasius, for nothing could be further from the Athanasian conception of the Trinity. It is not orthodoxy but Arian heresy that, by Athanasius's lights, gives us an inert, barren—not to mention, unknowable—ground of being. For Athanasius, God is an eternal life of love and delight, for the Father delights in his Son, his image, and the Spirit eternally images the delight that the Son has in his Father.

Yet Rahner's rule leaves us with some unanswered questions. If, as Rahner insists, the immanent and economic Trinity are one, and if the economy of redemption is the epistemological source of our knowledge of the immanent Trinity, then it seems that one should be able to read the ontological character of the persons from the economic interactions. To support the idea that nothing in the economy is "purely economic," Hart appeals to the icon of the baptism of Jesus. This icon not only manifests the economic relations of the triune persons but also summarizes the whole drama of salvation and the immanent relations of the Trinity. Jesus's descent into the waters and his ascent from them presignifies his future death and resurrection, while the gift of the Spirit in the form of a dove is a foretaste of Pentecost, when the Spirit falls as wind and fire. But in summarizing the economy of redemption, this iconographic depiction also shows that within the eternal life of God, "in declaring himself, even in uttering himself eternally, God both addresses and responds." Christ both speaks with the authority of the Father and responds to him. In short, "if the economic Trinity is God in himself, graciously extending the everlasting 'dance' of his love to embrace creation in its motion, then one dare not exclude from one's understanding of the Trinity the idea, however mysterious, of a reciprocal Thou."[34]

This is not, Hart argues, "a purely social trinitarianism," nor does this mean that the Son's response is somehow "alongside the Father's expression of his essence in the simplicity of the eternal Logos." Still, the baptism indicates that "one must still acknowledge this distance of address and response, this openness of shared regard."[35] To the baptism, one might add many other episodes of the Gospel narrative: Jesus's praise of his Father for hiding and revealing the things of the kingdom (Matt. 11:25–26); his "high priestly" prayer (John 17); his anguished prayer in Gethsemane (Matt. 26:36–46). If, as Robert Jenson has put it, a person is "one whom other persons may address in hope of response,"[36] then, to judge from the Gospel narrative, Father and Son at least appear to be "persons" in a fairly straightforward sense. They do, after all, *talk* to each other.

We might address this question with the Athanasian *skopos* of Scripture, the principle that the Scriptures speak of the Son in a twofold manner, as Logos and according to the assumed flesh. But I believe another Athanasian insight is more fruitful. Above, I suggested that Athanasius's trinitarian theology is more radically trinitarian than that of Augustine, since the latter appears to leave space to consider the Father "in himself," not sheerly as Father of the Son. To use Athanasius's terminology, Augustine does not grasp as clearly as Athanasius that the Son is "proper" to the Father, as intimate and intrinsic to the Father's being as any wisdom or power the Father could call his "own." Augustine finds it nonsensical to say that the Father can beget his own wisdom, unless he has some prior wisdom of his own to confer. But that, it seems, is to fall into an Arian paradigm, and to run into

Athanasius's critique of the "double wisdom" of Asterius. If the Father has "his own" wisdom, which is eternally conferred on the Son, which is then also his Wisdom, then we are multiplying Wisdoms. That will not do. God is one, and his Wisdom must be one.

Yet Athanasius's appeal to 1 Corinthians 1:24 still requires refinement, a refinement that involves working through the *mutuality* of the relations more consistently than Athanasius himself did. We can put it this way: is the Son dependent on the Father? Yes; the Father begets the Son, so the Son is Son only because the Father has begotten him. This is an eternal begetting, and so the Son always was, but the Son's always-existing is an always-existing that is from the Father, that depends on the Father. The Son as Wisdom and Power of the Father is dependent upon the Father. Yet, and at the same time, we must ask: is the Father dependent upon the Son? Yes; the Father is not Father except as he has a Son. The Father's always-existing as Father depends on the eternal existence of the Son, and, for Athanasius, the Father's eternal Wisdom and Power is precisely his eternal Word.

Dependence thus goes both ways, but the dependence is not symmetrical or identical. At least we can say that the Son depends "filially" on the Father, and the Father "paternally" on the Son. That is not saying much, though. We might also say that the Son's dependence on the Father is the dependence of begottenness; the Son does not "beget" the Father, except in some highly attenuated sense that all relations of dependence are relations of "begetting." The Father does not depend on the Son as one begetting him but depends on the Son for his status as Father. He depends on the Son as the one who does his will so fully that he is the living will of the Father, and he depends on the Son as his image, his radiance, and the exact representation of his glory.

Add the Spirit. Then what? The Father begets the Son in the Spirit; the Father speaks the eternal Word through the breath of the Spirit; the Father gives the Spirit to the Son as the Son's eternal and eternally complete inheritance. The Son gives the Spirit to the Father as well, but as the return gift, the inheritance "enhanced"; the Word spoken by the Father in the Spirit reverberates back to the Father; the Son begotten in the Spirit of love loves the Father with the love that is the Spirit. Surely there are better ways to say this, but the general point is the asymmetry of the relations: the Father and the Son share the Spirit, but they do not "hold" or "give" the Spirit identically, symmetrically. We can, in fact, start the meditation all over again beginning with the Spirit. As the one by whom the Father begets the Son, the Spirit gives fatherhood to the Father and sonship to the Son, so that the Father and the Son are both dependent on the Spirit, but asymmetrically.[37] The Spirit is the one by whom the Father speaks his Word, and so the Spirit gives the Father articulation and the Word beauty and rhetorical power. The Spirit is the love by which the Father loves the Son, so that the Spirit is the one who makes the Father a loving Father and the Son a beloved Son. Or, considered from the other direction, the Spirit is the love that the Son returns to the Father, and so is it through the Spirit that the Son is the loving Son and the Father the beloved Father.

What does this mean? I suggest that it is the failure to reckon with the asymmetry of the relations that has sent certain forms of social trinitarianism down a blind alley. The Trinity is not, as social trinitarianism has suggested, a modern egalitarian democracy, made up of distinct but identical individuals. The persons are indeed equal, but not identical. At its best, though, social trinitarianism has been a plea to take the personhood of the persons seriously; it has been a plea for a scriptural exposition of the ontological life of the Trinity in which the persons converse together as they do in the Gospel story. But the response to Trinity-as-democracy should not be the implicit subordinationism that has infected some traditional trinitarianism; we do not need to resort to a unilateral hierarchical Trinity, paternal monarchianism or paternal causality, to avoid the problems of social trinitarianism. An asymmetrical account of triune life takes the pleas of social trinitarianism seriously, and can get at all the dynamism and personal interactivity that social trinitarianism wants, without threatening to collapse into tritheism.

This is, in the end, consistent with the lines of Athanasius's teaching on the Trinity. The Father's Word is proper to his essence; without that Word, the Father would be *alogos*, powerless, wisdomless, as ineffective as a light source without rays of light. That Word would not be Word, power, Wisdom, if he were not the Word of the Father. They are mutually dependent, living in the Spirit in an eternal fellowship of infinite love and joy and shared delight. Precisely in their mutual dependency, which is also mutual infinite power, they are thus persons, a communion of persons, capable of saying, each to the other, "In your light I see light."

4

Beginnings

Word and World

"I believe in God the Father Almighty, Maker of heaven and earth."

The second half of the first article of the Apostles' Creed is arguably as central to Athanasius's theology as his formulations of trinitarian theology or Christology. Creation gave him a number of his most fundamental metaphysical convictions. The doctrine of creation implied an ontological distinction between Creator and creature, a distinction that remains intact, no matter how intimately God unites himself with human nature or how elevated human beings are in grace. God remains God and creation remains created. To be created is to be dependent, and creation manifests its own dependence, thus providing a kind of negative proof for the existence of an independent Creator. God created out of his goodness,[1] not from need, so that creation is a pointer to God's generosity. Creation is orderly and thus manifests not just God in general but the "logic" of God, that is, the eternal divine Logos. The good God creates a world that is good, and all that is participates in his goodness. Body and soul are both created, both equally contingent and dependent, both equally susceptible to change and decay. Bodies are not evil. Evil, for Athanasius as much as for Augustine, is no substance, but a breach with the source of existence and therefore a move toward non-existence. Sin is "decreation."[2] If the doctrine of the Trinity is at the center of the patristic "evangelization of metaphysics," the doctrine of creation is close by its side. The doctrine of the Trinity is about the character of ultimate reality; creation is the fundamental statement about the metaphysics of visible and contingent reality. For Athanasius, the two doctrines are intimately related: only a Triune God can create.

Creation might appear to be common ground between Athanasius and his opponents, but Athanasius certainly does not think so. Arius makes creation impossible, because he distances the Creator from the creature through a "throng" of mediators: if the Son is a created mediator, he is created through another created mediator, and that mediator through another, and another, receding to infinity (*Discourses* 2.26). Athanasius insists that God himself creates, the Father working through the eternal divine Son and the eternal divine Spirit. For Athanasius, this is an assertion not only about the creation but also about God, a God who is not proud, a God who is not so high and mighty that he disdains little things. If the Arians "assign the toil of making all things as the reason why God made the Son only, the whole creation will cry out against them as saying unworthy things of God." But if "God made the Son alone, as not deigning to make the rest, but committed them to the Son as an assistant, this on the other hand is unworthy of God, for in Him there is no pride." On the contrary, Jesus himself points to the Father's care for the smallest detail of his creation: "Are not two sparrows sold for a cent? And yet not one of them will fall to the ground apart from your Father" (Matt. 10:29). The Father is concerned with food and clothing; he feeds the birds of the air and invests the grass with clothing more glorious than Solomon's. "If then it be not unworthy of God to exercise His Providence, even down to things so small, a hair of the head, and a sparrow, and the grass of the field, also it was not unworthy of Him to make them." Providence and creation go together: "What things are the subjects of His Providence, of those He is Maker through His proper Word" (*Discourses* 2.25).

Far from agreeing with each other about creation, Athanasius and the Arians even disagree about who the Creator is. In contrast to the Arians, who believe that the creating Word is made by the Father, Athanasius insists that the Son is in "no wise a thing originate"; rather, he is the one who "changes everything else, and is Himself not changed" (see Heb. 1:12). He is different from all "things originate," which "being from nothing, and not being before their origination, because, in truth, they come to be after not being, have a nature which is changeable" (*Discourses* 1.36). The Son is begotten, and this is not a coming-to-be; it is an eternal begetting.

> The creatures began to be made; but the Word of God, not having beginning of being, certainly did not begin to be, nor begin to come to be, but was ever. And the works have their beginning in their making, and their beginning precedes their coming to be; but the Word, not being of things which come to be, rather comes to be Himself the Framer of those which have a beginning. And the being of things originate is measured by their becoming, and from some beginning does God begin to make them through the Word, that it may be known that they were not before their origination; but the Word has His being, in no other

beginning than the Father, whom they allow to be without beginning, so that
He too exists without beginning in the Father, being His Offspring, not His
creature. (*Discourses* 2.57)

Because the Son is eternal and does not come-to-be, he is capable of creation. Athanasius recognizes that, in a certain sense, human beings make,
but they cannot be "efficient" or "making causes" (*poiētikon aition*). They
cannot be such because they are "separate and divided from the only God,
and other in nature," so that "being works, they can neither work what God
works" nor "give grace with Him" (*Discourses* 3.14). Human beings cannot
make things that are not, but can only arrange and put together matter into
different forms: "None of things which are brought to be is an efficient cause,
but all things were made through the Word: who would not have wrought all
things, were He Himself in the number of the creatures" (*oude poiēsei pote
to mē on eis to einai . . . tautēn tēn hylēn syntithēsi kai emetarrythmizei*). Not
even angels can create, since they are creatures, nor the sun nor any other created thing. Rather, "God is He who fashions man in the womb, and fixes the
mountains, and makes wood grow; whereas man, as being capable of science,
puts together and arranges that material, and works things that are, as he has
learned; and is satisfied if they are but brought to be, and being conscious of
what his nature is, if he needs anything, knows to ask it of God" (*Discourses*
2.21). Even Moses was only a minister of words. He did not create the people
of God: "To minister is of things originate as of servants, but to frame and
create is of God alone, and of His proper Word and His Wisdom" (*Discourses*
2.27). Human words, in contrast to divine words, do not make, and human
wisdom is not creative either (*Discourses* 2.35; 2.79). Since the Word is the
Truth that is at the heart of created things, "it follows that the Word is not a
creature, but alone proper to the Father, in whom all things are disposed, and
He is celebrated by all, as Framer" (*Discourses* 2.20).

Athanasius's view of the Son and Word as eternal God, "proper" to the
being of the Father, leads him to a view of the relation of Creator and creation different from that of the Arians. Arians teach or imply that the Father
cannot have any direct relation with his creation, since finite things cannot
withstand the touch of the infinite Creator. The Father begets or creates the
Son in order to have a mediator, a sidekick who can carry out his purposes
safely. The Son serves as a buffer between God and creation. In Athanasius's
view, there is no such buffer. God is immediate to the creation. Though he is
utterly beyond creation, and even beyond thought, that Plotinian apophatic
point does not, for Athanasius, rob God of his contact with the world. On the
contrary, because God is truly transcendent, he is immediate to the world.[3]

As the work of the Father through the Word, the creation is "enfolded" in
the Father-Son relation, the common object of their delight.[4] It is the common
object of delight, however, because the world bears the imprint of the Son.

As the Word of the Father, the Father's living will and "image," the Word is also the pattern and "archetype" of creation.[5] There is a logic, a rationality to the creation, and that rationality is the work of the Word and the impress of the Word on the creation. The Father loves the world because it is made in the image of his image, the Son.

Many of the basic themes of Athanasius's creation theology appear in his work *Against the Pagans*, originally written in tandem with the treatise *On the Incarnation*. *Against the Pagans* is Athanasius's one extant contribution to the literature of apologetics that was popular in the first four centuries of the Christian church. The book divides into two large sections, the first section a refutation of paganism, and the second an outline of Athanasius's understanding of the Christian view of reality.[6] Athanasius treats creation in a christological and trinitarian context in *Discourses against the Arians*. Together, these treatises provide us with a sketch of Athanasius's understanding of the nature of things.

It is the nearest thing to overt metaphysics that Athanasius ever wrote, but Athanasius claims at the beginning of *Against the Pagans* that the whole treatise, not only the companion piece on the incarnation, is an apology for the cross of Jesus.[7] As John Behr explains it, Athanasius responds to criticism that the Christian faith is *alogon*, "irrational," by showing that the cross is the revelation of the Logos of God. Idolatry is the true irrationality, and by expelling idolatry the logic of the cross is vindicated:

> Athanasius thus uses idolatry, especially that of the body, as a kind of barometer, measuring the perversity into which humans have fallen, the degree to which their knowledge of God has been lost, and the extent to which the image of God in them has been obscured, the consequence of which is corruption and death. The prevalence of such idolatry, to which the bulk of *Against the Pagans* is given over to describing, demands the drastic solution presented in *On the Incarnation*. The death of idolatry since the advent of Christ demonstrates the power of Christ and the Cross. . . . The Christian faith therefore does indeed have its own *Logos*.[8]

It is all about Christ. It is a Christic metaphysics. Even when Athanasius is exploring the nature of created reality, the cross and the Christ of the cross remain in the forefront of his mind.

From Nothing

According to Athanasius, creation is *ex nihilo*. For Athanasius, origin determines nature. Nature, *physis*, is simply the way something comes-to-be, the way it is born. God has an eternal nature because he is without beginning, and the Son has the specific character as Son because he is begotten from the

Father. Creation, arising from nothing, arises from transition; before it *is*, it *becomes*, and it becomes in order to be. Becoming, movement, changeability, corruptibility are thus the fundamental character of created existence.[9] Anything that has once not existed might pass away, like the syllables of an utterance: "And man's word is composed of syllables, and neither lives nor operates anything, but is only significant of the speaker's intention, and does but go forth and go by, no more to appear, since it was not at all before it was spoken; wherefore the word of man neither lives nor operates anything, nor in short is man. And this happens to it, as I said before, because man who begets it, has his nature out of nothing" (*Discourses* 2.35).

Athanasius acknowledges, based on the text of Genesis 1–2, that God created some things by using preexisting matter. Adam was formed from the dust of the ground, but it is still the case that Adam was not before he originated:

> He that is, can make things which are not, and which are, and which were before. For instance, carpenter, and goldsmith, and potter, each, according to his own art, works upon materials previously existing, making what vessels he pleases; and the God of all Himself, having taken the dust of the earth existing and already brought to be, fashions man; that very earth, however, whereas it was not once, He has at one time made by His own Word. If then this is the meaning of their question, the creature on the one hand plainly was not before its origination, and men, on the other, work the existing material; and thus their reasoning is inconsequent, since both "what is" becomes, and "what is not" becomes, as these instances show. (*Discourses* 1.24)

This line of thought is the basis for Athanasius's explanation of why the creation is not eternal. The point is not the simple, logical one that creation is not eternal if it originated; rather, his argument is from the nature of originated things. Because originated things arise from nothing and are more fundamentally becoming than being, they do not possess the stable nature of eternal things. Thus, "if they curiously inquire why God, though always with the power to make, does not always make . . . they must be told, that although God always had the power to make, yet the things originated had not the power of being eternal." Since created things "are out of nothing, and therefore were not before their origination," they cannot logically "coexist with the ever-existing God." Thus God, considering what was good for them, then made them all when he saw that, when originated, they were able to abide (*Discourses* 1.29). God in his wisdom, through his living Wisdom, brought things into being when it was best for them, and beyond that we can say nothing.

Created things are all essentially the same in that they came-to-be, but Athanasius also recognizes the vast diversity of the creation. Reviewing the days of creation, he notes that each thing has its essence and remains in the essence in which it was made:

For is any one of the creatures just what another is, that you should predicate this of the Son as some prerogative? And all the visible creation was made in six days:—in the first, the light which He called day; in the second the firmament; in the third, gathering together the waters, He bared the dry land, and brought out the various fruits that are in it; and in the fourth, He made the sun and the moon and all the host of the stars; and on the fifth, He created the race of living things in the sea, and of birds in the air; and on the sixth, He made the quadrupeds on the earth, and at length man. And the invisible things of Him from the creation of the world are clearly seen, being understood by the things that are made (Rom. 1:20), and neither the light is as the night, nor the sun as the moon; nor the irrational as rational man; nor the Angels as the Thrones, nor the Thrones as the Authorities, yet they are all creatures, but each of the things made according to its kind exists and remains in its own essence, as it was made. (*Discourses* 2.29)

Created things must be multiple because they are limited and lacking, so that each one makes up the limits and weaknesses of the other. Through this differentiation and mutual support, the universe forms a single entity, a "body" made of many members, the body of the world.[10] When we look at creation, we find "many lights, and not the sun only, nor the moon only, but each is one in essence." Each light shines so that their service is "one and common" and so that "what each lacks, is supplied by the other, and the office of lighting is performed by all." Mutual service and limitation go hand in hand: "The sun has authority to shine throughout the day and no more; and the moon through the night; and the stars together with them accomplish the seasons and years, and become for signs, each according to the need that calls for it." Similarly, the earth does not provide everything that other creatures need. It provides fruits, but it provides no light. So too "the firmament is to divide between waters and waters, and to be a place to set the stars in. So also fire and water, with other things, have been brought into being to be the constituent parts of bodies; and in short no one thing is alone, but all things that are made, as if members of each other, make up as it were one body, namely, the world" (*Discourses* 2.28). Differentiated created things harmonize into a cosmic liturgy (*mia de kai koinē pantōn estin hē leitourgia*).[11] For Athanasius, creation's diversity is not a defect. It is part of the glory of creation to be constituted by limited and dependent parts, all of which have their place and contribute to the whole, like the organs of the body of Christ.

These created things are differentiated, but these differences are not such that created things are lords over other created things. Some are greater than others. Following Paul (1 Cor. 15), Athanasius notes that "star . . . differs from star in glory, and the rest have all of them their mutual differences when compared together," but for all this differentiation, it is not the case that "some are lords, and others servants to the superior." Nor is it the case that some are "efficient causes" by which "others . . . come into being." It is the nature of created things to be created, and that means they all owe their existence to the Creator and to him alone: "All have a nature which comes to be and is created, confessing in their own selves their Framer" (*Discourses* 2.20). Creation is not made up of lords and servants but exists in all its bounteous differentiation to sing in harmony the praises of its one Lord, the Son through whom the Father made the world. David says that "the heavens are telling of the glory of God; and their expanse is declaring the work of His hands" (Ps. 19:1), and that means that "the whole earth hymns the Framer and the Truth" (*Discourses* 2.20).[12] There is only *one* Lord.

Createdness is multiplicity, and createdness also means mutability and fragility. Even souls are mobile (*Against the Pagans* 4), and human beings are created in such a way that the soul can move, and move the body, toward God. That is God's purpose in creating. He makes human beings good, but also makes them mutable, so that they can progress in godlikeness, advance toward deification. This involves a "transcendence" of the body, not because the body is evil but because the body is what is "nearest" to humans, the locus of personal identity and the means for attachment to the things of this world. The soul transcends the body not by becoming detached from it but by driving it, like a charioteer, toward God, by turning the body from idolatrous infatuation with creation to bow and kneel and sing before the Creator, blessed forever. It is in this context that Athanasius speaks of human beings made in the image of God. The image is not a thing or substance, but has to do with participation in God. So long as a man participates in God, his soul moves toward, and moves the body toward, union with God. Sin breaks that participation and thus damages the image.[13]

Yet, for all its mutability and instability, creation is good. Athanasius's *Letter to Amun* (354) is a striking meditation on purity and defilement that affirms with surprising bluntness the goodness of bodily processes. Defilement, he argues, occurs "when we commit sin, that foulest of things." That is what Jesus meant when he said that we are defiled by what comes out—out of the heart. Bodily functions, by contrast, do not defile in the least. Athanasius rivals Luther in his unabashed affirmation of the goodness of bodies and bodily secretions: "What sin or uncleanness," he asks, is there "in any natural secretion—as though a man were minded to make a culpable matter out of the cleanings of the nose or the sputa from the mouth. And we may add also the secretions of the belly, such as are a physical necessity of animal life." There can be no sin in natural bodily functions if "the Master who made the body willed and made these parts to have such passages." We are made by God's hands, and "how could any defiled work proceed from a pure power?"

Because creation comes from nothing, it inherently drifts toward non-being. This raises a question about the goodness of creation: is a creation that threatens to snuff itself out at every moment a *good* creation? It appears to imply that the creation has some power that is not dependent upon a participation in the life of the Creator. That is, if creation tends toward non-being, and God has to continuously rescue it from the precipice, creation must have its own negative power to undo itself. But the creation has no power except what it is given, and so any tendency toward non-being would have to be a gift of the Creator, and why would the Creator give such a power to creatures? A drift toward non-being also suggests a fairly impersonal framework for understanding God's relation to creation. Of course, creation is utterly dependent upon the sustaining power of God, but since he is good he will not withdraw that power. And that leads us back again to the first point: if God does not withdraw his sustaining gift of existence, how can the world be straining against him?[14] Most likely, speaking of the creation's tendency toward "non-being" is, for Athanasius, a dramatic way to underline the fact that creation persists only through the continuous overflowing goodness of the Creator.

Sin and evil are a contingent intrusion into the creation, not an essential aspect of the creation's makeup. But they do feed on the inherent mutability of creation. As a result of Adam's fall, mutable and fragile humans turn away from God to the sensible world around us. The mobile soul is increasingly bound up with the physical and material creation, which, although good, is not God. Through sin, human beings are "divested of the contemplation of the Divine" and turn to created things (*Against the Pagans* 3). Souls devoted to created things are "subject to anxiety, fear, pleasure and thoughts of mortality," and human society descends to "murder" and "injustice" (*Against the Pagans* 3). Since God is the only stability in a world that is inherently unstable, human beings who turn from God lose all fixity and slip toward non-being.

> Turning away from the good [the soul] necessarily considers the opposite. For it cannot completely strip its motion, since it is, as I said before, in its nature easily moved. And knowing its free will, it sees that it can use its bodily members in both directions toward what is and toward what is not. What is is the good, and what is not is the evil. And I call the good what is, since it has its exemplars from God who is. And I call the evil what is not, since, having no reality, it has been fashioned by the imagination alone. (*Against the Pagans* 4)[15]

As the soul becomes fixed on creation, it becomes fixed on things that are slipping toward nothing, toward death. Idolatry of the creation is a form of necrophilia, and the soul takes death into itself. Death becomes the "way of life" of the soul in sin, and dead souls drive bodies to murder and the grave.

This account of the fall is open to question. The fall is an act of disobedience, but Athanasius seems to ontologize it. Has Athanasius confused an ethical lapse—sin—with a metaphysical drift, that is, tendency toward non-being? Athanasius can be defended by suggesting that by "non-being" he simply means a defection from true or full humanity, or a true or full fulfillment of created purpose. When war and vengeance and hatred fill social and political life, there is a movement toward "non-being" in the sense that more and more human beings are not—since they are dead. When human beings bow down to idols and come to resemble the senseless pieces of metal (or paper, or pieces of ideology) they worship, that too is a movement toward non-being: humans are meant to be sentient beings, and idolaters lose their sentience (cf. Ps. 115:8). And so on. Human beings under the dominion of death and sin, Athanasius says, move toward non-being, that is, they become "brute beasts." Here, non-being is not non-existence, but a fall from the fullness and abundance of human life under the Lord Jesus.

Further, Athanasius is emphasizing the fact that human beings are not created in their complete and final state. There is nothing inherently wrong with the creation. On the contrary, it is good. Yet creation as it comes from the mouth of God at the beginning is not yet fulfilled. It is created mobile and mutable, and thus designed to move from glory to glory. When church fathers like Athanasius say that the creation is fragile, balanced on the edge of existence, not stable, they are pointing to the fact that creation has a built-in eschatology.[16]

Eternal Power and Divine Nature

Insofar as creation hymns the praises of God, it reveals his character. Athanasius begins *Against the Pagans* with the premise that the truth about God and the universe is not so much taught as "made known" by the universe itself: "Every day it almost loudly proclaims itself through its works." To be sure, the truth about God "displays itself more clearly than the sun through the doctrine of Christ," but that is not because God has refused to show himself (*Against the Pagans* 1). In countless ways, God has shown himself in creation.

Humanity itself displays the Creator's "goodness" and "supreme beauty," since God created human beings in his likeness so that we "may rejoice in and communicate with the Divine living the true immortal life which knows no sorrows and is blessed" (*Against the Pagans* 2). God created human beings to know and delight in him, and he made them mobile so that they can move toward him, and this mobility reveals the stable and eternal Creator. The human mind's ability to ascend beyond and outside bodies is a specific hint of God's transcendence as Creator (*Against the Pagans* 2). More pointedly, Athanasius insists that humanity manifests the Logos of the Father in the fact that man is created *logikē*, rational. Only human beings reason about sensible objects. Only human beings think about the past and the future in addition to the present. Only human beings are capable of passing judgment on the things that present themselves to their senses (*Against the Pagans* 31). Human senses are like the strikes of a lyre: "When the senses of the body are put into harmony like a lyre when the understanding mind rules them, then the soul determines and knows what it makes and does" (*Against the Pagans* 31). Sociability is also a reflex of the divine Logos in man: "How does the body, having turned away from its nature, turn toward the counsels of somebody else and drive according to the nod of that other being?" (*Against the Pagans* 32).

Not only in man, but in the whole creation, the Son is known from his Father's works (*Discourses* 2.22). Like an artist who, "even if he is not seen, is known from his works," so the Maker and Creator is known "from the order of the cosmos . . . even if he is not seen by the bodily eyes" (*Against the Pagans* 35). The interdependence of creation is a sign of its overall dependence. No part of the creation can exist on its own, and it is unreasonable to believe that collective action by utterly dependent parts could produce an independent creation. The mutual dependency of parts points to the contingency and dependency of the whole.

Given the overpowering diversity and rich multiplicity of creation, one might expect it to be fragmentary and liable to dissolution. Instead one observes an intricate harmony everywhere, and in that "common order" we find a sign that "there is another Maker who orders them" (*Against the Pagans* 35). This is most dramatically seen in the fact that creation is not just a harmony but a harmony of opposites. Fire and water, dry and wet are united in "concordant harmony" and "make one thing as if the body consisted of one substance" (*Against the Pagans* 36). This not only reveals the existence of a harmonizer but also manifests his power: "That which is by nature conflicting and opposite by nature would not have been brought itself together, if He who had bound them together were not stronger than they and their master" (*Against the Pagans* 37). Why is not creation a scene of battle, "a great fight" between the opposing forces and elements? It must be the case that the stronger man has bound the strong elements.

God must be strong: his "eternal power" is manifest in creation (Rom. 1:18–20). God must also be one: "If there were many gods, there ought to be many worlds" since "it would not be becoming that the many produced only one world nor that the one world were made by many gods" (*Against the Pagans* 39). How can the world go in one direction without a single pilot? How can creation produce its harmonious sound unless it is played by a single artist? (*Against the Pagans* 39). In short, "because the world which has been made is one, one must also believe that its Maker is one" (*Against the Pagans* 39).

Through the order (*taxis*) and harmony (*harmonia*) of creation, we are able to see God as the Lord and Maker of all. "As the creation contains abundant matter for the knowledge of the being of a God," Athanasius writes, "and we learn from them without asking for voices, but hearing the Scriptures we believe, and surveying the very order and the harmony of all things, we acknowledge that He is Maker and Lord and God of all, and apprehend His marvelous Providence and governance over all things" (*Discourses* 2.32). The impress of God's wisdom, the living Wisdom that is the Son, is evident in everything that he has made:

> Such an impress then of Wisdom being created in us, and being in all the works, with reason does the true and framing Wisdom take to Itself what belongs to its own impress, and say, "The Lord created me for His works;" for what the wisdom in us says, that the Lord Himself speaks as if it were His own; and, whereas He is not Himself created, being Creator, yet because of the image of Him created in the works, He says this as if of Himself. And as the Lord Himself has said, "He that receives you, receives Me" (Matt. 10:40), because His impress is in us, so, though He be not among the creatures, yet because His image and impress is created in the works, He says, as if in His own person, "The Lord created me a beginning of His ways for His works." And therefore has this impress of Wisdom in the works been brought into being, that, as I said before, the world might recognize in it its own Creator the Word, and through Him the Father. (*Discourses* 2.78)

The Son is like a king who imprints his own name on every building in a new city. He is the "true Wisdom" speaking in Proverbs, who answers "those who admire the wisdom in the creatures" with "'the Lord created me for the works,' for my impress is in them; and I have thus condescended for the framing of all things" (*Discourses* 2.79).

Athanasius reaches for analogies that express the Word's orchestration of creation. The multiple and fragile originated things are harmonized like members of a choir: "As the choir consists of different men, children, women, old people and people who are still young, and as when the leader conducts each sings according to his nature and power, the man as a man, the child as a child, the old man as an old man, the young man as a young man, and all produce one harmony," so it is with the order of creation. Creation too is like a city whose citizens go about their diverse tasks for the betterment of the whole, "because of the presence of the one ruler and his orders" (*Against the Pagans* 43).

In contrast to some versions of neo-orthodoxy, Athanasius clearly teaches that the world manifests God's character and power, but in contrast to most modern natural theology, Athanasius insists that the creation reveals not some generic "deity" but specifically the Son. As Logos, the Son is the framer and arranger of the creation, and the fact that there is harmony in the creation is testimony that it was framed "logically," that is, by the Logos. Athanasius regularly interprets Romans 1:20 in the light of 1 Corinthians 1:24. The "power" and "divine nature" manifest in creation are not some generic divine energy, but the "wisdom" and "power" of God that is Christ, the *theotēs* that is the Father begetting the Son.

In some passages, Athanasius says that what is specifically evident in the creation is the difference and relation of the Father and the Son: "He is the

Word of the Creator God and is known from the Father's works which He Himself works, to be 'in the Father and the Father in Him,' and 'He that has seen Him has seen the Father,' because the Son's Essence is proper to the Father, and He in all points like Him" (*Discourses* 2.22). The Son is not only known from the Father's works but is known "to be 'in the Father and the Father in Him.'" The perichoretic relation of Father and Son is evident in the creation. Looking at the glories of the heavens, Athanasius says, we must "form an idea of the Word who orders this," but at the same time we must also "think of God His Father proceeding from whom He is rightly called Interpreter and Messenger of His Father" (*Against the Pagans* 45). If there is harmony in the universe, that points to a Harmonizer, a Logos; but the Logos must be the Logos *of* someone, the speech of the speaker who speaks forth the Word.

Athanasius also claims that creation itself is an act of grace. That is a controversial position, so before expounding Athanasius's own views on the subject, it will be useful to review the state of the debate in the early twenty-first century.[17]

Nature and Grace

Disputes about nature and grace, about the natural and supernatural realms, have been at the center of much of the theology of the past century. In the early decades of the twentieth century, the Catholic Church was disrupted by interconnected and sometimes acrimonious debates concerning the interpretation of Aquinas and scholasticism, the nature of the church, the theology of the Eucharist, the interpretation of Scripture, the relation between patristic and later Catholic tradition, and the problem of relating Catholic dogma to contemporary cultural and intellectual trends. At the center of these disputes were conflicting answers to the question of how nature and grace are related. This set of debates led to Vatican II and shaped the contours of contemporary Catholic thought.[18]

As a Protestant, this is my debate too. Within my own tribe, Michael Horton projects a particular version of the law-gospel distinction back into Eden, and this produces a Reformed version of the nature/grace dichotomy. According to Horton, Adam was not a recipient of grace at his creation. God's creation of Adam was an expression of "divine *goodness*," but Horton refuses to call it "divine *grace*."[19] Horton criticizes other Reformed theologians for suggesting that "grace is fundamental to any divine-human relationship,"[20] arguing that grace cannot "retain its force as divine clemency toward those who deserve condemnation" if the Adamic covenant is described as gracious.[21] Adam was created under law, not under grace. Law is "natural" and human beings are "simply 'wired' for it." Grace, however, is not natural and comes onto the stage only after Adam's sin.[22] It is not surprising that Horton claims that "Adam is created in a state of integrity with the ability to render God complete obedience," by which he could earn what Horton describes as his "right" to receive the tree of life.[23] Defending the proposition that the Adamic arrangements are rightly described as "covenantal," Horton says,

> Every covenant in Scripture is constituted by a series of formulae, most notably, oaths taken by both parties with stipulations and sanctions (blessings and curses). These elements appear to be present, albeit implicitly, in the creation narrative. Adam is created in a state of integrity with the ability to render God complete obedience, thus qualifying as a suitable human partner. Further, God commands such complete obedience, and he promises, upon that condition, the *right* (not the *gift*) to eat from the Tree of Life. While creation itself is a gift, the entrance into God's Sabbath rest was held out as the promise for loyal obedience in the period of testing.[24]

Lest anyone think that Adam's obedience was itself a gift of God, Horton insists that Adam's ability to obey comes from himself alone: "Created for obedience, he was entirely capable of maintaining himself in a state of integrity";[25] "Adam . . . was in a state of rectitude, perfectly capable of acceding to the divine mandate."[26] Adam was not created with free access to life but had all he needed to earn this access, working from his own natural capacities, apparently without any reliance on God's continuing assistance. His obedience was not the obedience of faith but the obedience of nature. For Horton, we might say that humanity begins Pelagian and falls into Augustinianism.

Among the ironies here is the fact that Horton is a strongly anti–Roman Catholic Protestant who formulates his views of the Adamic order in order to protect the gratuity of grace, against, so he thinks, a Catholic subversion of grace. Yet in the very act of maintaining an anti-Catholic view of the covenant, Horton offers a view of Adamic nature that separates nature and grace in a way that the Catholic Church has only recently questioned. In fact, Horton goes much further than many Catholics, for whom creation is a gift of grace and for whom a state of *natura pura* is hypothetical rather than actual. Horton's Adam existed in an actual state of pure nature, running on his own fuel and earning his access to the tree of life. Horton considers any deviation from this formulation a betrayal of the Reformation.

A more subtle duality of nature and grace is typical of Protestant soteriology. This is evident when we compare Protestant accounts of justification to that of Augustine. In book 19 of *City of God*, Augustine discusses the nature of justice and answers the question whether the city of man can be described as a just commonwealth. He concludes it cannot, arguing that the only just city is the one that gives God his due. Though he recognizes the order of the city of man as a good, he refuses to separate the relative justice of earthly polities and the absolute justice of the city of God. The reason, according to Oliver O'Donovan, is that in Augustine's work *iustitia* has a theological and not merely a political meaning; it is God's justice manifested in making people just. For Augustine, in other words, *iustificare* is embedded in a theology of *ius* and *iustitia*, and these themes are so intricately intertwined that Augustine pauses to digress at length about the Pelagian controversy in book 19, a section of the *City of God* primarily devoted to moral and political theology.[27] Though the Reformers were arguably closer to Augustine on this, the Augustinian integration of justice and justification is today virtually absent from much Protestant theology. For many Protestants, justification is concerned with the spiritual reality of our standing with God, while justice is a civic/natural concern outside the proper region of theology.[28] A nature/grace duality confines the Protestant doctrine of justification to a specifically "religious" realm.

So a discussion of nature and the supernatural, or nature and grace, is a catholic debate in the largest and loosest sense of that word. Still, Roman Catholic theologians after the Reformation and in the twentieth century have doubtless devoted more direct, sustained, and careful attention to these questions than anyone else. This is not surprising. In post-Reformation Catholic theology, the nature/grace scheme became a cornerstone of anti-Protestant polemics and dogmatics, offering a middle way that avoided the dangerous shoals of both Pelagianism and Lutheranism,[29] and revisions of the neoscholastic consensus concerning nature and the supernatural were at the root of the tumult of twentieth-century Catholicism that produced Vatican II. Protestants and Orthodox, therefore, do well to pay attention to what Catholics have had to say on this subject.[30]

In what follows, I use Matthias Joseph Scheeben as a representative of the type of theology to which twentieth-century theologians such as Henri de Lubac were responding. Scheeben is in some ways a revisionist in this tradition, in that he integrated the pneumatological emphasis of the Eastern fathers into a Western scholastic framework and arrived at formulations that burst out of the Aristotelian idiom he adopted. Yet twentieth-century theologians like de Lubac looked to Scheeben as a key representative of the tradition they challenged. After looking at Scheeben's theology of nature and grace, I will summarize the main contours of de Lubac's position, before returning to Athanasius to shed fourth-century light on a twentieth-century debate.

Scheeben on Nature and Grace[31]

The overriding concern of Matthias Joseph Scheeben's 1861 treatise, *Nature and Grace*,[32] is to counter what he identifies as the Pelagianism inherent in modern rationalism. For rationalists, "man's nature carried within itself at least the seed of all good which he could ever reach, including the Christian good." Scheeben concludes that the "crisis" of rationalism "will not be settled until the supernatural order is frankly, adequately, and radically distinguished from the natural order." On the other side, he rejects Protestantism and Jansenism, which claimed that grace "displaces and destroys nature," thus impossibly separating God as Redeemer from God as Creator. Scheeben strives for a theology in which the "praise of God's grace does not require any depreciation of nature."[33] Scheeben believes that combating these dangers requires a much more detailed and precise delineation of the differences between nature and supernature than most theologians had offered. Scholastics employed metaphysical categories to explain the natural order, but he argues that "in the supernatural order this point is often neglected." As a result "no foundation analogous to nature is looked for, and that is the reason why a clear, sound idea of the supernatural order is so rarely achieved."[34]

According to R. R. Reno, Scheeben's strategy for elaborating a more precise account of supernature is one of "separation" of human nature as such from the supernatural faculties and powers that come by grace. Scheeben thinks he can enumerate the faculties and powers that belong to supernature by siphoning off natural powers and examining what remains:

> With respect to the rule for determining what belongs to nature or to supernature, the general norm is to observe which powers nature has, how far these powers extend, and what end must be appointed for them if nature is to reach its suitable development and achieve rest and perfection . . . whatever is outside this list—hence the powers that do not emanate from the essence, and in general all that is unattainable by the unelevated powers from the essence—is supernatural, and if it pertains to a symmetrically organized life, counts as supernature.[35]

What powers does a "nature" have? Beginning with an etymology of Greek and Latin words for nature, Scheeben argues that "nature" includes everything that a being receives by its origin. One might almost identify "nature" with "essence," but more precisely nature is essence regarded from a particular angle, as the vital moving principle of a thing, the principle that impels a being toward its perfection and end. Natural faculties, powers, and acts are those acts, powers, and faculties that arise from the being's own essence, left to itself. "Supernatural" realities, by contrast, are those that surpass the capacities of nature itself, "everything that does not belong to the essence of a thing or is not found on the essence."[36] A supernatural "cause," for instance, is one "not tied down to the laws of matter," and a supernatural "effect" is an effect directly caused by God."[37] Following Suárez, Scheeben also uses the noun "supernature" to describe a complete transformation of human nature. Human beings can receive supernatural "adornments" that go beyond nature and are given directly by God, but "supernature" is human nature transfigured from top to bottom through sharing in divine essence, a "second nature" analogous to acquired habits that we describe as "second nature."[38] Though supernatural abilities and transfigured supernature are not natural in the sense that they arise from human nature in itself, they are not unnatural. Humans are created with obediential potentiality that makes them fit beings to receive supernatural endowments and to be transfigured into supernature.

Scheeben gives only passing attention to human natural endowments, focusing mainly on limitations. Existence itself, he says, is a gift of grace,[39] but the gifts of natural existence are not sufficient to bring human beings to their supernatural end. Left to themselves, people can know God only through God's works, and this knowledge is very imperfect. Scheeben devotes much fuller attention to the character of the supernatural and supernature. Supernatural life is sharing in the very life of God,[40] a participation impossible for human beings in their purely natural state. Before humans can share in the divine life in this way, they must receive a new nature, a nature above nature, a supernature. Supernature does not evacuate nature but is added to it in order to fulfill it.[41] Scheeben movingly expounds on the character of supernature in terms of divine begetting and adoption. Adam was created as a menial servant of God, but by supernatural grace he was to be transformed into a son, begotten in a manner similar to the begetting of the divine Son. By adoption and divine begetting, human beings share in the essence of God to the extent that they are capable of doing so. As fire enters into iron and communicates its essence without destroying the essence of the iron, so God's divine light and heat enter us and divinize us without destroying our humanity.

Scheeben develops his understanding of adoption in biblical and mystical terminology, but he also provides a more precise metaphysical description of supernatural existence. He insists that supernature is more than an intensification of natural moral and personal capacities, like knowledge and love, but involves a "physical" participation in God's own life and being. Supernatural effects like faith, hope, and love are caused directly by God, and they are possible because when nature is transfigured into supernature, God's essence becomes something like the "nature" or "substance" of the transfigured human being. God's essence itself becomes a quasi-substantial "substratum" that produces effects for which human nature has no capacity if left to itself.

Scheeben's detailed treatment of supernatural spirituality gives a glimpse of how this works. Human beings are composite beings, constituted of matter and form, of body and spirit. Though we are spiritual beings by nature, the development of our spiritual capacities is hampered by the confining shackles of matter, whose massiveness and ponderousness exert a kind of gravitational pull toward animality. Further, by comparison with the pure spirituality of God, created spirit has a certain "materiality" because created spirits are composed of act and potency, existence and essence. In the condition of supernature, however, the Holy Spirit becomes our spirit, and as a result the obstacles and obstructions of spiritual nature are "abolished":

> All these imperfections, which are the reason why the created spirit is related to God somewhat as animal life is related to natural, spiritual life, will be abolished

by the higher spirituality that is imparted to the soul when it is admitted to participation in the divine nature. This higher spirituality will endow the soul with the simplicity and the immortality of eternal life; with light and glory in a higher degree, in the way that God possesses them; with freedom and spiritual desire in the noblest sense of the word . . . the spirit will become truly spiritual, that is, simple and immortal, intelligent and free, when it is raised above its quasi-materiality and is given a share in God's spirituality, which alone is spirituality in the truest and fullest sense of the term.[42]

Scheeben devotes much of his work to the task of distinguishing natural and supernatural, nature and supernature, but in the end he divides in order to reunite, and in brokering this reunion he breaks out of the confines of his metaphysical apparatus. Reno notes that Scheeben cannot account for human participation in supernature without abandoning the Aristotelian framework that he wishes to maintain.[43] Scheeben sticks to the theological intention to describe a "mixed" existence—with both natural and supernatural features— and abandons Aristotle. In the closing chapters of his book, he examines the union of nature and supernature in marital and Marian terms. "Can there be a greater similarity," he asks, "can a more perfect parallel be drawn out, than between the marriage of the Virgin with the Holy Spirit and that of nature with grace?"[44]

Scheeben thinks that only this construction can counter rationalism and Lutheranism. By maintaining the integrity of nature, he counters Lutheran pessimism; by insisting that nature has limited capacities, he counters Pelagian optimism. The natural/supernatural scheme offers a middle way through the contested terrain of nineteenth-century Christianity.

De Lubac and the Nouvelle Théologie

In his *Brief Catechesis on Nature and Grace*, French Jesuit and eventual cardinal Henri de Lubac (1896–1991) cites Scheeben's use of "supernature" as the linguistic climax of a centuries-long "deviation of thought."[45] In de Lubac's reading, the neoscholastic view represented by Scheeben juxtaposes two realities, or levels of reality, in such a way that each is impenetrable to the other. It is questionable whether this is a fair representation of Scheeben's theology as a whole.[46] Fair or not, de Lubac claims that Scheeben's separation of nature and supernature is a typical example of the destructive dualisms that had plagued neoscholastic theology.[47] De Lubac's early work, *Surnaturel*, later clarified in *The Mystery of the Supernatural* and *Augustinianism and Modern Theology*,[48] assaults what became known as the "extrinsicism" or "extrinsicity" of neoscholastic thought, the notion that grace is alien to human nature rather than a fulfillment of it.

Like Scheeben, de Lubac is concerned with rebutting rationalism and secular atheism, but in de Lubac's view, neoscholasticism's notions of "pure nature" and its extrinsic view of the supernatural had contributed to the triumph of atheism by making the supernatural superfluous to man's existence. Scheeben's strategy of separation is part of the problem, not a solution, and only a more integral yoking of natural and supernatural can really combat the twin errors Scheeben has identified.

Much of de Lubac's response to the extrinsicism of neoscholasticism takes the form of historical investigation, though his historical research is theologically motivated and presses toward theological conclusions. De Lubac deals with three interconnected concerns: the natural desire for the supernatural, the notion of pure nature, and the notion of double finality. He argues that during the post-Reformation period and in response to Protestantism, Thomists abandoned Thomas Aquinas on all three points, all the while claiming the mantle of Thomas.[49]

Thomas Aquinas repeatedly affirms that intelligent beings have a natural desire for the vision of God (*omnis intellectus naturaliter desiderat divinae substantiae visionem*).[50] Thomists after Cajetan denied this or, like Scheeben, acknowledged the fact that Thomas taught it but explained it in a way that conformed with a preconceived dualistic framework.[51] When de Lubac tipped over the domino of natural desire, it fell onto the domino of pure nature.

"Pure nature" is human nature devoid of revelation or supernatural influence of any kind. Originally, scholastics developed the notion of pure nature to rebut Protestant views concerning original depravity and the "extrinsicism of the idea of imputed alien righteousness." (Dominic Soto writes of considering human nature "*in puris naturabilis mente concepto.*") What started as a "thought-experiment" became a "material principle at the heart of revived Scholastic theology."[52] For post-Reformation scholastics, "pure nature" became not just a hypothetical, possible state of man, but an actual state of man. De Lubac argues that if human beings naturally desire a supernatural end, their nature cannot be "pure nature," since it was already shot through with the disposition toward the supernatural.

De Lubac's position on *natura pura* is partly motivated by an existential orientation to the concrete and actual character of human life, human life in the world as it really now is. He admits the possibility that "a universe might have existed in which man, though without necessarily excluding any other desire, would have his rational ambitions limited to some lower, purely human, beatitude."[53] If Christianity is true, however, this is not the world that we have: "In me, a real and personal human being, in my concrete nature—that nature I have in common with all real men, to judge by what my faith teaches me, and regardless of what is or is not revealed to me either by reflective analysis or by reasoning—the 'desire to see God' cannot be permanently frustrated without an essential suffering."[54] A hypothetical man without a supernatural end cannot teach us anything about the kind of beings we actually are, since the difference between the two is not "one of individuation, but one of nature itself."[55] In other words, once doubts about natural desire and affirmation of pure nature collapse, the whole edifice of double finality is bound to topple as well. Again at this point, Thomists often stood against Thomas. Where Thomas believed that man has a single finality in the vision of God, Thomists spoke of a double finality, one natural and one transcending nature. But this whole paradigm collapses if human nature as created is oriented toward a supernatural finality.

Dualism is de Lubac's main target. He does not deny the distinction of nature and the supernatural, nor does he abandon what he calls the "ancient concept of *natura pura*."[56] He does, however, deplore the "system which has grown up around it,"[57] not least because it fails to achieve its stated aims. The notion of a double finality does not preserve the supernatural; it destroys it. Once a double end is introduced, then "everything, from the first beginning, from the very appetite for happiness, is thus seen in a kind of double way." Doubleness runs from beginning to end, so that some neoscholastics speak of a double beatitude: "*Duplex est beatitudo hominis.*"[58] But if nature has its own finality, then men can lead fulfilled human lives while ignoring their Creator. The dualism of neoscholasticism makes the supernatural superfluous.

Worse, it aids and abets secular atheism. On neoscholastic premises, natural human life is detached from grace and the supernatural, and human nature is presented in a way little different from "rationalist philosophies—both ancient and modern: a being sufficient to himself, and wishing to be so; a being who does not pray, who expects no graces, who relies on no Providence; a being who, depending on one's point of view, either wants to continue as he is, or seeks to transcend himself, but in either case stands boldly before God . . . in a proud and jealous determination to be happy in himself and by his own powers."[59] In *Catholicism*, de Lubac writes:

> For about three centuries, faced by the naturalist trends of modern thought on the one hand and the confusions of a bastard Augustinianism on the other, many could see salvation only in a complete severance between the natural and the supernatural. Such a policy ran doubly counter to the end which they had in view. For on the one hand they failed to observe that the more you separate the less do you really *distinguish*. . . . Thus the supernatural, deprived of its organic links with nature, tended to be understood by some as a mere "super-nature," a "double" of nature. Furthermore, after such a complete separation what misgivings could the supernatural cause to naturalism? For the latter no longer found it at any point in its path, and could shut itself up in a corresponding isolation, with the added advantage that it claimed to be complete. No hidden dissatisfaction could disturb the claim of its splendid equilibrium. . . . Such a dualism, just when it imagined that it was most successfully opposing the negations of naturalism, was most strongly influenced by it, and the transcendence in which it hoped to preserve the supernatural with such jealous care was, in fact, a banishment. The most confirmed secularists found in it, in spite of itself, an ally.[60]

De Lubac's interpretation of Thomas leaves him open, however, to the charge that he has undermined the graciousness of grace, which is the whole point of the neoscholastics' use of pure nature and their denial of the natural desire for the vision of God. If human beings have a natural desire for a supernatural end, then, it was argued, it would be unjust for God to refuse to fulfill that desire. The supernatural finality of human existence would be "owed" or "exacted," since God could not leave that desire unfulfilled without denying the nature that he had made. To protect the gratuity of grace, it is necessary to separate nature and grace, or nature and the supernatural, as rigorously as possible.

De Lubac works hard to parry this charge. Negatively, he argues that neoscholastic dualism undermines gratuity as much as it undermined the supernatural itself:

> Those . . . who have decided that it is necessary to posit first of all a certain "purely natural" human order in which that call is not heard, go on to admit, not realizing that by doing so they are destroying the essential of what they want to save, that in the actual, historical and concrete order, this call places God under an obligation in our regard by actually giving us a right—leaving aside the intervening problem of sin—to demand that he give us grace, and, eventually, if we are faithful, the light of glory. Thus, not content with having imagined an order of things in which our relationship with the Creator might have been ruled solely by the laws of commutative justice, they seem to imagine those same laws as being the basis for the order we actually have, since God has made the decision to "raise us up." Surely, for all they may say of gratuitousness, this in fact does away with it completely. Surely, too, it abolishes hope, or at last makes it relate only to our present sinful state—for anyone who thinks a thing is his due does not hope, but simply demands.[61]

De Lubac also tries to show that his position is compatible with the fundamental truth of God's freedom in grace. He affirms the gratuity of the original creation but distinguishes "the fact of the creation of a spiritual being" from "the supernatural finality imprinted upon that being's nature" and both of these from "the offer presented to his free choice to share in the divine life." The three gifts are to be distinguished in order to avoid hindering "God's utter independence."[62]

With this debate before us we can return to Athanasius: what does he teach about nature and grace?

Grace, Creation, and Participation

According to Athanasius, the Father's Wisdom is imprinted on the creation so that the Father may be found by his creatures, specifically by human beings who are involved in the creation but destined for communion with the Creator. Creation is thus itself an act of "condescension" and grace. Apart from the Son, who shares the nature of the Father, everything is "unlike in essence" and "external" to the Father, and thus made "at His grace" and can cease to be if he pleases (*Discourses* 1.20). This is necessarily the case. It cannot be that God needed creation, nor that the creation is an extension of the essence of God. If the Word made it "possible for [things originate] to come to be," it must have been an act of grace (*Discourses* 2.64). In creating the world, Wisdom condescends to impress himself on creation, giving it unity and concord (*homonoein*), so that the creation can be a single body. Coming-to-be is, in short, the gracious existence from the Father through the Son:

> For if there were no unity, nor the Word the own Offspring of the Father's Essence, as the radiance of the light, but the Son were divided in nature from the Father, it were sufficient that the Father alone should give, since none of originate things is a partner with his Maker in His givings; but, as it is, such a mode of giving shows the oneness of the Father and the Son. No one, for instance, would pray to receive from God and the Angels, or from any other creature, nor would any one say, "May God and the Angel give you"; but from Father and the Son, because of Their oneness and the oneness of Their giving. For through the Son is given what is given; and there is nothing but the Father operates it through the Son; for thus is grace secure to him who receives it. (*Discourses* 3.12)

Creation must be through the Son because the Father's light can be spread only by its radiance, which is the Son. And the same can be said of the Father's providential oversight of the creation once made. Deploying his light-radiance paradigm, Athanasius gives a trinitarian account of Providence. "If the radiance itself should say," he writes, "'All places the light has given me to enlighten, and I do not enlighten from myself, but as the light wills,' yet, in saying this, it does not imply that it once had not, but it means, 'I am proper to the light, and all things of the light are mine'; so, and much more, must we understand in the instance of the Son." This is because "the Father, having given all things to the Son, in the Son still has all things; and the Son having, still the Father has them; for the Son's Godhead is the Father's Godhead, and thus the Father in the Son exercises His Providence over all things" (*Discourses* 3.36). The Father providentially guides his creation in that he shares all things with his Son.

What is true of creation as a whole is true also of the creation of human beings, the crown of creation. Originating from nothing, humans are changeable, corruptible creatures, as inherently mortal as any other created thing, kept in existence only by the Word of the Father (*Discourses* 2.33). They are created in the image of the Father, or more accurately, according to the image of the Father. They are images of the Image, the eternal Image that is the Father's Word and Wisdom and radiance. They are children not by nature, as the Son is, but by imitation. For Athanasius, the nature/grace distinction is not a line that runs through the creation, distinguishing one created reality from another.[63] All created reality is a product of condescension; all existence is a gift of sheer grace. "Nature" describes instead what is proper to God (*Discourses* 3.19).

Given this account of creation as a whole, it is not surprising that Athanasius would claim that Adam was primordially in a state of grace. Adam "received grace from the first, and upon his creation was at once placed in paradise, differed in no respect either from Enoch, who was translated there after some time from his birth on his pleasing God, or from the Apostle, who likewise was caught up to paradise after his actions; nay, not from him who once was a thief, who on the ground of his confession, received a promise that he should be immediately in paradise" (*Defense of the Nicene Definition* 3.6). Not only human beings, but everything is and persists in existence by its participation in the life-giving Spirit:

> If then, as you say, "the Son is from nothing," and "was not before His genera-
> tion," He, of course, as well as others, must be called Son and God and Wisdom
> only by participation; for thus all other creatures consist, and by sanctification
> are glorified. You have to tell us then, of what He is partaker. All other things
> partake of the Spirit, but He, according to you, of what is He partaker? Of the
> Spirit? Nay, rather the Spirit Himself takes from the Son, as He Himself says.
> (*Discourses* 1.15)

All things "partake according to the grace of the Spirit" that comes from the Son (*Discourses* 1.16). Things originated "by partaking of Him . . . are sancti-fied by the Spirit" (*Discourses* 3.1). There is no hint of extrinsicism here, not a whiff of the idea that grace is alien to human life. Grace is operative as soon as Adam is in the garden. Created existence is originated existence, and thus corruptible and changeable existence; it is also, essentially and necessarily, graced existence.

The risk Athanasius runs, of course, is that this position will minimize the newness of redemptive grace, and particularly the newness of the incarnation and the redemption achieved in Christ. But here is one of Athanasius's most important and brilliant theological moves. While he insists that grace is inher-ent in the human situation from the first fiat of creation, he also recognizes the difference between the grace of participation enjoyed by Adam in the garden and the grace that is now bestowed through the Last Adam, the Son made flesh. Arguing, as always, against the Arians, he notes that if the Son is not "proper" to the Father, then the grace we receive through him is still "external." The Son is not one with the Father in the same way that other creatures are one with the Father. A Son who is one only in that sense has only the "grace in common with all" (*Discourses* 3.3).

The Son becomes a creature, is created for us, so that we might be recreated in him. Expounding on Proverbs 8, Athanasius writes,

He says, "The Lord created me," being a creature, He was not created for us; but if He was not created for us, we are not created in Him; and, if not created in Him, we have Him not in ourselves but externally; as, for instance, receiving instruction from Him as from a teacher. And it being so with us, sin has not lost its reign over the flesh, being inherent and not cast out of it. But the Apostle opposes such a doctrine a little before, when he says, "For we are His workmanship, created in Christ Jesus" (Eph. 2:10), and if in Christ we are created, then it is not He who is created, but we in Him; and thus the words "He created" are for our sake. For because of our need, the Word, though being Creator, endured words which are used of creatures; which are not proper to Him, as being the Word, but are ours who are created in Him. (*Discourses* 2.56)

The trinitarian and incarnational logic examined in other chapters of this book is essential here. The Son is intrinsic to the Father's being; he is "proper" to the Father's essence. So too the flesh is "proper" to the Son in the incarnation; it is his own flesh.[64] Both steps of this double intrinsicism are essential for grasping the gospel. What the gospel announces is not the first movement of grace. The Father moved in grace from the moment he spoke his Word and light appeared. In fact, grace was shown even before the first word of the creation. Rebutting the Arian interpretation of Proverbs 8, Athanasius insists that the "founded" Word refers to the incarnation, but to an incarnation that was "founded" before the foundation of the world. "Founded" and "created" in Proverbs 8 refer not to the ultimate origin of the Son but "to the Economy according to the flesh." Athanasius finds in this text evidence that the grace of the incarnation, while recent in realization, is yet prepared from before the world (*Discourses* 2.75).

But the incarnation offers greater grace, the grace of deeper participation in the communion of the Triune God, because the proper Son of the Father takes our flesh and makes it his own. God offers grace from "inside."[65] As Athanasius puts it,

When then received He the works to perfect, O God's enemies? For from this also "He created" will be understood. If you say, "At the beginning when He brought them into being out of what was not," it is an untruth; for they were not yet made; whereas He appears to speak as taking what was already in being. Nor is it pious to refer to the time which preceded the Word's becoming flesh, lest His coming should thereupon seem superfluous, since for the sake of these works that coming took place. Therefore it remains for us to say that when He has become man, then He took the works. For then He perfected them, by healing our wounds and vouchsafing to us the resurrection from the dead. But if, when the Word became flesh, then were given to Him the works, plainly when He became man, then also is He created for the works. Not of His essence then is "He created" indicative, as has many times been said, but of His bodily generation. For then, because the works had become imperfect and mutilated from the transgression, He is said in respect to the body to be created; that by perfecting them and making them whole, He might present the Church unto the Father, as the Apostle says, "not having spot or wrinkle or any such thing, but holy and without blemish" (Eph. 5:27). Mankind then is perfected in Him and restored, as it was made at the beginning, nay, with greater grace. (*Discourses* 2.67)

The movement of redemptive history is the movement from the "extrinsic" grace of creation and of Adamic humanity to the "intrinsic" grace of the incarnation and the humanity of the new Adam.

In response to Arian questions, Athanasius explains that this is why the incarnation was necessary in the first place. It was not enough for God to speak again, to give a new command that would undo the effects of Adam's sin, the reign of death, the corruption of the human race. That would simply have restored us to the position of Adam:

> Accordingly He came, not "that He might be ministered unto, but that He might minister," and might work our salvation. Certainly He was able to speak the Law from heaven, but He saw that it was expedient to men for Him to speak from Sinai; and that He has done, that it might be possible for Moses to go up, and for them hearing the word near them the rather to believe. Moreover, the good reason of what He did may be seen thus; if God had but spoken, because it was in His power, and so the curse had been undone, the power had been shown of Him who gave the word, but man had become such as Adam was before the transgression, *having received grace from without*, and not having it united to the body; (for he was such when he was placed in Paradise) nay, perhaps had become worse, because he had learned to transgress. Such then being his condition, had he been seduced by the serpent, there had been fresh need for God to give command and undo the curse; and thus the need had become interminable, and men had remained under guilt not less than before, as being enslaved to sin; and, ever sinning, would have ever needed one to pardon them, and had never become free, being in themselves flesh, and ever worsted by the Law because of the infirmity of the flesh. (*Discourses* 2.68, emphasis added)

Athanasius and Residual Extrinsicism

De Lubac attempts to maintain both poles of what he calls a "paradox." On the one hand, human beings have an inherent, natural desire for and orientation toward the supernatural fulfillment. At the same time, the fulfillment of this desire is not owed or exacted. Rather, it comes as a gift of sheer grace, fulfilling the natural desire in a transcendently supernatural fashion. This paradox moves Christian faith out of the realm of any philosophy. As de Lubac sees it, ancient philosophy treated nature as a kind of boundary; the potencies of any being are the potencies of its nature, no more. It has within itself all that it needs for its own fulfillment. Of humankind, however, Christianity asserts that humanity's fulfillment is a fulfillment that surpasses anything we might have in ourselves. To be ourselves is to be drawn out of ourselves; to gain life we must lose it.

In my view, the new account of nature and the supernatural does not quite achieve what it aims to achieve. De Lubac's laudable goal is to overcome the "extrinsicism" of neoscholasticism, but he himself speaks of nature and the supernatural as being in a relation of "opposition."[66] This appears to be an effort to preserve the gratuity of the supernatural, but it has the effect of reverting to extrinsicism. If nature stands in an oppositional relation with the supernatural, then they must be external to each other, and how is this externality distinguishable from extrinsicism? Rahner complains that the *nouvelle théologie* collapses into an intrincisism that endangers the gratuity of grace, but my complaint is the opposite: the *nouvelle théologie* does not escape a residual extrinsicism. John Milbank mounts a similar complaint against Rahner. The supernatural existential provides "another level of grace-given desire for grace," but Milbank says this "does absolutely nothing to reconcile gratuity with non-extrinsicism." He charges that Rahner simply restores "the neo-scholastic scheme of two parallel supernatural systems," and that Rahner's combination of *natura pura* and the supernatural existential leaves us "with extrinsicist doctrinal formulas confronting an account of human aspirations and human ethical norms which is thoroughly naturalized."[67]

Rahner's discussion of the gratuity of grace in relation to created spirit supports this conclusion. He distinguishes between "being ordered to grace" and "being directed to grace in such a way that without the actual gift of this grace it would all be meaningless." He affirms the first, not the second. A created spirit "is essentially impossible without this transcendence, whose *absolute* fulfillment is grace, yet *this* fulfillment does not thereby become due."[68] But the italics (which are Rahner's) indicate that there is a more relative fulfillment, a fulfillment of created spirit that does not involve grace. For Rahner, human beings who are created with an orientation to supernatural fulfillment can still have a meaningful existence even if this supernatural fulfillment is never reached. Hypothetically, if not actually, there is a rest other than rest in God. This is different from neoscholastic extrinsicity, but it is not clear how it avoids extrinsicity as such.

This residual extrinsicism raises a problem concerning God's relation to creation. De Lubac and Rahner, and even their neoscholastic opponents, acknowledge that existence is a completely unearned gift, but this is sometimes expressed in erroneous ways. De Lubac and Rahner have improved on Scheeben, who describes material reality as a set of shackles, a constraint, an obstacle and obstruction, a confinement of spirit from which created spirit seeks escape. Still, their formulations do not completely dispel the sense that man as a created being is distant from God and somehow flawed simply by virtue of being created. Citing Blondel, de Lubac says that there is a "natural heterogeneity" and an "abyss" between God and humans, an abyss that must be bridged by the supernatural fulfillment.[69] But this is not true. Augustine was right to recognize that God is more deeply in us, more near to us, than we are to ourselves, and Athanasius would have agreed. Scheeben recognizes this, and de Lubac and Rahner would not deny it. But if this is true, then it is simply incoherent to describe the relation of God to creation as if God were "foreign" or "alien" or on the other edge of an "abyss" from creation.

This raises the more general complaint that natural/supernatural constructions often tend to treat God as "external" to creation. While it is certainly true that God is "above" and "in heaven" and "exalted," it is also the case that he is immanent to every creature in every moment of time. Again, Athanasius has something to offer here, with his profound grasp of the proximity and intimacy of the Creator's presence to his creation. His theology is able to say, with Paul, "in Him we live and move and exist" (Acts 17:28). On the other hand, Yahweh forms the world as a temple to dwell in, so that we not only live and move in him but he also lives and moves among us. Creation is in perichoretic relation with the Triune God, indwelling and indwelt by the Creator.

Explicitly in Scheeben and more implicitly elsewhere, "nature" is a boundary, a limitation. A "nature" is a principle of movement or a set of capacities and ends that belong to that thing from its origin as a member of a species. Humanity has a nature because it can do thus and such and no more, because it can receive this much and nothing in addition, because it can go this far and no farther. But is this compatible with the Christian doctrine of creation? It would seem not. Created beings have only the limits that God places on them; created beings have no "independent" boundaries, no autonomous limits. David Bentley Hart is on the right track when he emphasizes (following Gregory of Nyssa) that each of us is "a vessel endlessly expanding as it receives what flows into it inexhaustibly," so that we become "ever more capacious and receptive" of God.[70] If this is what human "nature" *is*, then we are no longer using the word "nature" in its classical sense, and—as de Lubac admits—the terminology of nature and supernatural is misleading. To suggest that humanity has a "nature" that limits its capacities and ends suggests that humans have some independent capacity to resist, some power to push back against what God intends to do with it and, to be other than God decrees, some power that does not come from God. This impression is strengthened by the notion that "nature" is what humans are capable of "if left to themselves." Since we are never left to ourselves, and would cease to exist if we were, this notion of nature is empty. It appears implicitly nihilist.

If human "nature" expands to receive the increasing inflow of God's self-communication, then we no longer need something additional to nature, something "supernatural," to reach the beatific vision. The beatific vision is an infinite expansion of our capacity to receive God but does not require the replacement of our existing "nature" with another "nature." It demands not an "exaltation" above nature but the fulfillment of the "nature" that we have been given. Rahner actually defines "created spirit" as "openness to infinite being," a definition that eliminates definition.[71] By virtue of being the nature that he is, man is flexibly capacious enough to receive the Spirit of God. Again, Athanasius is on firmer ground in his thoroughly participationist conception of created and especially of human existence. Nature for him is not a confining boundary but involves participation in the life and energy of the Father and his proper Son and Spirit.

The fact that the natural/supernatural scheme does not move in this direction suggests that it operates with assumptions that are alien to the Christian doctrine of creation. Why can we not simply say that God created man in such a way as to be receptive to his Word, presence, love? Why could God not create man as a being capable of being indwelt by the Spirit more and more fully? If this option is refused, perhaps it is because there is something inherent in creaturehood that prohibits it. Perhaps the underlying assumption is that there is some limitation, perhaps a limitation inherent in matter, that makes this impossible. Such an assumption is explicit in Scheeben, but it does not appear to me that de Lubac and Rahner, for all their anti-dualism, have entirely escaped it.

The natural/supernatural distinction, for all its interest in dynamism and movement toward finality, works in a more spatial than temporal framework. The very term "supernatural" suggests a realm "above" nature, and this spatial metaphor is reinforced by language of "exaltation" and "raising," used by neoscholastics, de Lubac, and Rahner alike. The spatial metaphor again implies boundary, a built-in limit to the capacities of created nature—but built in by whom or what? Following hints from Irenaeus, Athanasius's conception of nature and grace is thoroughly historical. God and his creation coinhabit each other; God is within his creation and his creation is "within" the divine fellowship of Father and Son. But what might be described as "supernatural" grace is the deeper grace of the incarnation. It is not grace coming so much from the outside in or from the top down. The grace of the incarnation is *later* grace. Once we put the question of nature and grace into a temporal framework, it looks very different. God graciously creates man as a mobile and changeable being, and man begins to grow (or, as it turns out, degenerate). The "supernatural" end is just what is at the end of this temporal progression, the final word that God speaks to a creature to whom he has spoken from the beginning, the final self-communication to a being that, as image of God, is built from the outset to receive God's self-communication.[72]

Conclusion

Athanasius provides the tools for a more satisfying treatment of nature and grace, since he offers a biblicization and evangelization of the metaphysics of creation. Everything is created from nothing and is therefore inherently fluid, unstable, and utterly dependent on the Creator. Creation is an act of gratuitous generosity, a product of the sheer goodness of God. Adam too received grace, the grace of existence and the grace of sharing in the divine image. Yet this was not the ultimate grace to which humanity was destined. In the incarnation, and in the death, resurrection, and ascension of Jesus, the extrinsic grace offered and given to Adam is rooted in the depths of human nature. Adam participated in the Holy Spirit, the grace of creation; we are destined to a higher achievement, the grace of deification, which depends on the incarnation.

To see the fundamental drive of Athanasius's understanding of grace, however, we need to return to our theme: creation is all about Christ as much as Trinity, incarnation, and redemption. It is all about Christ, not only in the sense that the Word of the Father is the Creator and that the creation is organized according to his logic. It is about Christ because Athanasius's standard for cosmological truth is not conformity to scientific discovery or metaphysical principles. We arrive at the truth about the cosmos when we test it by the measure of Christ and him crucified. As noted at the beginning of this chapter, Athanasius's discussion of creation is part of an apology for the cross. The fittingness of a cosmological scheme, of an understanding of the nature of created reality, of an understanding of the Creator-creature relation, is tested by the incarnation, by the gospel story of the enfleshment of the Word, his death on the cross, and his resurrection in glory. Christ, *that* man, is the measure of all things.

5

Middle

God for Us

Athanasius's treatise *On the Incarnation* bears few traces of the controversy with Arius. This has led some to conclude that he wrote the treatise very early, before the Arian controversy became intense, or at least before the Arians had been condemned at Nicaea. Alternately, the treatise has been dated in the mid-320s, after Nicaea and around the time of Athanasius's elevation to the see of Alexandria. It is, according to some scholars, young Athanasius's attempt to prove his theological mettle as a successor to Alexander.[1] Whatever the date or circumstances of the treatise, *On the Incarnation* has rightly become a theological classic, and, because of its generally nonpolemical format, it gives us insight into the basic motives and themes of Athanasius's theology. It provides a framework for considering Athanasius's more technical, metaphysical, and polemical treatment of the incarnation in the *Discourses against the Arians*.

What is immediately striking about *On the Incarnation* is that it remains almost completely within the frame of redemptive history.[2] Athanasius does not avoid metaphysical questions. He does not hesitate to describe the Word as eternal God. The "Word of the Father" takes a body that is not "proper to His own nature" since "as the Word He is without body" (*asōmatos ōn tē physei*) (*On the Incarnation* 1).[3] In creating the world, the Father gave human beings "a grace which other creatures lacked," that is, "the impress of His own image, a share in the reasonable being of the very Word Himself" (*On the Incarnation* 3). Such metaphysical hints are sprinkled through the treatise, but the main thrust and structure are taken from the history of redemption. Adam was created mutable and, like every other creature, with a susceptibility to decay and death (*On the Incarnation* 4), "by nature subject to corruption" (*On the Incarnation* 5). As a result of Adam's sin, humans are plunged into a chaos of violence, betrayal, greed, and pleasure-seeking. Human evil was perversely progressive, ingeniously and creatively wicked: "They had gone on gradually from bad to worse, not stopped at any one kind of evil, but continually, as with insatiable appetite, devising new kinds of sins" (*On the Incarnation* 5). Human beings were undone, slipping slowly back to the nothingness from which they came.[4]

Not only did Adam's sin and the mayhem it produced throw the human race into misery, but it also presented a challenge to the Creator. Athanasius presents this as a double challenge to the faithfulness and reliability of God.[5] On the one hand, the Creator had threatened Adam with death—dying, you shall die—and it was not possible for him simply to withdraw the threat. God took humans, and human sin, too seriously for that solution. On the other hand, for Athanasius, it was equally unthinkable that the Lord Creator should leave death and chaos, corruption and nothingness, to have their way in his world. He had said Yes in creating the universe at the beginning, and sin and death could not turn his divine Yes to No. What was the point of giving existence to the universe in the first place if he was simply going to turn his back on it? "Surely," Athanasius argues, "it would have been better never to have been created at all than, having been created, to be neglected and perish." Besides, it would tarnish the goodness of God if the "ruin of His own work" were allowed to win out. Athanasius puts it strongly: "It was impossible [*oukoun edei*] . . . that God should leave man to be carried off by corruption, because it would be unfitting and unworthy [*aprepes kai anaxion*] of Himself" (*On the Incarnation* 6).[6] This is not an impossibility imposed by external limits on God's action. It is instead an impossibility rooted in the character of God. God is good; he created out of that goodness, and if he is going to be and prove himself good, he must see that through to the end. He must bring creation to the perfection he planned for it.

It is also fitting for God to rescue the creation because humanity is impressed with his own image. If he was going to allow that image to be defaced and destroyed, what was the use of having made human beings in his own image originally? It was not right that those who share God's image become nothing, and so God could only "renew His image in mankind, so that through it men might once more come to know Him" (*On the Incarnation* 13). It was equally fitting that this restoration be carried out by the one who is eternally and unchangeably the Father's image and Son: "He, the Image of the Father, came and dwelt in our midst, in order that He might renew mankind made after Himself" (*On the Incarnation* 14). As we saw in the last chapter, Athanasius works with a "relational" understanding of the image of God. It is not identical to the soul, or to any quality of man, but points to the relation of humans to the Creator, a relation of archetype and copy, reality and image. Restoring the image of God, then, means restoring humanity's relation to God so that human beings become accurate images of the God they are created to reveal.

God will rescue his creation, and especially the human race. It is fitting that the demiurgical Word himself, the Word who is proper to the Father, carry out this task, since he is the image. The question is, how is it to be done? What is the fitting "method" of redemption? Repentance alone would not do. Repentance is a change of direction and behavior, but it leaves man's basic corruption untouched. To restore creation, God must not only turn human beings to himself but must also arrest the process of decay and death to which they are enslaved. Only an incorruptible Savior can liberate the human race from corruption, and he must do it from the inside. Thus it is the Word's part, "His alone, both to bring again the corruptible to incorruption and to maintain for the Father His consistency of character with all." Since he is the Word of the Father, the Word by which the Father created, he is "both able to recreate all, and worthy to suffer on behalf of all and to be an ambassador for all with the Father" (*On the Incarnation* 7). So the Word comes in a new way to the world he already inhabited, the world he upheld from the beginning (*On the Incarnation* 8), uniting to human nature in unprecedented intimacy, so that divine life might be infused into human existence, so that the corrupt might put on incorruption, and the mortal immortality, and the instable creation become permanent.[7]

In assuming and appropriating our flesh, the Son does not cease to be what he always was. Athanasius emphasizes this point in various ways. On the one hand, he insists—in a way that anticipates Barth's profound meditations on the lordly incarnation of the Lord—that the body of the Son is "not a limitation" but instead an instrument. Anticipating what is wrongly called the "extra-Calvinisticum," he also argues that the Son continues to fill all things even as he exists in the body: "Existing in a human body, to which He Himself gives life, He is still source of life to all the universe, present in every part of it, yet outside the whole." At the same time he was "in" the body, he was both "in all things, and outside all things, resting in the Father alone" (*On the Incarnation* 17).

At the same time, Athanasius rejects all docetic dodges. Out of his pity for the human race,

> He took to Himself a body, a human body even as our own. Nor did He will merely to become embodied or *merely to appear*; had that been so, He could have revealed His divine majesty in some other and better way. No, He took our body, and not only so, but He took it directly from a spotless, stainless virgin, without the agency of human father—a pure body, untainted by intercourse with man. He, the Mighty One, the Artificer of all, Himself prepared this body in the virgin as a temple for Himself, and took it for His very own, as an instrument through which he was known and in which He dwelt. (*On the Incarnation* 8)

His emphasis on the reality of the body (*sōma*) or flesh (*sarx*) and his comparative silence about the soul of the incarnate Son have led some to conclude that Athanasius's Christology was Apollinarian. Apollinaris of Laodicea, a friend of Athanasius, taught that the Logos occupied the "place" of the human soul in the soulless human nature of Christ. The Cappadocians later condemned this view on the presupposition that "what is not assumed is not redeemed." If the Son's humanity lacked a soul, then the soul is not delivered from corruption and death, and since, for Athanasius, the soul is one of the basic sources of the instability of human life, a human with an unredeemed soul is simply unredeemed. Two treatises attributed to Athanasius take an explicitly anti-Apollinarian stance, but their authenticity is doubtful.[8] An authentic anti-Apollinarian statement, though, comes from the *Tome to the People of Antioch* (chap. 7). The Savior "had not a body without a soul, nor without sense or intelligence." In fact, it is "not possible, when the Lord had become man for us." Athanasius's gives two reasons for this impossibility. First, his body could not be "without intelligence." Second, salvation is salvation of the whole person, body and soul: "Nor was the salvation effected in the Word Himself a salvation of body only, but of soul also."[9] Still, it is true that Athanasius says little about the human soul of Christ, doubtless because he puts so much stress on the activity of the Word that he leaves little room for an active human soul. For Athanasius, Christ had a human soul, and it is redeemed and deified, but he has trouble figuring out what it might do. Stressing the union of the Word with the flesh is also a way of stressing the depth of the Word's condescension in the incarnation. Our bodies are closest to what we are as humans, and by taking the body the Word embraces human nature in its totality.[10] For some, the relative absence of reflection on the incarnate Son's human soul is evidence of Athanasius's adherence to what has come to be characterized as a "Word-flesh" model of the incarnation, supposedly prevalent at Alexandria.[11] Word-flesh Christologies maximize the confession that the eternal Word is the personal subject of the incarnate Son and minimize his full humanity. At the heretical extreme, this model is Apollinarian.

Athanasius does use the word "flesh" (*sarx*) to describe the humanity that the Son assumes and makes his own, but this, in my judgment, has less to do with any hedging on the full humanity of the Son and more to do with Athanasius's adherence to biblical categories. "Soul" and "flesh" in Scripture, after all, do not match up with the way these terms are used either in popular Christian piety or in much historical theology. In Genesis 1, "soul" (Heb. *nephesh*) is simply an animating principle for all living and mobile things. Adam is created a living soul when the dust is infused with divine breath (Gen. 2:7), but before Adam was created the world was already full of "souls"—water creatures (1:20–21), cattle and creeping things and beasts on earth (1:24), whatever eats plants and moves on the earth or in the sea (1:30).[12] On this understanding, "soul" is simply whatever it is that gives a creature life, not the mind or some

sort of Cartesian "thinking substance" within a human being. More striking is Athanasius's use of the word "flesh." This stands for him as a global
description of the humanity that the Son assumes and carries connotations
of weakness, frailty, possibility, corruptibility, and so on. That is precisely the
character of "flesh" in Scripture, where *sarx* describes the condition of man
fallen in Adam, including both the decaying human body and the concupis-
cent human soul. Aloys Grillmeier finds it bizarre that Athanasius makes "the
'flesh' of Christ the physical subject of experiences which normally have their
place in the soul,"[13] but Paul would have understood Athanasius perfectly
well. "Deeds of the flesh," after all, include not only sexual immorality and
idolatry, but anger, jealousy, envy, and other evils that typically "have their
place in the soul" (Gal. 5:19–21).

This is not at all to suggest that Athanasius had a fully worked out, analyti-
cal, systematic biblical anthropology that is applied to the specific example of
Jesus Christ. His use of "flesh" and, to a lesser extent, "soul" is much more
instinctive and loose. Yet we see in that usage one aspect of the project of the
church fathers—the project of evangelizing and, we might say, "biblicizing"
metaphysics.

God in a Space Suit?

In the third of his *Discourses against the Arians*, Athanasius addresses the
problems surrounding the incarnation in a more polemical context. Though
his main goal is to refute Arian confusions about the eternal Son, along the
way he makes some salient points about issues that later theologians addressed
under the rubric of "Person of Christ."

Arians stumble, Athanasius argues, when they come to the human attributes
of Jesus. They demand to know, If he is the Son and exhibits such human attributes, how can he be equal to the Father? They point to passages where Jesus
speaks of his reception of all things from the Father, and the Arians ask how a
Son who receives all from the Father can possibly be equal to the Father. Jesus
says, "All authority . . . has been given to me" (Matt. 28:18), and the Father
judges no man, "but He has given all judgment to the Son" (John 5:22). He
also says, "The Father loves the Son and has given all things into His hand"
(John 3:35), and "all things have been handed over to me by my Father" (Matt.
11:27). How then can the Son be from the Father by nature (*Discourses* 3.26)?

Athanasius's general response to these questions is in terms of what he
calls the *skopos* of Scripture, the double teaching concerning the Son. Scripture speaks of the Son in terms of his eternal and essential nature and also in
terms of his assumed humanity. Assuming this double teaching concerning
the Son, he argues that if the Arians were consistent, they would have to raise
questions about incarnation itself. If the Son can become flesh, certainly he

can become *receptive* flesh (*Discourses* 3.27). In doubting the eternal sonship of the Son, they are casting doubt on the central claim of the gospel, that the Word became flesh. Arians are mistaken to have "low thoughts concerning the Son of God" because of his human attributes. If they think the Son lowly from his appearance and body, they could just as well consider him the Word from the Father on account of his works. If they recognize the humanity of his form, they should acknowledge the divinity of his actions (*Discourses* 3.55).

Athanasius also works out his understanding of the relation of the Word and His flesh by comparing it with apparently similar events in the Old Testament. Incarnation, he insists, is something new. The Word came "into" men in the past, but in the incarnation he becomes flesh. The Word became man and did not simply come *into* man. This distinction is necessary to prevent the leveling of old and new, of Jesus and the prophets. It is the only interpretation of Jesus's life and death that makes sense of the gospel story. The Jewish reaction to Jesus's claims to sonship shows that he is claiming something new. If "He only appeared in a man, it were nothing strange, nor had those who saw Him been startled, saying, Whence is He? And wherefore do You, being a man, make Yourself God? For they were familiar with the idea, from the words, 'And the Word of the Lord came' to this or that of the Prophets" (*Discourses* 3.30). In the past, the Word came "individually" to men, but in the incarnation we have the unique instance of the Word himself said to become man, to suffer, to be begotten as a man. "Of old time He was wont to come to the Saints individually, and to hallow those who rightly received Him; but neither, when they were begotten was it said that He had become man, nor, when they suffered, was it said that He Himself suffered" (*Discourses* 3.31). Athanasius thus shows a deep sense of the eschatological character of the incarnation. Christ takes flesh "at the end of the ages for the abolition of sin" (*Discourses* 3.31).

At times, he speaks of the flesh as an "instrument" (*organon*) of the Son (cf. *On the Incarnation* 17, 44) by which the Son accomplishes his work.[14] He comes to die, but he cannot die in his own divine nature; therefore, he takes flesh, which exists functionally to enable the Son to accomplish redemption. These sorts of statements have led some to conclude that Athanasius offers a semi-docetic account of the incarnation. R. P. C. Hanson compares Athanasius's incarnate Christ to "God in a space suit": "Just as the astronaut, in order to operate in a part of the universe where there is no air and where he has to experience weightlessness, puts on an elaborate space-suit which enables him to live and act in this new, unfamiliar environment, so the *Logos* put on a body which enabled him to behave as a human being among human beings. But his relation to this body was no closer than that of an astronaut to his space-suit."[15] Athanasius also frequently seems to be hedging his christological statements by describing them as linguistic protocols. The Word "is said to be" flesh, "said" to hunger, "said" to suffer. To which one is tempted to reply, "Perhaps we can 'say' it; but is it *true*?"

Athanasius's treatment of the Gospel narratives also appears to border on a Christology that would later be condemned as "Nestorian," as his hesitations about attributing any limitations to the eternal Word force his readings of the specifics of the biblical text. When Jesus heals Peter's mother, Athanasius says, we must distinguish between the human action and the divine power. Jesus stretched out his hand humanly (*anthrōpinōs*) but healed divinely (*theikōs*; *Discourses* 3.32). Redemption and glorification are human and therefore they are attributed to the humanity of the Word and not the Word as Word: "If then (as has many times been said) the Word has not become man, then ascribe to the Word, as you would have it, to receive, and to need glory, and to be ignorant; but if He has become man (and He has become), and it is man's to receive, and to need, and to be ignorant, wherefore do we consider the Giver as receiver, and the Dispenser to others do we suspect to be in need, and divide the Word from the Father as imperfect and needy, while we strip human nature of grace?" (*Discourses* 3.39). Jesus fears death not as God but as man (*Discourses* 3.55). In sum, the "human things" must be imputed to the humanness and not to the Godhood (*Discourses* 3.41). The Word's affections (*pathē*) are not proper to the nature of the Word (*physis tou logou*) "as far as He is word," but instead the Word was "in the flesh which was thus affected" (*Discourses* 3.55).

This apparent Nestorian "two-step" leads Athanasius into some tortured exegesis, particularly when dealing with the problem of Jesus's questions and professed ignorance. Jesus asks where Lazarus is entombed (John 11:34), but asking questions, Athanasius is quick to point out, does not necessarily imply ignorance. One may ask questions for other reasons—to teach, for instance, rather than to learn. Though he asks about Lazarus, he already knows where Lazarus is and what he will do, and from this incident Athanasius draws more general conclusions. "When the Lord asks, He does not ask in ignorance, where Lazarus lies, nor again, who men do say that He is; but knowing the thing which He was asking, aware what He was about to do." This is sufficient to explode the "clever point" made by the Arians. If they insist on saying Jesus was ignorant, then "they must be told that in the Godhead indeed ignorance is not, but to the flesh ignorance is proper, as has been said" (*Discourses* 3.37). The Word did not cease to be God when he became flesh, and as Word (*autos ho logos*), he knew even those things he claimed not to know: "Therefore this is plain to every one, that the flesh indeed is ignorant, but the Word Himself, considered as the Word, knows all things even before they come to be. For He did not, when He became man, cease to be God; nor, whereas He is God does He shrink from what is man's; perish the thought; but rather, being God, He has taken to Him the flesh, and being in the flesh deifies the flesh" (*Discourses* 3.38).

Jesus's explicit profession of ignorance about the day of his coming (Matt. 24:36) raises more difficult questions. This is not a question, so Athanasius cannot deal with this as he deals with Jesus's questions at the grave of Lazarus. Instead, Athanasius insists in several ways that Jesus cannot be taken at face value. Despite his explicit profession of ignorance, Jesus must have known. After all, he predicted the signs that would precede his coming, and "He who speaks of what precedes the day, knows certainly the day also, which shall be manifested subsequently to the things foretold." Athanasius compares Jesus's professions of ignorance to a man "who, by way of pointing out a house or city to those who were ignorant of it, gave an account of what comes before the house or city, and having described all, said, 'then immediately comes the city or the house,' would know of course where the house or the city was (for had he not known, he had not described what comes before lest from ignorance he should throw his hearers far out of the way, or in speaking he should unawares go beyond the object)." In the same way, "the Lord saying what precedes that day and that hour, knows exactly, nor is ignorant, when the hour and the day are at hand" (*Discourses* 3.42).

Not only does Jesus give specific predictions about the day of his coming, but he must, as the demiurgical Word of the Father, the Lord of all ages and the measure of all intervals, have *determined* that day along with his Father. As "Framer of the universe," he "knows of what nature, and of what magnitude, and with what limits, the Father has willed it to be made; and in the how much and how far is included its period." The relation of Father and Son also argues for Jesus's knowledge of the day: "If all that is the Father's, is the Son's (and this He Himself has said), and it is the Father's attribute to know the day, it is plain that the Son too knows it, having this proper to Him from the Father" (*Discourses* 3.44). Citing Matthew 11, Athanasius says, with mounting exasperation, "If the Son knows the Father, how can He be ignorant of the day of His coming? And if the Son, who knows the Father so intimately, is Himself ignorant, what does that say about the Father? Is the Father also ignorant of the day?" (*Discourses* 3.44). In short, Jesus knows as God, though he is ignorant as man: "In like manner also about Lazarus He asks humanly, who was on His way to raise him, and knew whence He should recall Lazarus's soul; and it was a greater thing to know where the soul was, than to know where the body lay; but He asked humanly, that He might raise divinely" (*Discourses* 3.46).

Athanasius's most egregious forced reading on this point is an interpretation of 2 Corinthians 12:2, where Paul also professes ignorance of something that Athanasius thinks he too must have known.

What now say ye? Knew the Apostle what had happened to him in the vision, though he says "I know not," or knew he not? If he knew not, see to it, lest, being familiar with error, you err in the trespass of the Phrygians, who say that the Prophets and the other ministers of the Word know neither what they do nor concerning what they announce. But if he knew when he said "I know not," for he had Christ within him revealing to him all things, is not the heart of God's enemies indeed perverted and "self-condemned?" for when the Apostle says, "I know not," they say that he knows; but when the Lord says, "I know not," they say that He does not know. For if since Christ was within him, Paul knew that of which he says, "I know not," does not much more Christ Himself know, though He say, "I know not?" The Apostle then, the Lord revealing it to him, knew what happened to him; for on this account he says, "I knew a man in Christ." And knowing the man, he knew also how the man was caught away. (*Discourses* 3.47)

Paul cannot be truly ignorant, not only because Paul himself experienced the visions he describes, but also because Christ is in him. If Paul was ignorant, and if he received his revelation from the Son, then the Son would be ignorant too. But the Son cannot be ignorant, and therefore Paul knows. Somehow, Paul's professed ignorance is inverted by appeal to the certain fact that Jesus knows—but this is precisely the point in debate! By some hermeneutical magic, Jesus's profession of ignorance, combined with Paul's own profession of ignorance, produces the certainty that both knew what they claimed not to know. Two negatives, apparently, yield a positive.

There is a fair bit of playacting here. Paul is not genuinely ignorant but only pretends to be. He knows that Jesus professed ignorance, and he knows that the disciples cannot be above the master, so he acts ignorant in order to teach a lesson in discipleship. In fact, Paul is imitating Jesus very closely when he pretends to be ignorant, since Jesus pretended to be ignorant too. Jesus was not really ignorant either but professed ignorance "as showing His manhood." Since ignorance is proper to the flesh, the Son put on a show of ignorance to demonstrate that he had really taken flesh (*Discourses* 3.45). In addition to violating the plain sense of Jesus's statement, Athanasius's explanation ends up in convoluted contradictions. After all, if the Word had to pretend ignorance to prove that he was truly human, then he was not really sharing the ignorance that flesh is heir to. Perhaps his assumption of flesh was mere pretense as well?

"His Own" Flesh

Despite such statements used to support Hanson's interpretation, Athanasius's fundamental Christology is far more robust.[16] For starters, we should remind ourselves of the framework that Athanasius employs and the intention of his work. As we noted in the last chapter, Athanasius conceives the relation of Creator to creation in the context of *creatio ex nihilo* and the affirmation that the Word of the Father is "proper" to the Father's being. This, rather than the notion of the Son's body as *organon*, or commitment to a "Word-flesh" model of the incarnation, is the key to Athanasius's

Christology.[17] According to Athanasius, the Creator is immediately present to the creation, always and necessarily. Without the immediate presence of the sustaining Logos, creation could not persist (*menein*). In a sense, Athanasius dispenses with all manner of "mediations" between God and creation. That relation to creation does not change in the incarnation. God remains in direct contact with the creation, and in fact deepens that contact by assuming flesh, by making flesh "His own" (see further below). Through the incarnation, a human race that is inclined toward death comes to know God through the "immediate mediation" of the incarnate Word. The flesh of the Word is thus no screen between God and his creation; there has never been such a screen, and there is no need for one. Rather, the flesh is the medium through which he touches and embraces creation, and it brings the Word into such close relation to the world that the incarnation can be described as an *epiphaneia* of God.[18] When Athanasius says that the Word acted "through the body," the body might be taken as a distancing instrument—an eternal extender that enables a God who is too prissy to touch matter to interact with his creation and yet keep his distance; or it can mean that the body has become transparent to the Word, who is the power and Wisdom of the Father. Clearly, Athanasius means the latter, for, as he never tires of reminding his readers, God is not proud.[19]

Athanasius's intentions must also be specified. His aim is not to provide a technical analysis of the relation of Word and flesh in the incarnate Son,[20] any more (as we shall see in the next chapter) than he intends to provide a technical analysis of the mechanics of atonement. He is far more interested in the fact of the incarnation and the results of the death and resurrection of Jesus than he is in explaining how it could all happen. When he writes about the incarnation, in fact, he is not merely speaking about the fact that the Word assumed flesh. For Athanasius, "incarnation" is the person *and* the work, the person who is known to be the incarnate Word precisely by what he can do. John Behr writes, "Assuming, anachronistically, that 'Incarnation' refers solely to the birth from Mary of the divine Word in or as Jesus tends to lead . . . to an approach which holds that the proper task of Christology is to analyze the composition of the being of Jesus Christ, to determine whether he has the requisite elements of a true human being, or whether the divine Word has replaced the soul, the question which has beset modern scholarship on Athanasius."[21] For Athanasius, "incarnation" describes not merely the event of the Son becoming flesh but the whole life and work of Jesus. We will distort Athanasius if we understand the term too narrowly.

Finally, the question has been skewed through projecting an "Antiochene" or even Nestorian framework onto Athanasius. Athanasius does insist on the *skopos* of Scripture, as we have seen, the "double" account of the Savior. But this is not the same as saying that he follows a dualist reading of the Gospel narratives. Frances Young notes,

While it is true that the Antiochenes would use Athanasian passages . . . to good effect to defend their own dualistic exegesis . . . Cyril's appeal to Athanasius reflects his mind better: the Alexandrian way was to distinguish the Being or Essence of the Word from what the Word accepted in the "Economy," that is, the providential saving plan of God worked out in the incarnation. So undergirding Athanasius's exegesis is the unitive story or plot which is the mind of scripture expressed in its many words and images, and of which the one "Son" is the subject.[22]

When Athanasius sees a "double" reality in the Gospel story, it is not because some actions are done by the humanity and some events happen to the humanity, while divine actions are done by the divine nature. Rather, all that Jesus does is what the Word does, and the Word does all that he does through and in and by the *organon* of the flesh. The Word of the Father, who is the Father's Power and Wisdom, heals through the flesh and hungers in the flesh, walks on water in the flesh and thirsts in the flesh. Athanasius's distinction is not between the Word and the human nature that accompanies and does the creaturely business. The distinction is between the single subject of all the Gospel narratives—which is always the Word—and the actions that he performs in the economy.

Athanasius insists, in short, that the humanity of the Son is the Son's own (*idios*). He writes, "Whereas He was ever God, and hallowed those to whom He came, and ordered all things according to the Father's will, afterwards for our sakes He became man, and 'bodily' (Col. 2:9), as the Apostle says, the Godhead dwelt in the flesh; as much as to say, 'Being God, He had His own body, and using this as an instrument, He became man for our sakes.'" And he then adds,

On account of this, the properties of the flesh are said to be His, since He was in it, such as to hunger, to thirst, to suffer, to weary, and the like, of which the flesh is capable; while on the other hand the works proper [*idios*] to the Word Himself, such as to raise the dead, to restore sight to the blind, and to cure the woman with an issue of blood, He did through His own body. And the Word bore the infirmities of the flesh, as His own, for His was the flesh; and the flesh ministered to the works of the Godhead, because the Godhead was in it, *for the body was God's.* (*Discourses* 3.31, emphasis added)

The terminology used here is similar to that used to describe the Son's relation to the Father. The Son is the Father's own, proper (*idios*) Word and Wisdom, not an extrinsic or attached word or wisdom. To say that the Son is "proper" to the Father is to say that the Son is as necessary to the Father's existence as any of the Father's "attributes" or "properties." The Son is not an extraneous added accident but is of the substance of the Father. Similarly, the Son's flesh is the Son's own flesh (*idia sarx*), and the intimacy of the relation is such that Athanasius can state, with pithy power, "God's was the body" (*theou ēn sōma*). Flesh is now joined to the Word with something like the intimacy that the Word eternally has with the Father.

Because the Son takes flesh and makes that flesh "his own," he carries our infirmities. Citing Isaiah 53:4 ("He remedied our infirmities"), Athanasius argues that this healing is only possible on the basis of the incarnation. The Son had always healed, but he healed "as being external to the body" and thus left men "subject still to death." If he is going to overcome death and the infirmity of flesh once and for all, then he must be as we are: "He carries our infirmities, and He Himself bears our sins, that it might be shown that He has become man for us, and that the body which in Him bore them, was His own body; and, while He received no hurt Himself by 'bearing our sins in His body on the tree,' as Peter speaks, we men were redeemed from our own affections, and were filled with the righteousness of the Word" (*Discourses* 3.31). The direction of Athanasius's argument here is determined by the anti-Arian polemic; it sounds as if the Word carries infirmities in order to provide support for orthodox Christology and to refute the Arians. But the fundamental theology is still clear: the eternal Word, without ceasing to be eternal Word and divine in his own nature, takes on flesh and truly makes it his flesh.

Even the sufferings of the flesh are as much his own as the flesh itself: "When the flesh suffered, the Word was not external to it [*ouk ēn ektos*]; and therefore is the passion said to be His [*autou legetai kai to pathos*]: and when He did divinely His Father's works, the flesh was not external to Him, but in the body itself did the Lord do them" (*Discourses* 3.32). The passions (*pathē*) of the Son's flesh are his, since passions are proper to the flesh and the flesh is proper to the Son: "For on this account has the Apostle himself said, 'Christ then having suffered,' not in His Godhead, but 'for us in the flesh,' that these affections may be acknowledged as, not proper to the very Word by nature, but proper by nature to the very flesh" (*Discourses* 3.34). "It became the Lord," he writes, "in putting on human flesh, to put it on whole with the affections proper to it." On account of this, "as we say that the body was His own, so also we may say that the affections of the body were proper [*idios*] to Him alone, though they did not touch Him according to His Godhead [*ei kai mē hēpteto kata tēn theotēta autou*]." Since "the flesh is the Word's (for 'the Word became flesh'), of necessity then the affections also of the flesh are ascribed to Him, whose the flesh is." In the flesh, and because the flesh is his, we ascribe affections to him, "such namely as to be condemned, to be scourged, to thirst, and the cross, and death, and the other infirmities of the body." These are just as much his as "the triumph and the grace." It is consistent and fitting that "such affections are ascribed not to another, but to the Lord" (*Discourses* 3.32).[23] The Son's exaltation as well as his passion are "his own" because the body to which the suffering and exaltation happen is "proper" to him. "When the flesh advanced," he writes, "He is said to have advanced, because the body was His own, so also what is said at the season of His death, that He was troubled, that He wept, must be taken in the same sense" (*Discourses* 3.54). Again, the similarity to the language of the trinitarian discussions is remarkable: there Athanasius insists that the Son is not "external" (*ektos*) to the Father's *ousia*, and here the flesh is not external to the Son. It is an analogy, but the analogy holds: the Son is to the Father as the flesh of the Son is to the Son. Both are intrinsic relations, not extrinsic ones, though one is an eternal "natural" intrinsic relation and the other a temporal "graced" intrinsic relation.

The analogy of Trinity and incarnation extends to the pattern of perichoresis. Just as the Father is in the Son and the Son in the Father in the eternal divine life, so in the incarnation, the flesh is in the Son and the Son is in the flesh. "When the flesh receives," Athanasius writes, "since that which receives is in Him, and by taking it He has become man, therefore He is said Himself to have received" (*Discourses* 3.38). As he writes,

> For these belong not to the Word, as the Word; but are proper to men and, as when He spat, and stretched forth the hand, and called Lazarus, we did not say that the triumphs were human, though they were done through the body, but were God's, so, on the other hand, though human things are ascribed to the Savior in the Gospel, let us, considering the nature of what is said and that they are foreign to God, not impute them to the Word's Godhead, but to His manhood. For though "the Word became flesh," yet to the flesh are the affections proper; and though the flesh is possessed by God in the Word, yet to the Word belong the grace and the power. (*Discourses* 3.41)

That statement bears repeating: the flesh is in him because the flesh is *divinely possessed in the Word* (*theophoreitai en tō logō*). In sum, "He was Very God in the flesh, and He was true flesh in the Word" (*alēthēs sarx ēn en tō logō*; *Discourses* 3.41). Again, the analogy is striking. In trinitarian theology, perichoresis expresses the exhaustive mutual relation of the Father, the Son, and the Spirit, their exhaustive mutual infinitely intimate indwelling. Through the incarnation, human flesh has been graciously assumed into that intimate communion.

Pressing Athanasius's point, we can put it in these terms: since the Word is in the flesh and the flesh in the Word, and since the Father is in the Son and the Son in the Father, so the flesh is in the Father and the Father in the flesh. Flesh is taken up into God, and this is the ground not only for Athanasius's doctrine of deification (see chap. 6) but also the background for Jesus's own awe-inspiring promises: "I in them and you in me" and "that they also may be in us" (John 17:21–23). Through the incarnation, human beings are assumed within the intimate joy and delight of the Father and the Son and become objects of that delight.

God for Us

Despite some "God in a space suit" twists and turns, Athanasius's fundamental Christology is very different, providing thoroughly theological explanations for the limits and passions of Jesus in the Gospel story. At the heart of this account, Athanasius insists that the Son's every action and limitation in the incarnation are undertaken for our sake. Because of this, even the human statements about Christ have a proper "religious" (*eusebēs*) meaning (*Discourses* 3.37).

For instance, Athanasius describes the purpose of the incarnation as an exchange of origin. The Son has an eternal heavenly origin; we originate from the earth and are of the earth, that is, earthy. By assuming our nature and our origin in flesh, he intends to take us to heaven with him so that we can be born again from above:

> Whence also, whereas the flesh is born of Mary Bearer of God, He Himself is said to have been born, who furnishes to others an origin of being; in order that He may transfer our origin into Himself, and we may no longer, as mere earth, return to earth, but as being knit into the Word from heaven, may be carried to heaven by Him. Therefore in like manner not without reason has He transferred to Himself the other affections of the body also; that we, no longer as being men, but as proper to the Word, may have share in eternal life. For no longer according to our former origin in Adam do we die; but henceforward our origin and all infirmity of flesh being transferred to the Word, we rise from the earth, the curse from sin being removed, because of Him who is in us, and who has become a curse for us. And with reason; for as we are all from earth and die in Adam, so being regenerated from above of water and Spirit, in the Christ we are all quickened; the flesh being no longer earthly, but being henceforth made Word, by reason of God's Word who for our sake "became flesh." (*Discourses* 3.33)

This "for us" guides Athanasius's explanation of passages that speak of the Son's receptiveness as well. Jesus says that "power is given to me" and asks the Father to glorify him. All this is said "humanly because of the body." In his divine nature, he had "no need," but he is said to receive humanly for our sake, to ensure that the grace of God remains (*menein*) with us: "The grant is lodged with Him, the grace may remain sure." When man receives grace, "he is liable to lose again (as was shown in the case of Adam, for he received and he lost), but that the grace may be irrevocable, and may be kept sure by men, therefore He Himself appropriates the gift" (*Discourses* 3.38). Similarly, the power Jesus receives after the resurrection is not new to him, since he had already demonstrated his authority over Satan during his ministry. That power is already apparent in "His driving away the demons, and from His unbinding what Satan had bound, as He did in the case of the daughter of Abraham; and from His remitting sin, saying to the paralytic, and to the woman who washed His feet, 'Your sins be forgiven you;' and from His both raising the

dead, and repairing the first nature of the blind, granting to him to see."
What is new is that he receives the power "humanly," and this power is now
exercised *for* us and even *by* us: "What He had as Word, that when He had
become man and was risen again, He says that He received humanly; that for
His sake men might henceforward upon earth have power against demons, as
having become partakers of a divine nature; and in heaven, as being delivered
from corruption, might reign everlastingly" (*Discourses* 3.40). He took flesh,
died in the flesh, rose to new life in the flesh, so that the power of God might
become now a power of the flesh, so that we who are in the flesh can trample
Satan beneath our feet, so that we can triumph over death in him. .

In *On the Incarnation*, Athanasius describes the Word as a "good teacher
with his pupils," who comes "down to their level" and uses "simple" and
suitable means. In sin, the human race had turned from the invisible God to
sensible things, devoting themselves to idols, which can bring not stability and
incorruption but only further decay. To deliver them from this infatuation and
slavery to sensible things, the Word became sensible: "The Savior of us all, the
Word of God, in His great love took to Himself a body and moved as Man
among men, meeting their senses, so to speak, halfway. He became Himself
an object for the senses, so that those who were seeking God in sensible things
might apprehend the Father through the works which He, the Word of God,
did in the body" (*On the Incarnation* 15).

Creation, as we saw in chapter 4, is already imprinted by the Word of the
Father, its harmony of opposites a pointer to a divine Orchestrator. That is
not enough for God. He fills the creation with himself, then speaks to Israel,
and then comes in his Son, so that God himself becomes "an object of our
senses." This is to show forth the Word in every dimension of creation: "Above,
in creation; below, in the Incarnation; in the depth, in Hades; in the breadth,
throughout the world. All things have been filled with the knowledge of God"
(*On the Incarnation* 16). Since God is complete in himself—the Father with
his proper Son and Spirit has always already reached his *telos*—the accolades
of creation do not add to God's glory or pleasure. But it is for the good of
creatures, since praising God is what creation is designed for. Humans are
formed for doxology, with hands to lift in prayer, tongues to sing, knees to
bow. The incarnation re-tunes bodies for praise so that we can fulfill our *telos*
as well. Thus, even when the Father acts through his Word to elicit praise for
himself, he is not proud. Even then, he acts for us.[24]

Specific actions of Jesus were also designed to meet human needs and address
the myriad forms of human rebellion, disobedience, and ignorance. For those
who were "awe-struck by creation," the Son came as a creature who was also
Lord of the creation. Humanists who exalt human capacity find a unique man
in Jesus, whose "works marked Him, alone of men, as Son of God." Those
who are misled by evil spirits learn from Jesus's mastery of the demons that
these spirits are no gods. Those who devote themselves to "hero-worship and

the cult of the dead" find that faith inverted by the resurrection. Whatever deities men have adopted are exposed and undone by the Word made flesh (*On the Incarnation* 15).

At times, Athanasius applies this logic to his explanation of Jesus's ignorance. When the Son takes our flesh, he takes all the limits of flesh to himself, shares in them, in order to burst through them. He assumes our ignorance to reveal to us the knowledge of the Father: "Carrying our ignorance, He might vouchsafe to us the knowledge of His own only and true Father, and of Himself, sent because of us for the salvation of all, than which no grace could be greater" (*Discourses* 3.38). Of course, for this to work, the ignorance has to be the Son's own ignorance, as much his own as his flesh in general.

Some of the "for-us" reasons Athanasius gives for Jesus's ignorance are moralistic, even quaint. Jesus's profession of ignorance prevents his disciples from inquiring too curiously into the times and seasons of things to come. Where God has been silent, curiosity should cease and we should accept God's silence (*Discourses* 3.43). We also get a glimpse of God's condescending love, demonstrating that God descends from the brightness of his knowledge into fleshly ignorance for us. The timing of the Word's ignorance is important. He is not said to be ignorant "when the heaven was made by Him, nor when He was with the Father Himself, the Word 'disposing all things,' nor before He became man did He say it, but when 'the Word became flesh.'" Since ignorance is proper to humans, Jesus's ignorance is "proper to the Savior's love of man." Having been made human, "He is not ashamed, because of the flesh which is ignorance, to say 'I know not,' that He may show that knowing as God, He is but ignorant according to the flesh" (*Discourses* 3.43). He also suggests that the ignorance of the Son is eschatologically qualified. That is, the ignorance pertains to the state of Jesus prior to the resurrection. Though he takes our ignorance when he takes flesh, the goal of that assumption is not to remain in ignorance but to transform ignorance into knowledge. Athanasius points to the difference between Jesus's words in the Olivet Discourse and his response to the disciples' question about the restoration of the kingdom to Israel (Acts 1). In the latter passage, Jesus does not say that he is ignorant of the timing but instead tells the disciples that it is not expedient for them to know. This implies that Jesus knows the answer but refuses to give it for the sake of his disciples: "Now the flesh had risen and put off its mortality and been deified; and no longer did it become Him to answer after the flesh when He was going into the heavens; but henceforth to teach after a divine manner" (*Discourses* 3.48).

Athanasius insists that the ignorance of the Son is the best thing for his people. Jesus said, "I know not," even though he did know, but he did it "for our profit." Both his knowledge and his ignorance secure "our advantage." On the one hand, he told us enough so that when apocalyptic signs appear "we might not be startled nor scared, when they happen, but from them may expect the end after them." At the same time, he kept us in the dark about the day and hour, "lest [the disciples] should ask him further, and then either he should have to pain the disciples by not speaking, or by speaking might act to the prejudice of them and us all" (*Discourses* 3.48).

Jesus's ignorance is consistent with the entire aim of the incarnation: "Whatever He does, that altogether He does for our sakes, since also for us 'the Word became flesh'" (*Discourses* 3.48). All the limits that the Son assumes, he assumes for us:

> And further, not to know when the end is, or when the day of the end, is expedient for man, lest knowing, they might become negligent of the time between, awaiting the days near the end; for they will argue that then only must they attend to themselves. Therefore also has He been silent of the time when each shall die, lest men, being elated on the ground of knowledge, should immediately neglect themselves for the greater part of their time. Both then, the end of all things and the limit of each of us has the Word concealed from us (for in the end of all is the end of each, and in the end of each the end of all is comprehended), that, whereas it is uncertain and always in prospect, we may advance day by day as if summoned, reaching forward to the things before us and forgetting the things behind. For who, knowing the day of the end, would not be dilatory with the interval? But, if ignorant, would not be ready day by day? It was on this account that the Savior added, "Watch therefore, for you know not what hour your Lord does come"; and, "In such an hour as you think not, the Son of man comes" (Matt. 24:42; Luke 12:40). For the advantage then which comes of ignorance has He said this. (*Discourses* 3.49)

In addition to passages that speak of Christ's ignorance, the Arians highlighted passages describing the advancement of Jesus in glory, wisdom, or obedience. If the Son is equal to the Father, how can he grow? If he has had all glory with the Father from eternity and by virtue of his divine nature, how can he receive glory from the Father? If he is the eternal Wisdom of the Father, how can he be said to increase in wisdom? Part of Athanasius's answer is to agree that the Word and Wisdom of God cannot advance at all, insofar as we isolate him as the Word proper to the substance of the Father. Athanasius also appeals again to the *skopos* of Scripture, the hermeneutical rule that the Scriptures speak in a "double way" about the Son. When Scripture speaks of the Son's advance, it cannot be talking about his divine nature, since he eternally is all that he is. It must be speaking about the Son in the flesh.

The deeper point of Athanasius's response, though, again highlights the central thrust of his Christology, which is rooted in his theology proper. On Arian premises, Athanasius argues, the Son is elevated through taking flesh, living, dying, and rising again. The Son is more at the end of that series of events than he was at the beginning.[25] To Athanasius, this precisely reverses the intention of the incarnation. The flesh of Jesus is not an instrument of the Son's self-advancement. Rather, the Son takes flesh in order to advance the flesh:

But if He be God bearing flesh, as He truly is, and "the Word became flesh," and being God descended upon earth, what advance had He who existed equal to God? Or how had the Son increase, being ever in the Father? For if He who was ever in the Father, advanced, what, I ask, is there beyond the Father from which His advance might be made? Next it is suitable here to repeat what was said upon the point of His receiving and being glorified. If He advanced when He became man, it is plain that, before He became man, He was imperfect; and rather the flesh became to Him a cause of perfection, than He to the flesh. And again, if, as being the Word, He advances, what has He more to become than Word and Wisdom and Son and God's Power? (*Discourses* 3.51)

God is not proud, and God does not act in history for his self-advancement. He cannot advance, being the perfection of all perfections. Rather, he assumes flesh and acts so that we might be advanced, so that our humanity might be perfected: "The Son of God, since He could not advance, being perfect in the Father, humbled Himself for us, that in His humbling we on the other hand might be able to increase" (*Discourses* 3.52). The principle of double teaching about the Son is not simply a way of protecting the full divinity of the Son. It has direct soteriological import. The double teaching highlights the fact that the Son takes our condition to change our condition.

The Son's humanity advances "humanly," but there is also an advance in how fully the Son's flesh glows with the radiance of the Radiance who assumes it. The New Testament speaks of the body's advance, in order to emphasize that "in it advanced also the manifestation of the Godhead to those who saw it. And, as the Godhead was more and more revealed, by so much more did His grace as man increase before all men." As the Word advances in wisdom and stature, there is an advance in the "Word manifesting Himself" in the body (*proekopten en autō kai hē phanerōsis tēs thotētos tois hōrosin*; *Discourses* 3.52). Athanasius sometimes works this out in the context of a temple Christology. The human flesh of the Son advances, and this is a deifying advance, which increasingly shows the body as a temple: "The body increasing in stature, there developed in it the manifestation of the Godhead also, and to all was it displayed that the body was God's Temple [*hē tēs theotētos phanerōsis . . . hoti naos theou esti*], and that God was in the body [*theos ēn en tō sōmati*]" (*Discourses* 3.53). "He grew" means that the flesh of Jesus becomes ever more transparent to the Word and Wisdom that assumed it, and as we shall see in the next chapter, the Son does this also for us, as he makes *our* human flesh also transparent to divine light.

Impassible Sufferer

For contemporary theology and for fourth-century theology as well, the crux of the incarnation is the literal crux, the cross. Who is suffering on the cross?

Does God suffer and die? Does only the humanity of Jesus die? How can we make sense of the cross and the Jesus who dies there? For many contemporary theologians, Athanasius cannot make sense of it, because he assumes that the Word is impassible. For many theologians, impassibility stands as a roadblock to a full appreciation of the gospel. On this point, it is claimed, Athanasius fails his own test: having made the crucified Christ the measure of theological and metaphysical truth, Athanasius flinches, and on the central point.

For Athanasius, it is axiomatic that God is impassible, just as and just because God is unchangeable and eternal, so axiomatic that Athanasius never takes time to defend it. It is, after all, an assumption shared by Athanasius and Arius, and by everyone else in the early church, and thus requires no defense. Armed with this assumption, Athanasius sometimes appears to be engaged in an effort to distance the Son from the suffering of the body. The impassible Word seems to be the astronaut in the passible space suit of human flesh: "In the Body which was circumcised, and carried, and ate and drank, and was weary, and was nailed on the tree and suffered, there was the impassible and incorporeal Word of God. This Body it was that was laid in a grave, when the Word had left it" (*Letter to Epictetus* 5). When he is not hemming and hawing to insist on the impassibility of the incarnate Word, Athanasius, like the other fathers, seems to engage in a kind of double-talk: the impassible one suffered, yet did not suffer (*Letter to Epictetus* 6). The Word did not suffer in his own nature, but the suffering of the flesh is "ascribed" to him (*Letter to Epictetus* 6). Arians have an easier time of it. They share Athanasius's assumption about God's impassibility but resolve the issue by distancing not the suffering from Jesus, but the suffering Savior from the impassible God. For Arians, the passibility of the Savior is a crucial issue. They argue that only a suffering Savior could redeem, and this Savior could not be merely human. Since God himself cannot suffer, the suffering Christ must be someone less than God. Athanasius cannot resort to this expedient, but where he is incapable of creating a buffer between Son and Father, he creates a buffer between flesh and Word. So it seems.

Few patristic assumptions have come in for more extended and severe criticism in recent theology than the assumption of impassibility. Objections to impassibility have arisen in part from the scriptural portrait of God. Yahweh pities his people in their distress and comes to their assistance. He grieves and mourns over the sins of Israel and even of gentiles. He is so passionate in his love for his people that he says that his name is "Jealous" (Exod. 34:14).

Philosophical concerns also have pressured theologians toward divine passibility, and these concerns are most elaborately expressed by Hegel. To make sense of creation and incarnation, Hegel thinks we must presuppose some internal self-differentiation within God himself.[26] Creation and incarnation thus require a new sort of philosophy, a new basis. For Hegel, a substance philosophy cannot make sense of a God who remains unchanged and at the same time enters into a world of change without losing himself or alienating himself. Substance philosophies must be replaced by a philosophy of "spirit." Substance philosophies cannot incorporate relation and otherness as inherent qualities of a thing; for substance philosophies, relation is always extrinsic. A philosophy organized around spirit, however, places otherness and relationality at the center. As Anselm Min says, "What is required is a shift from a philosophy of 'substance,' which stresses simple self-identity, self-sufficiency, and essential immutability of being and allows activity, relation, and otherness only as something external to itself, to a philosophy of 'spirit,' which regards active mediation by otherness as internal to the constitution of self-identity in its concrete unity."[27]

Since God is Spirit, he is inherently, primordially relational. The Father "self-others" himself as the Son, and since the Son is the Father's own self-expression the Son "shares the totality of divine being." The Son, in Hegel's words, "unites the two qualities of being the totality in itself and of being posited as other."[28] The Father's infinity is not just the infinity of an infinite substance, which would mean his persistence as infinite in himself. Rather, "the Father is both Himself, that is, Father in his distinct self-identity and related and present to the Son in his distinct Otherness to the Father." This otherness and relation are not "external to the divine essence" but rather "something posited by the Father in his divine nature." The Father's identity and self-identity are thus "an identity mediated to itself by Otherness or a unity of identity and disidentity."[29] The same is true of the Son: his identity is "internally mediated by his relation to the Father." Further, the Father not only self-others himself and expresses himself in the Son, but also returns to himself as Spirit, as "concrete, dynamic, mediated identity." The Father "does not merely posit an Other but also has the power to sublate the Otherness of the Son, that is, to preserve that Otherness *as* Other, and at the same time transcend that Other as something posited by himself, whereby he mediates himself to himself." Thus the "Other is not a brute datum separating the Father from himself but a medium thoroughly open and transparent to the self-mediating action of the Father."[30] Creation is possible because of this self-othering, but for Hegel, the creation is not a free act of a God who is perfect and complete in himself. Rather, it is the necessary extreme self-othering of the God who is necessarily self-othering.

Hegel's conception of the incarnation builds on his account of the immanent Trinity "with its inner multiplicity and finality." Hegel does not consider the incarnation to be an afterthought, or even a "second" event successive to creation and necessary only because of the intervention of the fall. Human beings must be created to receive God, with a teleological orientation to union with God, otherwise the incarnation would be impossible: "Were created human nature simply other, alien, and opposed to the divine, the Incarnation would not mean genuine unity but mere juxtaposition of two heterogeneous elements. Unless human nature were created with an inner teleological relation to the divine, the Incarnation would mean only an external imposition of the divine on the human, which on its part would not need the divine and for which, therefore, the Incarnation would have no redemptive, reconciling significance."[31] The reconciliation and identification of God and man cannot take place outside the world that humanity inhabits. Humans are not pure spirits but embodied spirits, and so God must enter into this natural consciousness and follow the contours of human nature. In short, "the logic of reconciliation requires God's self-manifestation in a form that combines sensibility and self-consciousness, which can be found only in a particular, sensible individual."[32]

The incarnational and trinitarian aspects of Hegel's thought coalesce in an emphasis on the death of God on the cross, which in some ways is the center of his entire philosophy, the "speculative Good Friday." "As 'God in human form' or 'the concrete God,' Jesus is not 'the mere organ of revelation but is himself the content of revelation,' the ontological congeniality of human and divine."[33] In a more "Alexandrian" fashion, Hegel emphasizes that the gospel story is a story about God himself, but since he has already posited that God is in a relation of mutual conditioning with his creation, the history of the Son in the flesh is a history that modifies and fulfills God. "The history of Jesus is the history of God himself, and he alone is 'utterly adequate to the Idea.' In his death on the cross, 'God himself is dead,' and in subjecting himself to death, 'the uttermost pinnacle of finitude,' God experiences the sting of otherness at its most radical and proves his own humanity and his love for humanity."[34] In the cross, the God who self-othered himself in the Son, the God who created a world other than himself and entered that world in the incarnation, reaches the pinnacle of his self-othering self.

But the othering move is only one moment in the process, a moment that is sublated by the moment of resurrection:

> God does not remain dead in Jesus but has the power to sublate the otherness of death, that is, God has the power of Resurrection. No longer limited to the physical boundaries of a particular historical individual, God himself rises as the Holy Spirit from the particularity of finitude in a negation of negation and becomes a universal spiritual presence in the depth of human history, where he reconciles humanity with himself. For Hegel, otherness, negation, finitude—which is a moment of divine nature itself—is not the final word; reconciliation is. It is precisely the infinite power of God to subject himself to finitude and to overcome and triumph over that finitude and achieve reconciliation between himself and his Other.[35]

Understood in this way, the death and resurrection of Jesus is, for Hegel, "the whole of history," but it is essentially a "theology of Resurrection." Though Hegel says that finitude, negation, otherness are a moment within the divine life itself, it is not the final moment; rather, reconciliation and resurrection are the final word of God, which means that Hegel's theology is finally not tragic but a "theology of hope." God's infinity is not his immunity to suffering and negation and evil but the infinity of a "God who suffers yet overcomes."[36]

The death of God is the death of this kind of abstraction. It is the death of abstract transcendence, the infinite that, opposed to the finite, is itself finite. The death of God means that God is not opposed to the finite but incorporates the finite as a moment in his own being, his own realization. As Hegel writes,

> The death of this picture-thought contains, therefore, at the same time the death of the *abstraction of the divine Being*, which is not posited as Self. That death is the painful feeling of the Unhappy Consciousness, that *God himself is dead.* This hard saying is the expression of the innermost simple self-knowledge, the return of consciousness into the depths of the night of the "I" = "I," which no longer distinguishes or knows anything outside of it. . . . This Knowing is the inbreathing of the Spirit, whereby Substance becomes Subject, by which its abstraction and lifelessness have died, and Substance therefore has become *actual* and simple and universal Self-consciousness.[37]

What dies is classical theism's unrelated God, the God of substance philosophy. The absolute itself "must undergo a process of mediation with other, that is, become subject." That means that conflict and tragedy become "theological possibilities," and therefore he rejects the classical notion of God's impassibility. Death of God becomes a *theological* reality as pain, suffering, and tragedy are taken up in the life of God. In his 1827 *Lectures on the Philosophy of Religion,* Hegel says, "'God himself is dead,' it says in a Lutheran hymn, expressing an awareness that the human, the finite, the weak, the negative, are themselves a moment of the divine, that they are within God himself, that finitude, negativity, otherness are not outside of God and do not, as otherness, hinder unity with God. Otherness, the negative, is known to be a moment of the divine nature itself. This involves the highest idea of spirit." Love cannot be separated from "the infinite anguish of good Friday."[38]

Hegel's emphasis on God's passibility has been taken up most famously by Jürgen Moltmann. Moltmann has been deeply concerned with theodicy, but his theodicy renounces philosophical explanations and focuses on the cross. The cross does not explain suffering or evil; it manifests God's "loving solidarity with the world in its suffering" and manifests God's triumph over all that contradicts him. Radically, Moltmann "brings the dialectic of cross and resurrection within God's own experience."[39] Moltmann thus puts the cross at the center of his understanding of God: "The cross of the Son stands from eternity in the centre of the Trinity."[40] God identifies himself over against all other gods at the cross; at the cross, he shows himself to be the God who is revealed in his opposite, in godforsakenness. And it is not the Son only whose co-suffering with the world is evident on the cross, but the Father as well: "The grief of the Father is here as important as the death of the Son." He insists that "what happened on the cross was an event between God and

God. It was a deep division in God himself, in so far as God abandoned God and contradicted himself, and at the same time a unity in God, in so far as God was at one with God and corresponded to himself."[41] Moltmann also describes this as a loss and restoration of personal identity for the persons. The Son loses sonship by subjecting himself to abandonment, and the Father loses his fatherhood in losing the Son. But in the midst of that contradiction, they are united in love for the creation, a love that proceeds as the Spirit.[42]

Moltmann teaches that the persons of the Trinity are dependent on one another, and that they are mutually constituted by one another. As Veli-Matti Kärkkäinen points out, Moltmann denies that person can be reduced to relation, insisting instead that there "are no persons without relations, but there are no relations without persons."[43] The persons of the Trinity "ex-ist totally in the other: the Father ex-ists by virtue of his love, as himself entirely in the Son; the Son, by virtue of his self-surrender, ex-ists as himself totally in the Father."[44] Only in this way can trinitarian theology outwit the static categories of classical theism, too much hellenized: "Then only does the eternal life of the triune God become conceivable; its eternal vitality becomes conceivable too."[45]

God must be co-sufferer because he is love: "He suffers from the love which is the superabundance and overflowing of his being." Moreover, "a God who cannot suffer is poorer than any man. For a God who is incapable of suffering is a being who cannot be involved. Suffering an injustice does not affect him. . . . But the one who cannot suffer cannot love either. So he is also a loveless being."[46] Moltmann addresses the problem of God's freedom in terms of love: "God's freedom can never contradict the truth which he himself is," and that truth is love. The traditional idea of divine freedom is, Moltmann argues, based on the notion of domination and lordship, rather than the fundamental Christian revelation that God is love. God's freedom consists in the friendship that he offers creatures, and in this sense Moltmann says, "God 'needs' the world and man. If God is love, then he neither will nor can be without the one who is his beloved." More fully, "creation is the fruit of God's longing for his Other and for that Other's free response to the divine love. That is why the idea of the world is inherent in the nature of God himself from eternity. . . . And if God's eternal being is love, then the divine love is also more blessed in giving than in receiving. God cannot find bliss in eternal self-love if selflessness is part of love's very nature. God is in all eternity self-communicating love."[47] For Moltmann, creation is an act of self-humiliation and self-limitation. God clears out to create space for the world to be: to make something "'outside' himself, the infinite God must have made room for this finitude beforehand, 'in himself.'"[48] There is a sense in which creation itself is the zone of godforsakenness. The cross contradicts everything God is, and yet God is present there, embracing the godforsaken reality "to deliver from sin, suffering, and death." The cross is an intratrinitarian event "in which Jesus suffers dying in abandonment by his Father and the Father suffers in grief the death of his Son." At the point of their "deepest separation," the Father and the Son are yet "united in love for the world," and this love "spans the gulf which separates the godless and godforsaken from God and overcomes it."[49]

Hegel and Moltmann both charge that the axiom of impassibility is indebted to Hellenism, a sign of the hellenization of the church and a departure from the radical personalism of the biblical portrait of God. Yet there are powerful arguments in favor of impassibility. For the fathers and medieval theologians, impassibility is of a piece with God's unchangeability. God is not affected by things outside himself because God is unchangeably God, unchangeably himself. Unchangeability is not a limitation on God's life, nor does it imply that God is lifeless and inert. Quite the contrary: just *because* God is full of life and energy, he is unchanging. Creatures can only do this, and then that, and then that. We have to "die" to one activity in order to take up another. God is living, and indeed he is life, and thus cannot *not* be doing all that he does and is. Because God is simple, his being is identical to all his attributes, and since his being is always in act, his attributes are always fully engaged. God does not lay aside doing justice in order to take up the task of mercy. He is always doing and being all that he is. How can a being who is always doing all, always being all, "change"?

When the fathers speak of "impassibility," they are not claiming that God is incapable of action, that God's life is "uneventful." On the contrary, they are highlighting the sheer eventfulness of divine life. And, as a result, they are also emphasizing the responsiveness of God. God is not changeless in the sense that he is inert and unresponsive. He is changeless because he is infinitely responsive, because he is always and forever responding to everyone and everything. Humans can respond dexterously to visual and audible cues; we can sense the unsaid and the unseen and can act accordingly. But our sensitivity to these cues is limited and finite; God's is infinite. We never experience a momentary shift in mood without God being involved and responding accordingly. In our anguish, he is there; and when in the next moment anguish turns to elation, he is still there. But this is not because he has changed; if he is always all that he is, then he is always responding to everything and everyone.[50]

Word on the Cross

Yet, this does not yet get to the heart of the theological issue. Plato, Parmenides, and the Stoics, after all, believed that God, or whatever they called their ultimate principle, was timeless and passionless, but they had not heard Yahweh's grief over Israel's rebellions in the wilderness nor learned of the incarnation of the Son. If the Son of God came in the flesh and was raised on a cross, and if the Son of God is all that Athanasius says he is, then God's relation to time and flesh, his relation to creation and his ability to be acted upon, must be something different from anything the Greeks could have conceived. The defense of impassibility above to some extent infuses biblical conceptualities into the subject, but it does not yet arrive at an evangelization of metaphysics. We need to attend specifically to the cross. Christ, and him crucified, is the measure of metaphysics and theology, the measure of all.

Fortunately, the cross is just where Athanasius focuses his attention. His affirmation of impassibility is an *evangelical* affirmation. He does not flinch at the last moment. He assumes impassibility precisely in order to elucidate and preach the good news about the cross of the Word made flesh.

We can begin to see how by taking note of another recent theologian's objections to impassibility. Robert Jenson has also objected to the axiom of impassibility and seen it to some degree as a product of a residual Hellenism. At the same time, Jenson works from and within Nicene orthodoxy rather than abandoning it. He notes that the creeds of the church gradually closed off all avenues of escape from the evangelical claim that God in Christ was reconciling the world to himself on the cross. Nicaea shut down the Arian effort to separate the suffering Christ from God, and Chalcedon closed off the Nestorian escape hatch, which would have made the Sufferer on the cross the "humanity" in isolation from the divinity. For his own part, Jenson starts from a "simpleminded beginning": "If indeed the Christology is true whose slogan is that 'one of the Trinity suffered in the flesh,' then the God here referred to by 'the Trinity' is not impassible, in any use of the adjective that would occur to a native user of Greek, Latin, or English—or at least not to any such user who had mastered the relation of subject and predicate." The qualifying phrase "in the flesh" is "indeed important," but Jenson points out that it "does not displace the subject-object relation: with or without 'in the flesh' the subject of 'suffered' is God the Son/Logos."[51] On the other hand, Jenson insists that it will not do to say that "the biblical God is 'passible.'" According to Jenson, Moltmann follows Hegel down a blind alley. Luther's righteous "outrage at Erasmus was in considerable part driven by insistence that God is not going to react to our bad behavior by withdrawing his promises, that he cannot be affected in this way."[52]

Jenson argues that the question of passibility and impassibility must be asked and answered at different levels. Drawing on Origen's exposition of Yahweh's pity for Israel in Ezekiel 16 (in which Origen says, "*ipse Pater non est impassibilis*"), he asks, "Was God passible when he felt pity for the exposed newborn Jerusalem?" Yes, Jenson says, "since in fact he was affected and so manifested this dispositional property." Was God also "impassible in his commitment to the wayward foundling?" Yes again; borrowing a musical analogy from Jeremy Begbie, Jenson argues that God is impassible even when he shows pity "since at this level of the narrative's hyperbars he simply overrides all challenges to that commitment." What about more generally: "Is God, considered as the subject of his total history with us, impassible? By the testimony of Scripture, he is indeed—in any plausible sense of the word." But "happening upon a lost sheep" God is at the same time passible "in any plausible sense of the word." What about God in himself, "abstracted from all such tales"? Is he, considered thus abstractly, passible or not? Here Jenson sniffs out a "pseudo-question, since the abstraction cannot be performed on the biblical God." While we can reason about an immanent Trinity from the economy, we cannot "abstract" from the economic to the immanent, since one person of the immanent Trinity is *identical* to the person of Jesus, a person within the saving history. Thus we "cannot deny the hypostatic identity of the inner-triune relations, all of which have the Son as a pole, with narrative relations of the saving history."[53] It is not that Jesus is a particular illustration of a more general principle of divine life. Because he is Word made flesh, Jesus displays divine life within a human life. Jesus is the key to answering the question of the impassible God.

Though Jenson rejects impassibility and Athanasius affirms it, in my judgment they have much the same aim. Jenson wants to redefine impassibility, unchangeability, and other "metaphysical" attributes of God as descriptions of his commitment to redeem and fulfill his creation. Athanasius, I think, already does something similar.

In part, many of the objections to impassibility arise from a fundamental misunderstanding of what is meant by impassibility in the Christian tradition and in Athanasius in particular. John Behr writes,

> What is at stake for Athanasius is not whether Christ "felt" hunger, fear, and pain, whether he "really experienced" being human as we do, but the relationship between activity and passivity: Is Christ the active agent in this or the passive subject? "Suffering" here is to be understood in terms of "passivity," being acted upon, rather than in terms of "feeling" or "experiencing." In reverse, "impassibility" is not a lack of involvement, or an inability to change; if God is impassible, this means that he is not subject to anything, that he cannot be compelled.[54]

Thus the impassibility is "best understood in terms of the Word's active, willing acceptance of our human condition." Precisely because he is impassible, and *willingly* suffers all that we inescapably do, Jesus can "overturn the hold that it has on human beings."[55] For Athanasius, the Word *must* experience passions to overcome them, but he must do it freely.[56]

Thus, according to Athanasius, the *Word* takes on flesh and the sufferings of the flesh that come along with it. He is not touched by them in his divine nature, but they are as much his own as the body is his own. The eternal Son, who is one with the Father, "appropriates" (*idiopoieisthai*) flesh, and because of this one may legitimately apply "human predications to the subject of 'God the Word.'"[57] This is not merely "a manner of speaking." We can *say* that the Word suffered in the flesh because the Word did in fact take flesh. In his fullest statement of this point, Athanasius writes,

When the flesh suffered, the Word was not external [*ektos*] to it; and therefore is the passion said to be His [*autou legetai kai to pathos*]: and when He did divinely His Father's works, the flesh was not external to Him, but in the body itself did the Lord do them. . . . These things were so done, were so manifested, because He had a body, not in appearance, but in truth; and it became the Lord, in putting on human flesh, to put it on whole with the affections proper to it [*tautēn meta tōn idiōn pathōn autēs holēn endysasthai*]; that, as we say that the body was His own, so also we may say that the affections of the body were proper to Him alone, though they did not touch Him according to His Godhead. If then the body had been another's, to him too had been the affections attributed; but if the flesh is the Word's (for "the Word became flesh"), of necessity then the affections also of the flesh are ascribed to Him, whose the flesh is. And to whom the affections are ascribed, such namely as to be condemned, to be scourged, to thirst, and the cross, and death, and the other infirmities of the body, of Him too is the triumph and the grace. For this cause then, consistently and fittingly such affections are ascribed not to another, but to the Lord; that the grace also may be from Him, and that we may become, not worshippers of any other, but truly devout toward God, because we invoke no originate thing, no ordinary man, but the natural and true Son from God, who has become man, yet is not the less Lord and God and Savior. (*Discourses* 3.32)

As with everything pertaining to the incarnation, the Word takes on these sufferings *for us*, to make our sufferings lighter. Referring specifically to Jesus's anguish in Gethsemane, Athanasius writes,

Wherefore of necessity when He was in a body suffering, and weeping, and toiling, these things which are proper to the flesh, are ascribed to Him together with the body. If then He wept and was troubled, it was not the Word, considered as the Word, who wept and was troubled, but it was proper to the flesh; and if too He besought that the cup might pass away, it was not the Godhead that was in terror, but this affection too was proper to the manhood. And that the words "Why have You forsaken Me?" are His, according to the foregoing explanations (though He suffered nothing, for the Word was impassible), is notwithstanding declared by the Evangelists; since the Lord became man, and these things are done and said as from a man, that He might Himself lighten these very sufferings of the flesh, and free it from them. Whence neither can the Lord be forsaken by the Father, who is ever in the Father, both before He spoke, and when He uttered this cry. (*Discourses* 3.56)

The apparent double-talk of Athanasius is not double-talk at all. On the contrary, as Jenson recognizes, the Word is the subject of the sentence, "The *Word* suffered in the flesh," and Athanasius knows that

what the human Body of the Word suffered, this the Word, dwelling in the body, ascribed to Himself, in order that we might be enabled to be partakers of the Godhead of the Word. And verily it is strange that He it was Who suffered and yet suffered not. Suffered, because His own Body suffered, and He was in it, which thus suffered; suffered not, because the Word, being by Nature God, is impassible. And while He, the incorporeal, was in the passible Body, the Body had in it the impassible Word, which was destroying the infirmities inherent in the Body. But this He did, and so it was, in order that Himself taking what was ours and offering it as a sacrifice, He might do away with it, and conversely might invest us with what was His, and cause the Apostle to say: "This corruptible must put on incorruption, and this mortal put on immortality." (*Letter to Epictetus* 6)

He takes on flesh, which suffers terrors like all flesh. But he does not suffer these terrors in his divine nature, nor does he suffer them fruitlessly. He does not suffer simply to demonstrate his sympathy, his willingness to come alongside as co-sufferer. He suffers terrors so that we might be delivered from terror: "When He had become man, He had a flesh that was in terror. For the sake of this flesh He combined His own will with human weakness, that destroying this affection He might in turn make man undaunted in face of death" (*Discourses* 3.57). Though Jesus requests that the cup be removed, it is not, and he bows to the Father's will, receiving the terrors of the flesh. By suffering that terror in the flesh, he overcame terror, a fact demonstrable in the lives and deaths of the martyrs. Flesh no longer shrinks from the cup of woe. Jesus's flesh did not shrink, and that is the flesh the martyrs share (*Discourses* 3.57).

Athanasius's account of the cross follows precisely these lines. One of the sharp Arian protests against the orthodox arose from Jesus's cry of dereliction: "How can He be the own Word of the Father, without whom the Father never was, through whom He makes all things, as you think, who said upon the Cross 'My God, My God, why have You forsaken Me?'" (*Discourses* 3.26). Isaiah spoke accurately when he prophesied that the Savior would "carry" infirmities (Isa. 53:4). That is a stronger claim than the promise that the Lord would "heal." Healing can be done from a distance, while the Word is "external to the body." But bearing infirmity and sin requires that he "become man for us," and more, "that the body which in Him bore them, was His own body; and, while He received no hurt Himself by 'bearing our sins in His body on the tree,' as Peter speaks, we men were redeemed from our own affections, and were filled with the righteousness of the Word" (*Discourses* 3.31).

In the final analysis, Athanasius responds to the Arian view of the incarnation with the argument he uses at the beginning of *On the Incarnation*. Jews and Greeks scorn the incarnation, but for Christians it is the power and wisdom of God at work. Attending to the human attributes of the incarnate Son leads the Arians to "low thoughts" of the Son, but the result should be the opposite. The incarnation shows that God is even more fully God, more fully Lord of his creation, than we might have dared to believe. Through the incarnation, "the thing which they, as men, rule out as impossible, He plainly shows to be possible; that which they deride as unfitting, his goodness makes most fit; and things which these wise-acres laugh at as 'human' He by His inherent might declares divine" (*On the Incarnation* 1). In the cross, God, the living God, the creating Word, demonstrates what it means to be God, the God of life whom death cannot hold or stop or even slow. Jesus could suffer *triumphantly* only because his flesh was God's, only because the flesh was the proper flesh of the Word who is incapable of being terrified or defeated by pain or suffering. It was the flesh of the Word whose love *no* obstacle can block or frustrate, and thus in his suffering and death Jesus triumphs over death and suffering.

Conclusion

What is the world like? What is the ultimate nature of things? For Athanasius, I have argued throughout this volume, the answer to that metaphysical question always returns to Christ, the eternal Word of the Father who became flesh. The ultimate reality is the Creator God, the Father who creates and maintains all things through his own proper Word and Spirit. The ultimate reality of creation is from nothing, sustained and maintained only by the power of the Father's Word. And the ultimate meaning and crux of history is the incarnation, the Word taking flesh to do the works that the Father sent him to do.

Athanasius, despite some infelicitous turns of phrase and tendentious arguments, does not think that the Son is playacting when he enters the world he created and sustains it in order to become a creature among creatures. The little word *idios*—proper—tells it all. The Word is *idios* to the Father, proper to him, as intimate and intrinsic to the Father's being as any attributes of the Father. Nothing can be more intrinsic to the Father than his Word, Wisdom, radiance, expression. And then this Word, willingly and graciously, makes humanity *idios* to himself. Flesh is not eternally intrinsic to the Son's being in the way that the Son is eternally intrinsic to the Father. The assumption, the "making-proper" (*idiopoieisthai*), of flesh is a free act and a product of will in a way that the existence of the Word is not a product of will. With that qualification, however, we can say that the flesh of the Word is now intrinsic to the Word's being Word. Having assumed flesh *for us*, that flesh becomes a property of the Word, not an external possession or detached instrument, but as proper to the Word as his being the Word of the Father. That is what Athanasius means when he writes of an "impassible sufferer," the impassible Word on the cross. Jesus's death on the cross is the voluntary act of the Word who has taken all our anguish to himself and made it *his*.

Objections to impassibility often represent efforts to equalize the Word and the creature.[58] That is, to Athanasius, only another form of Arianism, a backdoor denial of the Word's nature as Word of the Father. As such, it is also a threat to the gospel. Unless the Word is God come to us in flesh, then we are still in our sins, then there is no "it is finished" at the cross and no triumph over death. A Christ who is merely equal to us is not a saving Christ, and the Arian "gospel" is no gospel. The true gospel is a "rhetoric of reversal."[59] That is, it reverses the terms of the Creator-creature distinction: the Creator becomes creature, the impassible suffers, so that passible creatures might triumph over death and suffering, so that the creature might be deified. For Athanasius, to say that "the impassible suffered" is simply to state the good news, that death has been trampled by this one death, that the corruptible has put on incorruption, the weak has put on strength, the dishonorable has been swallowed up in glory.

6

End

God Made Man, Man Made God

The grace of God is inherent in creation, because God is a God of goodness and kindness. God is not proud. He is a God of little things, who does not disdain to bring non-existents into being, who, with the gentleness of infinite power, sustains them in their fragility. But for Athanasius, creation is not the starting point of grace. Grace precedes creation. Even the incarnation, he intimates, has an origin before the creation, in that the Son was "founded" as incarnate Son before the foundation of the world (*Discourses* 2.75).[1] If the Son was "founded" before the foundation of the world, we too were "founded" in him. Athanasius deploys Paul's hymn to the electing God (Eph. 1) in an anti-Arian argument: "How then has He chosen us, before we came into existence, but that, as he says himself, in Him we were represented beforehand?" Further,

> How at all, before men were created, did He predestinate us unto adoption, but that the Son Himself was "founded before the world," taking on Him that economy which was for our sake? Or how, as the Apostle goes on to say, have we "an inheritance being predestinated," but that the Lord Himself was founded "before the world," inasmuch as He had a purpose, for our sakes, to take on Him through the flesh all that inheritance of judgment which lay against us, and we henceforth were made sons in Him? And how did we receive it "before the world was," when we were not yet in being, but afterwards in time, but that in Christ was stored the grace which has reached us? (*Discourses* 2.76)

The language of Proverbs 8 about the Son being "founded" is thus not about the creation of the Son, but about the determination of the Father to send the Word in human flesh, a determination arrived at before the mountains or the deep were formed.

> Therefore reason is there that the Word, on coming into our flesh, and being created in it as "a beginning of ways for His works," is laid as a foundation according as the Father's will was in Him before the world, as has been said, and before land was, and before the mountains were settled, and before the fountains burst forth; that, though the earth and the mountains and the shapes of visible nature pass away in the fullness of the present age, we on the contrary may not grow old after their pattern, but may be able to live after them, having the spiritual life and blessing which before these things have been prepared for us in the Word Himself according to election. For thus we shall be capable of a life not temporary, but ever afterwards abide and live in Christ; since even before this our life had been founded and prepared in Christ Jesus. (*Discourses* 2.76)

As we saw in chapter 4, this precreation grace of predestination is manifest from the beginning of creation. Creation itself is an act of grace; existence is a gift and depends on the continuing sustenance of the Word and the Spirit. Adam was the recipient of grace from the beginning, the grace of participation in the Spirit, the grace of the ordering Word, and the grace of the spoken word of a loving Father. Even in the midst of a world of death and sin, Israel remained in that grace throughout the history of the Old Testament. This grace is evident not only in the call of Abram and the promises given to the patriarchs, to Moses and to David, but also evident in the Lord's providential oversight of Israel's history. The Triune God orchestrated the history of Israel so that, like the creation itself, everything happened at just the right time. Just as God created things at just the right time, even so each event of the biblical history happened just when it was best: "Though He was able, even from the beginning in the time of Adam, or Noah, or Moses, to send His own Word, yet He sent Him not until the consummation of the ages (for this He saw to be good for the whole creation), so also things originated did He make when He would, and as was good for them" (*Discourses* 1.29).

God could have reversed the effects of sin by fiat, immediately after the fall, but this would not have been expedient. God does what is best for humanity. Not only in the incarnation but in all his actions in history, God has humanity's best interests in view. "We must consider what was expedient for mankind," Athanasius says, "and not what simply is possible with God." To be sure, he could have sent a flood before instructing Noah to build an ark, but he did it after the ark was ready. He might have brought Israel out of Egypt with a word; he had no need of Moses, "but it profited to do it through Moses." So too at the climax of the ages in the gift of the Son: "The Savior too might have come among us from the beginning, or on His coming might not have been delivered to Pilate; but He came 'at the fullness of the ages' (Gal. 4:4), and when sought for said, 'I am He' (John 18:5). For what He does, that is profitable for men, and was not fitting in any other way; and what is profitable and fitting, for that He provides." Jesus is merely doing what his Father does when he insists that he ministers to people rather than seeking their ministry. With regard to the incarnation, the rationale of God's timing is evident: "If God had but spoken, because it was in His power, and so the curse had been undone, the power had been shown of Him who gave the word, but man had become such as Adam was before the transgression, having received grace from without, and not having it united to the body; (for he was such when he was placed in Paradise) nay, perhaps had become worse, because he had learned to transgress" (*Discourses* 2.68). As we have seen in previous chapters, the grace of the new covenant is given "from within" the human race, and before this grace could be given intrinsically, Israel and the world had to be prepared for the human epiphany of the Word.

End of the Ages

For Athanasius, the incarnation marks the beginning of a new creation, the beginning of a new path for the world and for humanity. Explaining the phrase "beginning of ways" in Proverbs 8, he argues that it refers to the incarnation. "If a new creation has come to pass," he observes, "some one must be first of this creation; now a man, made of earth only, such as we have become from the transgression, he could not be." As there was a first man who set the world on the wrong track, there is one man who sets the world back to rights. The first creation had fallen into unfaithfulness, "and there was need of some one else to renew the first creation, and preserve the new which had come to be." The "beginning" of the new creation, the *archē*, is Jesus, sent from the love of the Father, to create a new way. Because of Jesus, it becomes possible that "man might walk no longer according to that first creation, but there being as it were a beginning of a new creation, and with the Christ 'a beginning of its ways,' we might follow Him henceforth, who says to us, 'I am the Way'" (*Discourses* 2.65).

The incarnation is not simply a remedy for human sin. It is truly the coming of a new creation, superior to the original creation. The Son is "created" in the incarnation, to share in the creature's lot, in order to restore everything. "Before the works were made, the Son was ever, nor was there yet need that He should be created," yet he became created after God's works were created and "need arose afterwards of the Economy for their restoration." Scripture points to this "condescension and assimilation to the works" in Proverbs 8, which says that the uncreated Wisdom was "created." Isaiah prophesies the same: "And now thus says the Lord, who formed me from the womb to be His servant, to gather together Jacob unto Him and Israel, I shall be brought together and be glorified before the Lord" (*Discourses* 2.51). The Son is the fitting agent of this renewal, since "He Himself is Framer of the creation, and His works are evidently later than Himself." Thus, "it became Him, being other than the works, nay rather their Framer, to take upon Himself their renovation, that, whereas He is created for us, all things may be now created in Him. For when He said 'He created,' He immediately added the reason, naming 'the works,' that His creation for the works might signify His becoming man for their renovation" (*Discourses* 2.53).

This new beginning involves a transition from shadowy types to the truth. Again, Athanasius's argument is set in an anti-Arian polemic. If the Son is merely another among the originated things, he had no more authority or power to make this new way, to be the beginning of ways, than angels. Since he is the Son of the Father, he is "better and His acts better and transcendent." What was revealed earlier was merely a "type," but "now the truth has been manifested." Hebrews provides Athanasius with many of the proof texts for the superiority of the new covenant: "'By so much was Jesus made a surety of a better testament' [7:22]; and again, 'But now has He obtained a more excellent ministry, by how much also He is the Mediator of a better covenant, which was established upon better promises' [8:6]. And, 'For the Law made nothing perfect, but the bringing in of a better hope did' [7:19]. And again he says, 'It was therefore necessary that the patterns of things in the heavens should be purified with these; but the heavenly things themselves with better sacrifices than these' [9:23]." If the covenant is so far better, it is because the mediator of the covenant is better than Moses and all the rest: "In the verse before us, then, and throughout, does he ascribe the word 'better' to the Lord, who is better and other than originated things. For better is the sacrifice through Him, better the hope in Him; and also the promises through Him, not merely as great compared with small, but the one differing from the other in nature, because He who conducts this economy, is 'better' than things originated" (*Discourses* 1.59).

The change effected by the incarnation is, for Athanasius, something that we might call an ontological change. Because the Son comes in a body and joins himself inseparably to human flesh that he makes his own, the new covenant is as much "better" than the old as the Son is "better" than earlier mediators. The first covenant came through angels, but "regarding the Word's visitation in the flesh, and the Economy which He then sustained, he wished to show that He was not like those who had gone before Him." Just as much as "He excelled in nature those who were sent afore by Him, by so much also the grace which came from and through Him was better than the ministry through Angels." Angels came to demand fruit from Israel, but the Son comes to "forgive the debts and to transfer the vineyard." Again the thrust of the argument is anti-Arian. If the covenant is so much better, the mediator must be too: "Certainly what the Apostle proceeds to say shows the excellence of the Son over things originate" (*Discourses* 1.59). But the argument works in reverse as well: since the mediator is better, the hope and achievement are so much the greater.

Human beings in the new covenant are capable of transcending the original Adamic nature in which they were made. As we have seen, Athanasius believes that Adam was created with a corruptible, unstable body directed by a mobile, equally unstable soul. Both soul and body were created *ex nihilo*, and so Adam was susceptible to change and decay, a decay that became all the more radical and insurmountable because of Adam's sin. Bodies are good, but since human beings are created with bodies, they have the potential to turn from contemplation and love of God toward sensible things, and to seek gratification of bodily pleasure more than obedience to the Creator. Now, however, the Son has come in the flesh and has lent human flesh some of his own power and stability. Human beings can be delivered from corruption through the work of the Son.

Athanasius often describes this change in terms of the Johannine image of adoption. The Son is the only begotten Son, uniquely Son, God existing as Son, but through the incarnate Son, creatures created as men are made into sons, begotten of God, not merely formed by him. As Athanasius notes, "the term 'begot' is here as elsewhere expressive of a Son, as He says by the Prophet, 'I begot sons and exalted them'; and generally, when the Scripture wishes to signify a son, it does so, not by the term 'created,' but undoubtedly by that of 'begot.'" This is what John means when he writes, "'He gave to them power to become children of God, even to them that believe in His Name; which were begotten not of blood, nor of the will of the flesh, nor of the will of man, but of God'" (*Discourses* 2.59). Athanasius highlights a remarkable Johannine formulation: the same John who declares that the Word is eternal God with God, only begotten God (or Son), utterly unique, uses the same language of "begetting" to describe the sonship of those who are joined to the flesh of the Son. One might gloss John in an Athanasian idiom: the Son who is begotten by nature took flesh so that human beings might participate by grace in his begotten-ness.

The Son who is the "only-begotten" of the Father from all eternity becomes the "firstborn," not the first one created but the firstborn of a new creation:

> He is called "First-born among many brethren," because of the relationship of the flesh, and "First-born from the dead," because the resurrection of the dead is from Him and after Him; and "First-born of the whole creation," because of the Father's love to man, which brought it to pass that in His Word not only "all things consist," but the creation itself, of which the Apostle speaks, "waiting for the manifestation of the sons of God, shall be delivered" one time "from the bondage of corruption into the glorious liberty of the children of God." Of this creation thus delivered, the Lord will be First-born, both of it and of all those who are made children, that by His being called first, those that come after Him may abide, as depending on the Word as a beginning. (*Discourses* 2.63)

Athanasius thus identifies the neat chiasm of redemptive history, not only in his well-known notion that "God became man that man might become God" and the Son was created body so that body could be renewed and deified (*Discourses* 2.47), but in his play with "being" and "being-made." The Son exists first, then is made man. But human beings are made first and then are raised up to become sons in the Son (*Discourses* 2.53).

> And here too the cautious distinction is well kept up, for first he says "become," because they are not called sons by nature but by adoption; then he says "were begotten," because they too had received at any rate the name of son. But the people, as says the Prophet, "despised" their Benefactor. But this is God's kindness to man, that of whom He is Maker, of them according to grace He afterwards becomes Father also; becomes, that is, when men, His creatures, receive into their hearts, as the Apostle says, "the Spirit of His Son, crying, Abba, Father." And these are they who, having received the Word, gained power from Him to become sons of God; for they could not become sons, being by nature creatures, otherwise than by receiving the Spirit of the natural and true Son. Wherefore, that this might be, "The Word became flesh," that He might make man capable of Godhead. This same meaning may be gained also from the Prophet Malachi, who says, "Hath not One God created us? Have we not all one Father?" (Mal. 2:10). For first he puts "created," next "Father," to show, as the other writers, that from the beginning we were creatures by nature, and God is our Creator through the Word; but afterwards we were made sons, and thenceforward God the Creator becomes our Father also. (*Discourses* 2.59)

This radical new beginning in the midst of history is the deeper point behind Athanasius's frequent insult that the Arians are "Jews," which in many instances looks like sheer name-calling. As noted in chapter 1, when he talks about Jews, Athanasius frequently employs the harsh unchristian rhetoric of his time. But he is making a serious theological point. The theological root of the charge is that the Arians cannot account for the new beginning of the world. Since they do not believe that the Son is God himself, they cannot believe that Jesus's appearance makes all that much difference. They are "Jews" in the sense that they remain trapped in a world before incarnation, the "lesser" world of created mediators and extrinsic grace (cf. *Discourses* 3.28).

Christ Died for Us

As we have noted in earlier chapters, there are hints that Athanasius sees this advance for humanity as a completion of the original destiny of Adam and creation, rather than as an extrinsic *telos* super-added to the original creation. Humanity deviated from that destiny because of sin, but the impassible God never wavered, and in the incarnation the Son comes to complete the creation and to complete the deification of man, not merely to deliver it from evil. Picking up a reference to John 17:14, Athanasius explains:

> Not of His essence then is "He created" indicative, as has many times been said, but of His bodily generation. For then, because the works had become imperfect and mutilated from the transgression, He is said in respect to the body to be created; that by perfecting them and making them whole, He might present the Church unto the Father, as the Apostle says, "not having spot or wrinkle or any such thing, but holy and without blemish" (Eph. 5:27). Mankind then is perfected in Him and restored, as it was made at the beginning, nay, with greater grace. (*Discourses* 2.67)

Created being is fragile and unstable, and can be made stable and persevere in the grace given if it is more deeply rooted, internally rooted, in God's own life. That is what the incarnation accomplishes: those created by God become founded by God; those already sustained by their participation in the Spirit now share in the Spirit of the risen Christ; and those who are in the flesh are joined to the flesh that is joined to the eternal Son, who will lose nothing of what he has been given.[2]

As was noted in the previous chapter, on Athanasius's account, the incarnation is entirely *for us*. The flesh of the Son does not promote or exalt the Son, since he shared the glory of the Father from the beginning. Rather, the Son takes flesh to promote the flesh, to give it a new origin and new life, to make a new beginning for humanity in the world. The Son became man not so that God could become more God; he became man in order to make men gods. Since the Son had all glory before the creation, "it follows that He had not promotion from His descent, but rather Himself promoted the things which needed promotion; and if He descended to effect their promotion, therefore He did not receive in reward the name of the Son and God, but rather He Himself has made us sons of the Father, and deified men by becoming Himself man" (*Discourses* 1.38). The Word had no need, and so he does not humble himself for the sake of any reward that he might receive (*Discourses* 1.40). Thus "the Word was not impaired in receiving a body, that He should seek to receive a grace, but rather He deified that which He put on, and more than that, 'gave' it graciously to the race of man" (*Discourses* 1.42). "As Christ died and was exalted as man," Athanasius writes, "so, as man, is He said to take what, as God, He ever had, that even such a grant of grace might reach to us" (*Discourses* 1.42).

This deification of humanity is not possible unless the Son is truly proper to the Father, and the flesh truly proper to him. No "external" (*ouk ontos ektos*) flesh could do the trick (*Discourses* 1.45). Virginia Burrus has suggested that for Athanasius the incarnation functions as a blood transfusion into the human race. The human race is corruptible, and under the dominion of death and sin is heading toward utter dissolution. Divine medication is injected through the flesh of the Son, and this begins to solidify the race and put things back together.[3] It is true that Athanasius sometimes writes this way. Yet this does not reflect the key features of his thought. It is not merely the Son's assumption of flesh that deifies but the whole set of actions performed by the Son in the flesh. Everything he does, he does for us, and the restoration of the human race is the end point of his life, death, and resurrection.

Expounding on Psalm 45, Athanasius insists that the Son is anointed with the Spirit for us (*Discourses* 1.46), so that his body could be sanctified by the Spirit, the body that is his: "He who, as the Word and Radiance of the Father, gives to others, now is said to be sanctified, because now He has become man, and the Body that is sanctified is His. From Him then we have begun to receive the unction and the seal" (*Discourses* 1.47). The incarnation is an ordination to priesthood analogous to the ordination of Aaron, but this ordination by itself does not accomplish atonement unless the priest offers sacrifice (*Discourses* 2.7–9). The uncreated Son was created as man, created for us, so that we might be recreated in him.

> He says, "The Lord created me," being a creature, He was not created for us; but if He was not created for us, we are not created in Him; and, if not created in Him, we have Him not in ourselves but externally; as, for instance, as receiving instruction from Him as from a teacher. And it being so with us, sin has not lost its reign over the flesh, being inherent and not cast out of it. But the Apostle opposes such a doctrine a little before, when he says, "For we are His workmanship, created in Christ Jesus" (Eph. 2:10), and if in Christ we are created, then it is not He who is created, but we in Him; and thus the words "He created" are for our sake. For because of our need, the Word, though being Creator, endured words which are used of creatures; which are not proper to Him, as being the Word, but are ours who are created in Him. (*Discourses* 2.56)

The climax of this series of actions "for us" was the Son's ascent on the cross, equally for us. Through the cross he defeated death and defanged the serpent, removing his poison. "The Word being clothed in the flesh," Athanasius writes, "every bite of the serpent began to be utterly staunched from out it; and whatever evil sprung from the motions of the flesh, to be cut away, and with these death also was abolished, the companion of sin." This is what Jesus meant when he declared of his death, "The prince of this world comes, and finds nothing in Me" (John 14:30) and what John meant when he explains, "For this end was He manifested that He might destroy the works of the devil" (1 John 3:8) (*Discourses* 2.69).

How does the cross achieve this? Athanasius's answer to that question does not easily fit into the traditional categories of atonement theology. He certainly sees Jesus as a representative of the human race and as a substitute for Adamic humanity. Yet he does not express this in terms of Jesus vicariously receiving the punishment we deserve. Instead, he tends to think in liturgical categories. Seeing that humanity was under the dominion of death, the Son was full of pity and compassion and so took on a body. His body was like all human bodies mortal, and so he too "surrendered His body to death in place of all, and offered to the Father" (*On the Incarnation* 8).[4] Like a king who comes to the rescue of a city that has been attacked by robbers, the Son "by the offering of His own body . . . abolished the death which they had incurred, and corrected their neglect by His own teaching" (*On the Incarnation* 10).

When we read *On the Incarnation* with its companion treatise, *Against the Pagans*, it becomes evident that the contrast of Adamic and redeemed humanity is a contrast between idolatry and true worship. As human beings turn from God toward sensible things, they begin to worship and serve the creature rather than the Creator, and this turn to the creature is manifested most plainly in the practice of idolatry, literally, worship of created objects—stones, statues, golden calves. Jesus is the new Adam, the beginning of a new race, because he offers the first act of true worship to the Father. By the Spirit communicated through baptism, men and women are caught up in that great liturgical offering, pulled from their obsession with the creation and their worship of idols and turned again to the living God. The Son, we might say, seizes humanity in the incarnation and in the cross entices it toward the heavenly sanctuary to worship the Father.

At times Athanasius explains the cross in terms of debt. The Son "assumed a body capable of death, in order that it, through belonging to the Word who is above all, might become in dying a sufficient exchange for all" (*On the Incarnation* 9). All men owe a debt of death: "All men were due to die," and the Word came in mortal flesh in order to "settle man's account with death and free him from the primal transgression." Because the Word's body was capable of death, he offered it in death, but because it was the body of the incorruptible *Word*, it could not remain in corruption. Thus "it happened that two opposite marvels took place at once: the death of all was consummated in the Lord's body; yet, because the Word was in it, death and corruption were in the same act utterly abolished." Death was unavoidable "that the due of all might be paid" (*On the Incarnation* 20).[5]

Whatever the "mechanics" of the transaction of the cross, the effect is evident. By his death, the Son overcomes death, and he overcomes death precisely in the flesh. As noted, because the Word is "in" the flesh that is offered on the cross, "death and corruption were . . . utterly abolished" (*On the Incarnation* 20). Hebrews 2:14–15 plays a crucial role in Athanasius's treatment of the effects of the cross. In the condition of sin and corruption, the human race is dominated by the fear of death. But through the cross, the Son has destroyed the one who has power over death, the devil, and thus delivered "them who all their lifetime were enslaved by the fear of death" (*On the Incarnation* 20). As Hebrews 2:14–15 makes clear, the triumph of the Son over death and his liberation of the human race from fear of death is accomplished by the Son's triumph over the devil, the one with power over death. Following Johannine hints (John 12:32), Athanasius argues that the very form of Jesus's execution signifies its purpose. He is lifted up into the air, the realm of fallen angels and demons and devils, so that he can conquer them on their own ground. By being lifted up in the air and defeating the demons, Jesus is also making a way for us, a way of return to the Father.

Athanasius gives a great deal of attention to the cross and its effects, but he does not neglect the rest of the story of the gospel. Jesus went to the cross as the incarnate Word, with flesh subject to death, but also as the Word, who was the Lord of life. Death could not hold him. In fact, the resurrection was already implicit in the cross: "Our resurrection is stored up" in the cross (*anastasis hēmōn en autō apokeitai*; *Discourses* 1.43). Rather than a transfusion, Athanasius sees the incarnation of the Son as the beginning of a rescue operation, the Son taking flesh to take it to the grave and raise it up again. It is

> as if some son, when the servants were lost, and in the hands of the enemy by their own carelessness, and need was urgent, were sent by his father to succor and recover them, and on setting out were to put over him the like dress with them, and should fashion himself as they, lest the capturers, recognizing him as the master, should take to flight and prevent his descending to those who were hidden under the earth by them; and then were any one to inquire of him, why he did so, were to make answer, "My Father thus formed and prepared me for his works," while in thus speaking, he neither implies that he is a servant nor one of the works, nor speaks of the beginning of His origination, but of the subsequent charge given him over the works—in the same way the Lord also, having put over Him our flesh, and "being found in fashion as a man," if He were questioned by those who saw Him thus and marveled, would say, "The Lord created Me the beginning of His ways for His works," and "He formed Me to gather together Israel." (*Discourses* 2.52)

Athanasius thinks that the exaltation of the Son in Philippians 2 might refer to the resurrection. All other men are born in Adam and under the dominion of death. Jesus, however, the man from heaven, was "not held under death." Thus, "though He humbled Himself, yielding His own Body to come unto death, in that it was capable of death, yet He was highly exalted from earth, because He was God's Son in a body" (*en sōmati huion tou theou*; *Discourses* 1.44). Death is proper (*idios*) to human nature, and the Son put on flesh to be put to death in flesh, so that he could quicken all men by his proper power (*Discourses* 1.44).

This humiliation is the beginning of a process of exaltation and deification. The Word humbled himself so that he could raise up our humanity. Due to death and sin, "man's nature [was] in want, because of the humble estate of the flesh and of death." Just as he took our flesh and offered himself to the Father, so also "as man, He is said because of us and for us to be highly exalted, that as by His death we all died in Christ, so again in the Christ Himself we might be highly exalted, being raised from the dead, and ascending into heaven." He goes as our forerunner, better than Aaron and the priests of old. For the Son, this is just a return to where he had been, as "Lord and Framer of the heavens." For us, though, everything changes: "For us therefore is that present exaltation written" (*Discourses* 1.41). In his ascension, the Son took our flesh into heavenly places. Angels continuously worship the Triune God, but they are astonished when human flesh is exalted to heaven and placed at the right hand of the Father: "Whereas the powers in heaven, both Angels and Archangels, were ever worshipping the Lord, as they are now worshipping Him in the Name of Jesus, this is our grace and high exaltation, that even when He became man, the Son of God is worshipped, and the heavenly powers will not be astonished at seeing all of us, who are of one body with Him, introduced into their realms" (*Discourses* 1.42).

Temples of the Spirit

Pentecost is as crucial to Athanasius's account as the cross and the resurrection. The Son receives the Spirit for us, as man, anointed so that we can come to share in the Spirit. He is not anointed to become God, nor to become king, since "He had the Kingdom eternally, existing as God's Image." He was anointed for us. Athanasius draws a typological analogy between the "becoming king" that happened with the coronation and anointing of Israel's kings and the "becoming Savior" that occurs when Jesus is anointed with the antitypical anointing of the Spirit: "The Israelitish kings, upon their being anointed, then became kings, not being so before, as David, as Hezekiah, as Josiah, and the rest; but the Savior on the contrary, being God, and ever ruling in the Father's Kingdom, and being Himself He that supplies the Holy Ghost, nevertheless is here said to be anointed, that, as before, being said as man to be anointed with the Spirit, He might provide for us men, not only exaltation and resurrection, but the indwelling and intimacy of the Spirit" (*Discourses* 1.46). As the Old Testament types are fulfilled in the antitype of Christ, so the great archetype and antitype impresses his character on us.

With the presence of the Spirit, redemption is a trinitarian action. We are made children of God by the incarnation of the Son, who comes from the Father, but this is not realized except as we participate in the grace of the Spirit. Creatures participate in the Spirit "naturally," but Athanasius insists that there is a different and full share in the Spirit that comes through the agency of the incarnate Son. We come to share in the perichoretic fellowship of the Triune God and know that we share in that life through the gift of the Spirit (1 John 4:13). Thus, "because of the grace of the Spirit which has been given to us, in Him we come to be, and He in us; and since it is the Spirit of

God, therefore through His becoming in us, reasonably are we, as having the Spirit, considered to be in God, and thus is God in us" (*Discourses* 3.24). In our corruption and sin, we are strangers and far off (*xenoi kai makran*), but through sharing in the Spirit we are brought near and "knit into the God-head" (*Discourses* 3.24). Through the Spirit, we come to love Christ, and as lovers of Christ we become Christ-bearers, a point that Athanasius makes in a cleverly chiastic formula: we are "lovers of Christ and Christ-bearers" (*hoi philochristoi kai christophoroi*; *Discourses* 3.45). Again, the emphasis is on the transition from an "extrinsic" to an "intrinsic" gift of grace. All things share in the Spirit, or they would have no being at all. But not all creatures are indwelt by the Son through the Spirit. All things are animated by the Spirit; not all things are filled with the Spirit.

Through the gift of the Spirit, Jesus himself is a human temple, bearing the indwelling Spirit, and so prepares our flesh also to be a temple of the Spirit: "It is very plain that the Spirit's descent on Him in Jordan was a descent upon us, because of His bearing our body. And it did not take place for promotion of the Word, but again for our sanctification, that we might share His anointing, and of us it might be said, 'Do you not know that you are God's Temple, and the Spirit of God dwells in you'" (*Discourses* 1.47). Because of the Son, we have become temples, that is, places of true worship of the true God. "The fact that the Lord, even when come in human body and called Jesus, was worshipped and believed to be God's Son, and that through Him the Father was known, shows," Athanasius believes, "that not the Word, considered as the Word, received this so great grace, but we." Given "our relationship to His Body we too have become God's temple, and in consequence are made God's sons, so that even in us the Lord is now worshipped, and beholders report, as the Apostle says, that God is in them of a truth" (*Discourses* 1.43). Human beings in sin turn to idols and become "places" of false worship. By the work of the Son and the Spirit, we are reconstituted as temples of the living God, turned in worship to the Father.

More specifically, the Spirit is the power by which the incarnate Son casts out demons. In themselves, humans do not have dominion over the demons but rather are subject to them. But through the Spirit that comes to us through the incarnate Son, we are given this divine power to cast out demons and trample them. In the Psalms, David teaches that "no otherwise should we have partaken the Spirit and been sanctified, but that the Giver of the Spirit, the Word Himself, has spoken of Himself as anointed with the Spirit for us." As a result, we "securely received it, He being said to be anointed in the flesh; for the flesh being first sanctified in Him, and He being said, as man, to have received for its sake, we have the sequel of the Spirit grace, receiving 'out of His fullness'" (*Discourses* 1.50). This Spirit gives us a share in the Son's conquest of demons. The Son always had power over demons, a power that Satan recognized in the first encounters between Jesus and the devil in the wilderness. The Son did not have to gain such power, except as he gains it for us:

And again, that what He said that He had received, that He possessed before receiving it, appears from His driving away the demons, and from His unbinding what Satan had bound, as He did in the case of the daughter of Abraham; and from His remitting sins, saying to the paralytic, and to the woman who washed His feet, "Your sins be forgiven you"; and from His both raising the dead, and repairing the first nature of the blind, granting to him to see. And all this He did, not waiting till He should receive, but being "possessed of power." From all this it is plain that what He had as Word, that when He had become man and was risen again, He says that He received humanly; that for His sake men might henceforward upon earth have power against demons, as having become partakers of a divine nature; and in heaven, as being delivered from corruption, might reign everlastingly. (*Discourses* 3.40)

In a sense, the Son takes on flesh to make flesh capacious enough to receive the Spirit. Because of the incarnation, human flesh is stretched enough to hold the Word, and by union with that flesh, our flesh is stretched to hold the flood of the Spirit that flows from him. By taking flesh, the Word made flesh capable of bearing the Word. Because "the ministry through Him has become better" than the law (Rom. 8:3), he made "the flesh capable of the Word; He made us walk, no longer according to the flesh, but according to the Spirit" (*Discourses* 1.60).

Theopoiesis

This is the reality that Athanasius describes as "deification," or "making-God" (*theopoiēsis*), something he also calls "son-making" (*huiopoioumetha*; *Discourses* 1.34). This has nothing to do with overturning the Creator-creature distinction or erasing the difference between the eternal Son and human beings, between the Son by nature and children by grace. Athanasius expended much of his theological energy erecting and maintaining the necessary walls between God and creation. It is not plausible that he would suddenly dispense with this labor in his doctrine of deification. For Athanasius, theopoiesis means that human beings are brought into the communion of Father, Son, and Spirit by the incarnation of the Son and the gift of the Spirit, and having been introduced into that communion we begin to share divine attributes in a creaturely fashion. Fragmented human beings are given integrity; changeable human beings are made stable; mortal human beings are made immortal; human beings subjected to passions transcend their passions. Through the incarnation and the gift of the Spirit from the exalted and still incarnate Son, human flesh takes on the qualities of divinity, and human beings created after the image of God become ever more transparent images of God.

Again, Athanasius's doctrine is typically set within a polemical context. The Arian Christ is incapable of deifying creatures. If the Son is not eternal

Son, he cannot make sons; if he is not eternal God, he cannot be the god-maker: "What then was before this, if then He was exalted, and then began to be worshipped, and then was called Son, when He became man? For He seems Himself not to have promoted the flesh at all, but rather to have been Himself promoted through it, if, according to their perverseness, He was then exalted and called Son, when He became man" (*Discourses* 1.38). Arianism amounts to an affirmation of the apotheosis of man, rather than the conde-scension and grace of God. The gospel is not about a Son who is rewarded with godhood but is about the God who becomes man to deify us (*Discourses* 1.39). Arian Christology fails here because it undermines the trajectory of the gospel narrative. The gospel is this: God became man so that man might become God; the Creator was created so that creatures might be joined to the Creator. Arian Christology cannot tell such a story but tells only a story of the Creator sending a high creature to rescue creatures and place them somewhat nearer to the Creator. The Arian Son cannot lead creatures behind the veil and into the divine fellowship because he is not part of it, since, in the end, there is no divine fellowship to be part of. The Arian Christ might look accessible and cuddly, but in fact, he exists precisely to keep the Creator God at a distance from us. The true living Word of the Father, though, is proper to the Father and makes flesh proper to himself so that we might become, by grace, "proper" to the life of God, internal to the divine fellowship, human beings fulfilled in our humanity by deification.

Deification in Athanasius's telling does not involve an ascent beyond embodied existence any more than it involves transcendence of creatureli-ness. Deification is about proper use of flesh, not about the destruction of flesh. Though he does not rely on it, Athanasius's thinking here is consistent with Paul's emphasis in Romans 6, where he moves from a declaration of baptismal union with Christ in his death and resurrection to the exhorta-tion to offer the members of our bodies as instruments of righteousness. That is what Athanasius is after: embodied human beings whose bodily parts are used for righteous purposes. Just as the Word took on flesh, so by the Spirit the flesh of Christians is devoted to right action. We are able to share in these divine perfections because he took a body and because we have become his body.

> For the grace which the Son gives from the Father, that the Son Himself is said to receive; and the exaltation, which the Son bestows from the Father, with that the Son is Himself exalted. For He who is the Son of God, became Himself the Son of Man; and, as Word, He gives from the Father, for all things which the Father does and gives, He does and supplies through Him; and as the Son of Man, He Himself is said after the manner of men to receive what proceeds from Him, because His Body is none other than His, and is a natural recipient of grace, as has been said. For He received it as far as His man's nature was exalted; which exaltation was its being deified. But such an exaltation the Word

Himself always had according to the Father's Godhead and perfection, which
was His. (*Discourses* 1.45)

Through the Son's incarnation, death, and resurrection, and through our union
with his risen flesh, we are made—in a remarkable formulation—"natural
recipients of grace" (*to physin echon tou dechesthai tēn charin*; *Discourses*
1.45). Grace is not alien and "supernatural." It comes from outside, that is,
from the Word, who is not a creature; but it comes from outside *in* and so
becomes constitutive of our existence as creatures. Because the Spirit and his
gifts have been poured out *within* us, we are naturalized to grace.

Athanasius's use of the light-radiance paradigm provides another description of deification. The Son is the radiance of the Father, proper to the eternal
light, and thus the grace of the Father must be bestowed through the Son. This
is evident in the baptismal formula, since we are baptized not only into the
name of the Father, but also into a share in the Son and the Spirit.

> Since the course of the discussion has led us also to mention holy Baptism, it is
> necessary to state, as I think and believe, that the Son is named with the Father,
> not as if the Father were not all-sufficient, not without meaning, and by accident;
> but, since He is God's Word and own Wisdom, and being His Radiance, is ever
> with the Father, therefore it is impossible, if the Father bestows grace, that He
> should not give it in the Son, for the Son is in the Father as the radiance in the
> light. For, not as if in need, but as a Father in His own Wisdom has God founded
> the earth, and made all things in the Word which is from Him, and in the Son
> confirms the Holy Laver. For where the Father is, there is the Son, and where
> the light, there the radiance; and as what the Father works, He works through
> the Son, and the Lord Himself says, "What I see the Father do, that do I also";
> so also when baptism is given, whom the Father baptizes, him the Son baptizes;
> and whom the Son baptizes, he is consecrated in the Holy Ghost. And again as
> when the sun shines, one might say that the radiance illuminates, for the light
> is one and indivisible, nor can be detached, so where the Father is or is named,
> there plainly is the Son also; and is the Father named in Baptism? Then must
> the Son be named with Him. (*Discourses* 2.41)

The grace of the Father's light and the Son's radiance form one grace, and
this grace is the one grace that dwells in those who are united to the flesh
of the Son. The Son comes with the Father and makes "Our abode" in him
(John 14:23). That is how it must be, since "the light must be with the ray, and
the radiance must be contemplated together with its own light" (*Discourses*
2.42). Deification is thus illumination—"illumination" not only in the sense
that our darkened intellects become illuminated but also in the sense that our
flesh begins to shine with the light of God. Illumination means that we are
made into the image of the Image, the Image that is the radiant image of the
light that is the Father. In the Radiance, we are made radiant. Drawing on the

account of Moses "horned" with the reflected glory of the Lord, Athanasius says that one who has studied the Scriptures "glitters with the sublime beams of the most high God."[6]

Deification is also completion, realization of the created destiny of humanity and creation. The Son "simply and without any condition is in the Father," a position he has "by nature." For human beings, though, "it is not natural," and therefore we need "an image and example." The Father and the Son provide that model of human perfection. When Jesus compares the perichoretic unity of Father and Son to that of the disciples ("You, Father, are in Me, and I in You"; John 17:21), he is saying that "unless I had come and borne this their body, no one of them had been perfected, but one and all had remained corruptible." Jesus's prayer to the Father is that he would "grant to them Your Spirit, that they too in It may become one, and may be perfected in Me." Through the perfecting of believers, it becomes apparent that the Father's "Word has sojourned among them; and the world seeing them perfect and full of God, will believe altogether that You have sent Me, and I have sojourned here." In short, Jesus works and prays so that "men, redeemed from sin, no longer remain dead; but being deified, have in each other, by looking at Me, the bond of charity" (*Discourses* 3.23).

Deification does involve gaining knowledge. The Son, as we have seen, shared in the ignorance of the flesh so that he could bring flesh to know God, to share in God's knowledge (*Discourses* 3.48). Through the incarnation, the body becomes a body of wisdom, an organ of wisdom through being made god. When Luke and Hebrews speak of the advance in the wisdom and knowledge of the eternal Wisdom and Knowledge, that advance cannot be the Word's as Word. He takes flesh and advances the flesh, so that the flesh takes on the Wisdom that He is, and participates in it. "Neither then was the advance the Word's, nor was the flesh Wisdom, but the flesh became the body of Wisdom." Wisdom did not advance "in respect of Itself; but the manhood advanced in Wisdom, transcending by degrees human nature, and being deified, and becoming and appearing to all as the organ of Wisdom for the operation and the shining forth of the Godhead." Thus "the advance is of the human nature" (*Discourses* 3.53).

Through all this, Athanasius says, human beings transcend their humanity. That might sound as if we are elevated beyond creaturehood, as if to "become gods" we must cease to be men. That is not what Athanasius means. He means, on the one hand, deliverance from sin, but, on the other hand, he is also talking about the maturation and completion of humanity. Creation is good from the beginning, but creation is not perfected from the beginning. Creatures are made temporal and hence changeable, precisely so they can advance beyond the childish state in which they were first created.

Concretely, what is involved in this "transcendence" of Adamic human nature through deification? Human beings are created passible, subject to external forces, liable to be derailed from lives of faithful obedience by fear of pain and death or expectation of pleasure. Deification is a triumph over human passions, which is possible because the Son took our passions on himself and delivered flesh from them (*Discourses* 3.32). The Son delivered us from the passions and limits of flesh in taking those passions and limits as his own, so that we might come to resemble the impassible God. Since the Word "appropriated [*idiopoieisthai*] what pertains to the flesh, no longer do these things touch the body, because of the Word who has come in it." Instead, "they are destroyed by Him, and henceforth men no longer remain sinners and dead according to their proper affections, but having risen according to the Word's power, they abide ever immortal and incorruptible" (*Discourses* 3.33). Again, Athanasius develops this in the context of an anti-Arian polemic. Only an impassible, divine Son can make us impassible in the flesh: "While He Himself, being impassible in nature, remains as He is, not harmed by these affections, but rather obliterating and destroying them, men, their passions as if changed and abolished in the Impassible, henceforth become themselves also impassible and free from them for ever" (*Discourses* 3.34).

This does not mean that deified humans lack feeling. It means that they are not subjected to and enslaved by their feelings. They are determined by their soul's fixed orientation to the unchangeable God, which directs the bodily actions toward God. It means that, like their Creator, no obstacle can frustrate their burning love for God and for others. They are impassible because of the overwhelming force of their passion to love and serve the Father and his Word. What does an impassible human look like? For Athanasius, he or she looks like a martyr.

Humans were created mutable. Human beings are never still, never one thing for very long. As a result, anything offered and given to human beings is likely to be forgotten and lost, as Adam lost the graces given to him at the beginning. If grace is not only to be given but to be retained, it requires a more stable foundation than human nature as such. In this sense too, the incarnation and work of the Son have "deified" man, providing the basis for human beings to mimic the divine immutability and faithfulness: "And as we said that He suffered in the flesh, and hungered in the flesh, and was fatigued in the flesh, so also reasonably may He be said to have advanced in the flesh; for neither did the advance, such as we have described it, take place with the Word external to the flesh, for in Him was the flesh which advanced and His is it called, and that as before, that man's advance might abide and fail not, because of the Word which is with it" (*Discourses* 3.53).

Finally, human nature is mortal, and in the condition of sin is fearful of its mortality. Deification is liberation from the fear of death, which is essentially a human form of immortality, to be consummated at the resurrection. Deliverance from death manifests itself in human overcoming of the passions of fear and timidity, a triumph that must, on Athanasius's premises, be manifest in flesh, in bodily action, and not simply in intellectual ascent. *On the Incarnation* points to the lives and deaths of martyrs as evidence that the Spirit of the incarnate Son, the Spirit of the crucified and risen deliverer, is beginning to pervade the human race: "Is it a slight indication of the Savior's victory over [death], when boys and young girls who are in Christ look beyond this present life and train themselves to die? Every one is by nature afraid of death and of bodily dissolution; the marvel of marvels is that he who is enfolded in the faith of the cross despises this natural fear and for the sake of the cross is no longer cowardly in the face of it" (*On the Incarnation* 28). Is it possible to doubt Christ's "conquest of death" after "so many martyrdoms in Christ and such daily scorn of death by His truest servants" (*On the Incarnation* 28)?

Whole societies had been devoted to death, violence, and murderous competition. Now all the deathliness that has corrupted human existence from within is being overcome in the Spirit. Barbarians "are naturally savage in their habits," and while they sacrifice to idols, "they rage furiously against each other." As soon as they hear the teaching of Christ, "they turn from fighting to farming, and instead of arming themselves with swords extend their hands in prayer" (*On the Incarnation* 52). Bodily actions change, as Christ, the one who fulfills the *typoi* of the prophets, impresses his image back onto the human race: "They shall beat their swords into ploughshares and their spears into sickles, and nation shall not take sword against nation, neither shall they learn any more to wage war" (Isa. 2:4, quoted in *On the Incarnation* 52).

Remade according to the Pattern

To be a Christian is to be joined in the Spirit to the flesh appropriated by the Son of God. Because the Son offered human flesh as a suitable sacrifice to the Father, he has overcome death, the demons, and everything else that stands in the way of human perfection. Jesus has dispelled death and demons, and hence he has dispersed the fear of death that made slaves of the human race before the incarnation. The demons who occupied the air have been cast down, and now we have the liberty to pass by them and ascend to heaven. Human flesh has been taken up into the life of God, and the life and light of God now dwell in flesh, so it is now possible for those who share in the life of the incarnate Son to overcome fleshly desires, to turn from the creation to the Creator, and to suppress fleshly passions. We can make all these same points in terms of "typology." Christ is the image of God, and as the Father imprinted that image on creation and humanity at the beginning, so he is re-impressing that image from the inside through the incarnation, death, and resurrection of Jesus. The *typos* is imprinted on us again. There is an aesthetic dimension to this: God, the great artist of creation, who impresses his beautiful image everywhere and in everything, does not give up when creation gets marred by sin and decay. He returns to reshape the world, especially the human race, in his image.

Human beings are not remade and fulfilled through sheer passive reception. According to Athanasius, the Christian life is a life of strenuous effort, renunciation, and voluntary self-control, as well as a grateful reception of a gift. Though he nowhere works out the details of this process, he would likely express the pattern in the words of Paul: "Work out your salvation with fear and trembling; for it is God who is at work in you, both to will and to work for His good pleasure" (Phil. 2:12–13). *Because* of the work of the Spirit of the Son, we are to labor toward perfection. The Son is Son by nature and thus does what he sees the Father doing as an expression of his essential being. We become sons by grace, and our growth in sonship comes about through grace-empowered effort, through imitation (*mimēsis*).[7]

Athanasius inherited an ascetic Alexandrian spirituality that emphasized the priority of contemplation and knowledge.[8] Sin produced ignorance of God, and the life of the Christian was seen as a life of contemplation in order to restore the knowledge lost in the fall. As might be expected, this highly intellectual spirituality was not for everyone, and earlier Alexandrian theologians accordingly mixed their intellectual asceticism with a gradation and ranking of Christian living. For the Alexandrians, there were several ranks of Christians, from the contemplatives at the height to the comparatively ignorant and incurious laypersons at the bottom.

Athanasius works within this framework but modifies it considerably on both of these points. In place of knowledge, Athanasius emphasizes the development of virtue. This is partly based on anthropological differences. Origen had taught that human beings were initially sheer minds that were later infused into bodies, but for Athanasius, the body is of the essence of being human. Bodies should be controlled by the mind, and the body's passions must be overcome. But bodies themselves—including, as we have seen, bodily emissions—are part of God's original, good creation. Given his emphasis on bodies and on the development of virtue, it is natural that Athanasius would also modify the hierarchy that he inherited from earlier Alexandrian teachers. There is still a hierarchy, with ascetic athletes like Antony at the top, but the difference between an Antony and a lay member of the church of Alexandria is "only in degree, not in fundamental character." Ascetic perfection is not mandatory for all Christians; "a life of moderate virtue was sufficient."[9]

In the first of his *Festal Letters*, which we examined in chapter 1, Athanasius expounds on this point by meditating on the different purposes of the trumpets that called Israel to worship. The trumpets of Israel were typical of the apostolic summons, which

> call us, at one time to war, as the blessed Paul says; "We wrestle not with flesh and blood, but with principalities, with powers, with the rulers of this dark

world, with wicked spirits in heaven" (Eph. 6:12). At another time the call is made to virginity, and self-denial, and conjugal harmony, saying, to virgins, the things of virgins; and to those who love the way of abstinence, the things of abstinence; and to those who are married, the things of an honorable marriage; thus assigning to each its own virtues and an honorable recompense. Sometimes the call is made to fasting, and sometimes to a feast. Hear again the same [Apostle] blowing the trumpet, and proclaiming, "Christ our Passover is sacrificed; therefore let us keep the feast, not with old leaven, neither with the leaven of malice and wickedness." If you would listen to a trumpet much greater than all these, hear our Savior saying; "In that last and great day of the feast, Jesus stood and cried, saying, If any man thirst, let him come unto Me and drink" (John 7:37). For it became the Savior not simply to call us to a feast, but to "the great feast," if only we will be prepared to hear, and to conform to the proclamation of every trumpet. (*Festal Letter* 1.3)[10]

The same trumpet calls different people to different actions and may even call the same person to different forms of Christian living at different times of his or her life.

The basic pattern of Christian living is, for Athanasius, a life of "innerworldly asceticism." Lay Christians need not renounce sex, as monks, virgins, and solitaries do, nor are they required to reject food and wealth with the same thoroughness as ascetics. Yet they are to practice a form of asceticism within the life that the Lord calls them to. Festival times provide common Christians with an opportunity to practice the disciplines of "true feasting," not the feast of malice and wickedness but a feast on the unleavened bread of charity and truth. Partly for reasons of ritual purity, Athanasius urges his congregation to refrain from sexual activity during the time leading up to the feast. If sexual intercourse was defiling in the old era (Lev. 15), how much more, Athanasius reasons, should Christians refuse to have sex "thoughtlessly" on the same day as a feast? In the time of grace, "a greater diligence in our way of life (*politeia*) is required." Consequently, Athanasius urges us to "purify ourselves when we are going to share in such awesome mysteries."[11] Christians should also use the festival times as opportunities to discipline themselves in their consumption of food and pleasures.

More than with food or sex, Athanasius is concerned with the temptation that wealth and property pose to Christian faithfulness. In *The Life of Antony*, Antony faces down sexual temptation and temptations regarding other pleasures and food; he confronts demons in various guises. But the temptation that lies on the boundary between the city and the desert is the temptation of wealth. Antony has to renounce his possessions in order to take up his life as an ascetic hero, and as he travels toward his home in the desert, he sees first "the apparition of a great silver dish" and then "no illusion, but actual gold thrown in his path." Though Antony "marveled at the amount," he passed on "as one stepping over fire" and soon came to his mountain fortress.[12] Here

Athanasius's instructions are not simply negative; he not only teaches his congregation to renounce greed but exhorts them to practice hospitality and generosity: "Since, therefore, this occasion for discipline is set before us [the Easter feast], and such a day as this is come, and the prophetic voice has gone forth that the feast should be celebrated, let us give all diligence to this good proclamation, and like those who contend in the stadium, let us compete with one another in the purity of the fast, in the watchfulness of prayers, in the study of the Scriptures, in distributing to the poor, and let us be at peace with our enemies" (*Festal Letter* 3).[13]

Disciplinary practices such as periodic fasting, almsgiving, and abstention from sex were a central part of Athanasius's program of discipleship, but at the very center of the program was the study of Scripture. The living Word, eternally with the Father, was communicated to Christians through the written word. The eternal image was impressed through meditation on the words of Scripture, and the original *typos* took shape in concrete human life as the Scriptures had their impact on Christians.

Athanasius provides a detailed overview of the book of Psalms and its right use in his epistle to the otherwise unknown Marcellinus.[14] In part, the letter is a review of the contents of Psalms, a book that contains all the parts of Scripture within it. The account of creation in Genesis 1–2 echoes in Psalm 18; Exodus and Numbers are summarized in Psalms 77 and 113; the cry of beleaguered Israel in the book of Judges appears in the Psalms of Ascent; prophecies fill the psalms, and the psalms celebrate the coming of the Savior, the "Word" who comes to heal and deliver (Ps. 106). Jesus's career is foreshadowed in some detail: the eternal nature of the Son is declared in Psalm 44, the joy that greets his birth in 86, the plot of the Jews in Psalm 2, and the attack of "dogs," the piercing of the Christ's hands and feet, the division of his garments in Psalm 21. The psalms do not leave Jesus in the grave, but describe his exaltation and his entry as "king of glory" into heaven (Psalm 23), where he sits at the right hand of his Father (Ps. 109). The psalms are a "garden containing things of all these kinds," from the Pentateuch, the prophets, and the Old and New Testaments.[15]

If the book of Psalms is a microcosm of the rest of Scripture, it is equally true that the contents of the book of Psalms are found everywhere else. All Scripture indwells the psalms; the psalms in turn indwell all of Scripture. Moses, Isaiah, and Habakkuk wrote hymns, just as David, Asaph, and others did. Prophecies and narratives are summarized poetically in the psalms, and the rest of Scripture expounds those same prophecies and narratives. There is one Spirit, and the Scriptures inspired by that Spirit manifest his unity. At the same time, all distinctions are from the Spirit, and the unity of Scripture is a differentiated unity, so that "the whole is in each" and the "distinctions of the Spirit pertain to all and to each severally." The psalms contain all the rest of Scripture, and yet the psalms add something unique to the full revelation of God in his written work: "The Book of Psalms thus has a certain grace of its own, and a distinctive exactitude of expression." Athanasius focuses on several of the distinctive features of Psalms. Most importantly, in contrast to other books, which record events, prophecies, laws, and institutions, Psalms records "the emotions of each soul," so that, in addition to learning from prophets about the coming of Christ or from the narratives about the deeds of kings, the hearer of the psalms "also comprehends and is taught in it the emotions of the soul."[16]

Hearing the psalms thus not only reveals events and prophecies, not only reveals the emotions of the soul, but is uniquely powerful for healing the soul, since the psalms show "how one must heal passion through speaking and acting." By providing words for each circumstance of life, the psalms give articulation and pattern to experience and the feelings of experience.

> In the Psalms it is written and inscribed how one must bear sufferings, what one must say to one suffering afflictions, what to say after afflictions, how each person is tested, and what the words of those who hope in God are. . . . There is a command to give thanks in all circumstances, but the Psalms also teach what one must say when giving thanks. Then hearing from others that as many as wish to live a godly life must be persecuted, from these we are taught how one must call out while fleeing, and what words must be offered to God while being persecuted and after being delivered subsequent to persecution.[17]

Beyond that, the book of Psalms, in contrast to other books, is designed to be sung by the faithful, not merely to be heard. Those who listen see themselves as "other than those about whom the passage speaks" and are inspired to imitation. The one who sings psalms takes on the words of Scripture as his or her own words and is "affected by the words of the Songs, as if they were his own songs." No one would dare utter the words of Abraham or Moses as his own, but "each sings [the psalms] as if they were written concerning him, and he accepts them and recites them not as if another were speaking, nor as if speaking about someone else. But he handles them as if he were speaking about himself." The words of the psalms become a "mirror" to the soul, in which each singer "perceive[s] himself and the emotions of his soul."[18]

The psalms are a mirror of the soul because they are a mirror of human experience—of suffering, desperation, exultation, thanksgiving, prosperity, adversity, garden and wilderness, isolation and communion, and on and on. They are a mirror of the soul also because they are a mirror of our emotional life, including every permutation of passion. More than a mirror, though: through our singing the psalms, the diverse passions of the soul, Athanasius argues, are trained and harmonized. Praising God "in well-tuned cymbals and harp and ten-stringed instrument was again a figure and sign of the parts of the body coming into natural concord like harp strings, and of the thoughts of the soul becoming like cymbals, and then all of these being moved and living through the grand sound and through the command of the Spirit so that, as it is written, the man lives in the Spirit and mortifies the deeds of the body." By "beautifully singing praises, he brings rhythm to his soul and leads it, so to speak, from disproportion to proportion."[19] The perfected soul is a symphony, harmonized by the Spirit through the discipline of psalm-singing. The psalms are expressions of deep passion, of anguish and fear, and soaring elation. Yet singing the psalms is actually a discipline in *im*passibility, for through the psalms we are trained to turn all circumstances and moods into worship. Those who sing and absorb the psalms will have a rich emotional life, but none of their passions will cause them to deviate from following the crucified Messiah. Through singing the psalms, we are conformed to the impassible sufferer, the Word made flesh.

Throughout this exposition of the meaning and power of the psalms, Athanasius is engaging in "typological" exegesis, but of a kind that combines christocentric allegory with christomimetic tropology. Christ is the perfect exemplar of virtue, a virtue that he "typified" (*etypōsen*) in his own life. Humans are unstable, since we are created from nothing and tend to be more fascinated by changeable creatures than by the unchangeable God. Stability comes only through conformity to Christ: "The Christian life requires 'continual formation [*typoun*] of the self through imitation' of the 'eternally consistent form or pattern [*typos*] provided by the divine Word.'"[20] By healing the passions of the soul and bringing it to harmony, the psalms are also molding the singer to the "mind of Christ."[21]

As we have seen, Athanasius believes that the incarnate Son has conquered the devil and demons. He was lifted into the air on the cross in order to defeat the demons whose power lodged there, and thus through the cross he weakened the demons and constructed a path, the path of the cross, back to the Father. Demons are now pathetic figures, like the shabby devil who makes his pitiful appeals to Ivan in *The Brothers Karamazov*. In Antony's lengthy discourse, recorded by Athanasius, he mocks the demons. If they had real power, they would not have to create "phantasms" or "work their fraud by being transfigured." Since they cannot do much of anything, they "play parts as if they were on stage, changing their forms and striking fear in children by the illusion of the hordes and their shapes"—child's play, Antony thinks, "antics" that earn them only ridicule as "weaklings" (*Life of Antony* 28).

Yet Antony's own encounters with demons are more intense than he lets on. He warns his disciples that demons will attack them with evil thoughts, then with "conspicuous and filthy pleasure," and then attempt to "frighten . . . by fabricating phantasms, transforming themselves, and imitating women, beasts, reptiles, and huge bodies of thousands of soldiers" (*Life of Antony* 23). Their final assault on Antony is a theater of horror worthy of Hieronymus Bosch or Cormac McCarthy. Seeing that they could not frustrate Antony's resolve by sexual temptation or beatings, they let loose.

When it was nighttime they made such a crashing noise that the whole place seemed to be shaken by a quake. The demons, as if breaking through the building's four walls, and seeming to enter them, were changed into the forms of beasts and reptiles. The place immediately was filled with the appearances of lions, bears, leopards, bulls, and serpents, asps, scorpions, wolves, and each of these moved in accordance with its form. The lion roared, wanting to spring at him; the bull seemed intent on goring; the creeping snake did not quite reach him; the onrushing wolf made straight for him—and altogether the sounds of all the creatures that appeared were terrible, and their ragings were fierce. (*Life of Antony* 9)

Wounded, Antony "groaned because of the pain felt in his body" but rebuked them: "It is a mark of your weakness that you mimic the shapes of irrational beasts" (*Life of Antony* 9). God suddenly appeared, as "the roof opened, as it seemed, and a certain beam of light descend[ed] toward him." The demons fled, his wounds healed, and the building was brought back to normal. When Antony asked God what had taken him so long, he received this answer: "I was here, Antony, but I waited to watch your struggle. And now, since you persevered and were not defeated, I will be your helper forever, and I will make you famous everywhere" (*Life of Antony* 10).

Antony was of course unique, Athanasius's supreme ascetic hero, and his battles with demons were accordingly unique. Yet Athanasius intends Antony's life to be a model, not only for monks and hermits, but for Christians in Alexandria, throughout Egypt, and beyond. They can learn to imitate, in a more moderate fashion, the heroic renunciations of the great hermit, and they should also learn from Antony's example that even defeated demons can mount their terrors. Christian living is an aesthetic project, God reshaping the human soul and body as each believer cares for himself or herself through the disciplines of Christian living. It is also warfare, a continuing battle, not only against temptation but also against demons and spiritual powers who, though weakened and destined for defeat, remain threatening to the slothful and unprepared. Be alert, be vigilant, Athanasius tells his congregation.

Through these disciples the Christian is being deified and progresses in being made god. For Athanasius, deification involves taking on divine attributes in a human way. God is impassible, and the deified Christian approaches impassibility so that he is not thrown about by his whims and feelings. God is deathless, and the deified believer no longer fears death. He will, at the resurrection, triumph over death. God is incorruptible, and Christians are deified as they overcome, in union with the eternal Son by the Spirit, the instability that is part of created human nature. And they overcome corruption ultimately when they attain the incorruptibility of the resurrection. This does not happen all at once. But already now, and increasingly through the practice of Christian disciplines, this mortal is putting on immortality, this corruptible putting on incorruption, as the Christian strives in hope of the fullness of deified life at the end.

Conclusion

For Athanasius, deification is not an isolated individual process. To be sure, he celebrates the isolated hermetic life of Antony, but he also recognizes that the end point of the incarnation and redemption accomplished by Christ is the formation of a community. Christians engage in their deifying disciplines together—together enjoying the true feast of fasting and the true fast of charity, together being molded according to the pattern of the Word through study of the Word. Christian living is a collective "way of life," a *politeia*. David Brakke points out that Athanasius uses the term frequently to describe "both the individual Christian life and the Church" as "the heavenly civic life."[22] The Christian way of civic life was prepared by the law and the prophets, the latter of whom were sent to the Jews but were "for all the world a holy school of the knowledge of God and the conduct of the soul" (*tēs kata psychēn politeias*; *On the Incarnation* 12.5). Monastic communities particularly express this pattern. As soon as Antony enters the wilderness, others come to take up what is no longer quite a solitary life: "From then on, there were monasteries in the mountains, and the desert was made a city by monks, who left their own people and registered themselves for the citizenship in the heavens" (*Life of Antony* 14).[23] But this citizenship is not confined to those who have renounced earthly citizenship. God's gifts in Christ are great: power over demons, adoption of children, knowledge of the Father and of the Son, the gift of the Spirit, and the "pattern of heavenly conversation" (*ouranou . . . politeias typos*; *Bishops of Egypt* 1.1).

In the incarnate Word, the type of heavenly society has come to earth and is being imprinted on the life of the church. Moses and Solomon built houses according to the pattern (*typos*) that they witnessed in heaven. Jesus has entered that heavenly sanctuary, the archetype of all human sanctuaries, and having entered brings that type to earth, in the form of a church celebrating a new and true feast:

> And this is a great proof that, whereas we were strangers, we are called friends; from being formerly aliens, we have become fellow citizens with the saints, and are called children of the Jerusalem which is above, whereof that which Solomon built was a type. For if Moses made all things according to the pattern showed him in the mount, it is clear that the service performed in the tabernacle was a type of the heavenly mysteries, whereto the Lord, desirous that we should enter, prepared for us the new and abiding way. And as all the old things were a type of the new, so the festival that now is, is a type of the joy which is above, to which coming with psalms and spiritual songs, let us begin the feast. (*Festal Letter* 45)

One of the key features of this Christian *politeia* is unity, and Athanasius stresses the link between the triune unity and the unity of the church. By looking to and contemplating the unity of Father and Son, the church is unified, since contemplation of a thing shapes the one contemplating to resemble that thing (*Discourses* 3.21). The unity of the church is part of its perfection as the people of God, in the sense that "perfection" means "full realization" or "eschatological completion."

> Wherefore the Son Himself, simply and without any condition is in the Father; for this attribute He has by nature; but for us, to whom it is not natural, there is needed an image and example, that He may say of us, "As Thou in Me, and I in You." "And when they shall be so perfected," He says, "then the world knows that You have sent Me, for unless I had come and borne this their body, no one of them had been perfected, but one and all had remained corruptible. Work Thou then in them, O Father, and as You have given to Me to bear this, grant to them Your Spirit, that they too in It may become one, and may be perfected in Me. For their perfecting shows that Your Word has sojourned among them; and the world seeing them perfect and full of God, will believe altogether that You have sent Me, and I have sojourned here. For whence is this their perfecting, but that I, Your Word, having borne their body, and become man, have perfected the work, which You gave Me, O Father? And the work is perfected, because men, redeemed from sin, no longer remain dead; but being deified, have in each other, by looking at Me, the bond of charity." (*Discourses* 3.23)

Athanasius sees this unification of the church as part of the eschatological work of the Son, the completion of the story of Israel. The Son exists first and is afterward created as man. His formation as man is not the "beginning of his being" but rather the beginning of his manhood, "where also He collects together the tribes of Israel" (*Discourses* 2.53; cf. 2.52). From Ephesians Athanasius draws the conclusion that the recreation of humanity in the Son involves the reunion of Jew and gentile:

> But if in Him the two are created, and these are in His body, reasonably then, bearing the two in Himself, He is as if Himself created; for those who were created in Himself He made one, and He was in them, as they. And thus, the two being created in Him, He may say suitably, "The Lord created me." For as by receiving our infirmities, He is said to be infirm Himself, though not Himself infirm, for He is the Power of God, and He became sin for us and a curse, though not having sinned Himself, but because He Himself bore our sins and our curse, so, by creating us in Him, let Him say, "He created me for the works," though not Himself a creature. (*Discourses* 2.55)

Renovating creation is like renovating a house, and the Lord who made the world at the beginning also made provision for its repair. The Son comes into the flesh as a temple, and through his death and resurrection transforms the community he gathers into a temple of the Spirit. Thus the Lord proves to be "as a wise architect, proposing to build a house, consults also about repairing it, should it at any time become dilapidated after building, and, as counseling about this, makes preparation and gives to the workmen materials for a repair; and thus the means of the repair are provided before the house; in the same way prior to us is the repair of our salvation founded in Christ, that in Him we might even be new-created. And the will and the purpose were made ready 'before the world,' but have taken effect when the need required, and the Savior came among us" (*Discourses* 2.77).

This Christian *politeia* is, for Athanasius, Christ's means for remaking the world. Though writing in the first flush of Constantine's conversion, Athanasius kept his sights on the incarnate Word as the one who would put down idolatry, overturn death, and stabilize humanity. *On the Incarnation* presents a "triumphalist" Christology, whose main proof of the rationality, the *logikē*, of the cross is the fact that it produces people who have no fear of death, who are "impassibly" determined to do good and serve and worship their Lord, no matter what the cost or what they suffer. Athanasius's great proof of the power of the cross is the martyr church. Some scholars have seen in this an implicit critique of imperial ideology, which, even in its Christian guise, offered a false gospel of salvation through political power.[24] Whether that was intentional or not, Athanasius is clear: there is only one Savior, one Lord, only one "way of life" that leads to life, and that is the way of the cross, the way of following the one who took flesh and trampled death by death.

Epilogue (Again in the Augustinian Mode)

What is the nature of things? What is their ultimate reality? What can we say about metaphysics?

You have taught us, O Lord, that it is all about Christ, the Word who is proper to your essence, who assumed flesh and made that flesh proper to himself. On the cross, your Word suffered and offered himself, his own flesh, as a suitable sacrifice, and since the flesh was the flesh proper to the Word, that flesh could not stay dead. Through your Spirit, the stability and power of that resurrected flesh is communicated to us who believe and are baptized, so that in our flesh, the flesh of the church, your Word, the Christ, can and will work out his triumph. He is the radiance of your eternal light, and he has shone through his own "proper" flesh, imprinted the image of his radiance on his flesh by works of power, and now through the Spirit is imprinting that image on the church. Through your Son and Spirit, the radiance that is your Word shines through the temple of the Spirit and through us is trampling death and Satan underfoot.

This you taught your servant Athanasius, and this you have taught us through him. You have taught us that your Word that is proper to your being, the Word that has made our flesh proper to himself, now makes us proper to himself, so that in your Son we become sons, in your Word we become proper to the Word. In the Word made flesh, our flesh is "worded."[1] By your Spirit, you taught your servant to say:

> As we are all from earth and die in Adam, so being regenerated from above of water and Spirit, in the Christ we are all quickened; the flesh being no longer earthly, but being henceforth made Word [*logōtheisēs*], by reason of God's Word who for our sake "became flesh." (*Discourses* 3.33)

Creatures "worded" in the Word: for your servant Athanasius, there can be no deeper metaphysics than this, no deeper account of the nature of things. For it is all about Christ, the eternal Word made flesh, the Truth, the Way, the Life, and the measure of all truth, all ways, all life.

So you have taught your servant; so you teach us. Beyond speaking that Word, you have taught us to say nothing, but only called us to turn our hands, our hearts, our tongues to you in grateful service and praise.

Notes

Chapter 1 Evangelizing Metaphysics

1. The opening pages of this chapter overlap considerably with my discussion of the origins of the Arian controversy in *Defending Constantine* (Downers Grove, IL: InterVarsity, 2010), though in that book my focus is on Constantine's role in the controversy. Recent scholarship presents a fairly radical revision of the fourth-century conflict—from the chronology of events and the reliability of sources, especially of Athanasius, to the context, background, and importance of Arius himself, the force of the Nicene formula, the effect of its creed, and the question of the relation of orthodoxy and heresy. The best recent treatments are found in Timothy D. Barnes, *Constantine and Eusebius* (Cambridge, MA: Harvard University Press, 1981), 191–244; Lewis Ayres, *Nicaea and Its Legacy: An Approach to Fourth-Century Trinitarian Theology* (Oxford: Oxford University Press, 2006), chaps. 2–3; Rowan Williams, *Arius: Heresy and Tradition*, rev. ed. (Grand Rapids: Eerdmans, 2001), 29–91; R. P. C. Hanson, *The Search for the Christian Doctrine of God: The Arian Controversy, 318–81* (Grand Rapids: Baker Academic, 2005), 13–273; T. D. Barnes, *Athanasius and Constantius: Theology and Politics in the Constantinian Empire* (Cambridge, MA: Harvard University Press, 1993), 1–33; John Behr, *Formation of Christian Theology*, vol. 2, *The Nicene Faith, Part 1* (Crestwood, NY: St. Vladimir's Seminary Press, 2004). Deft and still useful older treatments are found in Henry Chadwick, *The Early Church*, Pelican History of the Church (New York: Penguin, 1967), 129–36; W. H. C. Frend, *The Rise of Christianity* (Philadelphia: Fortress, 1984), 492–517. For scholarship on Athanasius up to 1984, see Charles Kannengiesser, "The Athanasian Decade, 1973–1984: A Bibliographic Report," *Theological Studies* 46 (1985): 524–41; studies since then can be found at http://www.athanasius.theologie.uni-erlangen.de/bibliographie. David S. Potter, *The Roman Empire at Bay, AD 180–395*, Routledge History of the Ancient World (London: Routledge, 2004), 401–22, is excellent on the history, but out of his depth on the theology.

2. The Melitian controversy is briefly summed up in Chadwick, *Early Church*, 124; Frend, *Rise of Christianity*, 493–94; Williams, *Arius*, 32–41. Potter, *Roman Empire*, 412, tells the story of the prison-house schism. Records list an "Arius" as a supporter of Melitius, and Frend, *Rise of Christianity*, 493, believes it is the same Arius who later emerged in conflict with Alexander, but recent scholars have doubted that the two are the same man (Williams, *Arius*, 40; Hanson, *Search*, 5).

3. Ever since I heard it from a student, I have thought of modalism as the "little hat" doctrine of the Trinity. According to modalism, there are no eternal distinctions among the persons; the

177

persons are just roles, the "little hats" that the one God dons at different times for different purposes.

4. Williams, *Arius*, 86–91.

5. Aloys Grillmeier, *Christ in Christian Tradition*, vol. 1, *From the Apostolic Age to Chalcedon (451)*, trans. John Bowden, 2nd ed. (Atlanta: John Knox, 1975), 138–49, 219. Ayres (*Nicaea and Its Legacy*, 21–22) cautions that Arius ought not be labeled an "Origenist," since all sides of the debate were influenced by Origen and there were other influences at work on Arius.

6. Quoted in Hanson, *Search*, 6–7.

7. Ayres, *Nicaea and Its Legacy*, 3 and passim, emphasizes the central importance of theories of "begetting" in the debate over Arius's views.

8. Both sides of the controversy claim to be following the footsteps of the "Fathers," and often with equal plausibility. This supports the contemporary view that the Arian controversy is not about the church defending a preexisting orthodoxy but is about the church groping toward orthodoxy.

9. Translation available online at http://www.fourthcentury.com/index.php/urkunde -chart-opitz/.

10. For discussions of the problems see R. D. Williams, "The Quest of the Historical *Thalia*," and S. G. Hall, "The Thalia of Arius in Athanasius's Accounts," both in *Arianism: Historical and Theological Reassessments*, ed. Robert C. Gregg (1985; repr., Eugene, OR: Wipf & Stock, 2006), 1–36, 37–58. Williams responds to G. C. Stead ("The *Thalia* of Arius and the Testimony of Athanasius," *Journal of Theological Studies* 29 [1978]: 20–52), who argues that the quotations of the *Thalia* preserved by Athanasius in the first of his *Orations* is, in Williams's summary, a "mixture of paraphrase, expansion (designed to bring out the unacceptable implications of what Arius actually says), and fragmentation quotation," and Stead turns to Athanasius's list of the "Blasphemies of Arius" (*On the Synods* 15) as a more reliable guide to Arius's own works. Williams's article defends the reliability of Athanasius's summary in *On the Synods*. Williams has more recently discussed the problems surrounding the dating and contents of the *Thalia* in *Arius*, 62–66.

11. See C. Kannengiesser, "The Blasphemies of Arius: Athanasius of Alexandria, *De Synodis* 15," in Gregg, *Arianism*, 59–78, for a literary analysis of this text and an effort to tie Athanasius's use of these quotations to the specific political circumstances of his time.

12. See Virginia Burrus, *Begotten, Not Made: Conceiving Manhood in Late Antiquity* (Stanford, CA: Stanford University Press, 2000), who highlights the sexual insults and stereotyping in Athanasius's rhetoric.

13. Williams, *Arius*, 98.

14. Barnes, *Constantine and Eusebius*, 203–4.

15. Frend, *Rise of Christianity*, 497.

16. The most complete recent biography of Athanasius is Barnes, *Athanasius and Constantius*. Briefer biographical introductions may be found in Thomas G. Weinandy, *Athanasius: A Theological Introduction* (Aldershot, Hampshire: Ashgate, 2007); Khaled Anatolios, *Athanasius*, The Early Church Fathers (London: Routledge, 2004); Alvyn Pettersen, *Athanasius* (London: Geoffrey Chapman, 1995); M. C. Steenberg, *Of God and Man: Theology as Anthropology from Irenaeus to Athanasius* (London: T&T Clark, 2009), 158–62; Behr, *Nicene Faith*, 163–68.

17. Barnes, *Athanasius and Constantius*, 10.

18. Barnes (ibid., 11) notes that Athanasius cites Plato explicitly only three times, and each of the citations is to a passage that was well-known in antiquity. E. P. Meijering makes it plain that Athanasius uses the thought patterns and terminology of Middle Platonism, but the depth of this indebtedness is still a matter of dispute; see Meijering, *Orthodoxy and Platonism in Athanasius: Synthesis or Antithesis* (Leiden: Brill, 1968). Khaled Anatolios, *Athanasius: The Coherence of His Thought* (London: Routledge, 1998), 7–13, provides a lucid summary of the philosophical context.

19. This translation of Gregory Nazianzen's *Orations* can be found at http://www.newadvent.org/fathers/310221.htm.

20. Barnes, *Athanasius and Constantius*, 10–14, on the background of Athanasius as a lower-class biblicist. See also Hanson, *Search*, 239–73; A. H. M. Jones, *Constantine and the Conversion of Europe* (Toronto: University of Toronto Press, 1978), 153.

21. Barnes, *Athanasius and Constantius*, 21; Potter, *Roman Empire*, 422; Jones, *Constantine*, 155–56.

22. Jones, *Constantine*, 156–57.

23. Ibid., 160–63. Athanasius never completely denied the charges of breaking a chalice or of intimidation. His response to the chalice episode was usually that it did not matter since Ischyras was not a priest and therefore the chalice was not holy. Anyone with small children will recognize the maneuver, a denial that is as good as an admission.

24. Socrates, *Ecclesiastical History* 1.34, 96. See also Hanson, *Search*, 263.

25. Hanson (*Search*, 263) notes that we do not know why Athanasius was exiled. Ayres (*Nicaea and Its Legacy*, 103) says that the last straw was the charge that Athanasius threatened to interrupt the transport of grain from Alexandria to Constantinople. See also Jones, *Constantine*, 163–64.

26. James Joyce, *Ulysses*, ed. Hans Walter Gubler (New York: Vintage, 1986), 32.

27. Raymond Van Dam, *The Roman Revolution of Constantine* (Cambridge: Cambridge University Press, 2008), 257.

28. Anatolios, *Athanasius*, 14.

29. It is typical of the rhetoric of the period that Athanasius highlights the persecution he and his allies endured. Arians did the same, as did the Donatists and virtually every other heretical group. All sides believed that the true church is the suffering church and positioned themselves as the genuine heirs of the martyrs.

30. Four orations are extant, but only the first three are genuinely Athanasian. At one time Kannengiesser expressed doubt about the genuineness of the third oration, but he has since modified his views. See Anatolios, *Athanasius*, 246n74. On the date, see David M. Gwynn, *The Eusebians: The Polemic of Athanasius of Alexandria and the Construction of the "Arian Controversy,"* Oxford Theological Monographs (Oxford: Oxford University Press, 2007), 21–26, who concludes that a date during Athanasius's second exile is most likely. Anatolios (*Athanasius*, 87) concludes the same.

31. Barnes, *Athanasius and Constantius*, 92.

32. Quoted in Behr, *Nicene Faith*, 165.

33. Quoted in ibid., 165.

34. Barnes, *Athanasius and Constantius*, 1. Anatolios, *Athanasius*, 33–39, discusses the various views of Athanasius through the centuries.

35. Anatolios, *Athanasius*, 35.

36. For an extended discussion of Athanasius's rhetorical construction of the "Eusebian party," see Gwynn, *Eusebians*. For a broader study of Athanasius's use of rhetorical techniques, see G. Christopher Stead, "Rhetorical Method in Athanasius," *Vigiliae Christianae* 30 (1976): 121–37. Gwynn neatly summarizes the results of the new scholarship: "The relative insignificance of Arius himself within the debates has been amply demonstrated, notably by Maurice Wiles, while Hanson among others has emphasized that the traditional image of a conflict between established 'orthodoxy' and manifest 'heresy' cannot be maintained. 'On the subject which was primarily under discussion there was not as yet any orthodox doctrine. . . . [The controversy] is not the story of a defence of orthodoxy, but a search for orthodoxy, a search conducted by the method of trial and error.' Furthermore the distortion inherent in Athanasius's presentation of his foes has likewise been acknowledged, for 'it was Athanasius's great polemical success to cast his opponents as Arians' [quoting M. R. Barnes and D. H. Williams]. No modern student of the so-called 'Arian Controversy' is now unaware of these problems of terminology and categorization. As Rowan Williams declares in his review of Hanson, 'the time has probably come to

relegate the term Arianism at least to inverted commas, and preferably to oblivion'" (*Eusebians*, 7). Ayres (*Nicaea and Its Legacy*) agrees that Arius was a marginal player (13) and argues that the central question was not about whether the Son was "God" but about the grammar of the use of the still-flexible word "God" (14), that the issue of how to understand divine generation played a crucial role (2), and that the debate was not between Origenists and anti-Origenists or between hellenizers and anti-hellenizers (20–21, 31–32), since all parties were indebted both to Hellenistic categories and to Origen. Behr draws the provocative conclusion that Christian orthodoxy is always about contemplating "the Christ who is still the coming one. The content of orthodoxy is not protological, but eschatological" (*Nicene Faith*, 15).

37. Williams, "Quest," 25.

38. Ibid., 8.

39. Ibid., 9–10. Ancient followers of Arius are not the only ones who have had difficulty with this point. In their study *Early Arianism: A View of Salvation* (Philadelphia: Fortress, 1981), Robert C. Gregg and Dennis Groh rest much of their account of Arius's soteriology on the notion that the Son comes to knowledge and advances in glory and sonship (cf. 61–63). While that may have been the view of some "Arians," it was not Arius's view.

40. Anatolios, *Athanasius*, 25.

41. Ibid., 27–28.

42. After summarizing the objections to the term "Arianism," Gwynn laments that "the assumption that it is possible to identify a theological position that can be described as 'Arian' remains highly persuasive, and no one has yet fully taken up the challenge that Williams laid down" (*Eusebians*, 7).

43. Maurice Wiles, *Archetypal Heresy: Arianism through the Centuries* (Oxford: Oxford University Press, 1996).

44. Williams, *Arius*, 86–91. Williams writes that before Constantine and Nicaea, "episcopal authority itself had its roots precisely in the *experience* of tradition, the continuity of teaching; yet it was one step removed from the authority of the *theodidaktos* in that it operated fairly strictly within the sacramental context. That is to say, it represented a focus of unity in a common *practice* of worship, centering upon the presence of the symbolic token of continuity and self-identity, the apostolically-validated bishop, rather than a focus on the *personality* of the teacher or of the distinctive *ideas* of a school" (86–87). Academic theology is defined by the charisma of the teacher; Catholic theology is institutionalized, ritualized, regularized, creedalized.

45. Gregg and Groh, *Early Arianism*.

46. Hanson, *Search*, 109–16.

47. M. F. Wiles and R. C. Gregg, "Asterius: A New Chapter in the History of Arianism?" in Gregg, *Arianism*, 132–38.

48. Adolf von Harnack, *History of Dogma*, trans. Neil Buchanan (New York: Dover, 1961), 1:17, quoted in William V. Rowe, "Adolf von Harnack and the Concept of Hellenization," in *Hellenization Revisited: Shaping a Christian Response within the Greco-Roman World*, ed. Wendy E. Helleman (Lanham, MD: University Press of America, 1994), 77–79.

49. Harnack, *History of Dogma*, 1:227–28, quoted in Rowe, "Harnack," in Helleman, *Hellenization Revisited*, 83.

50. Adolf von Harnack, *What Is Christianity?* trans. Thomas Saunders (New York: Harper & Row, 1957), 207, quoted in Rowe, "Harnack," in Helleman, *Hellenization Revisited*, 84–85.

51. Catherine Mowry LaCugna, *God for Us: The Trinity and the Christian Life* (San Francisco: Harper, 1973), 38–39.

52. Robert Jenson, "What Is the Point of Trinitarian Theology?" in *Trinitarian Theology Today: Essays on Divine Being and Act*, ed. Christoph Schwöbel (Edinburgh: T&T Clark, 1995), 37.

53. Ibid. Other theologians have also discovered other anti-Hellenistic motifs in early Trinitarian theology. John Zizioulas (*Being as Communion: Studies in Personhood and the Church*

[Crestwood, NY: St. Vladimir's Seminary Press, 1997]), for example, argues that the Cappadocians developed an unprecedented ontology of personhood.

54. Any assessment of Athanasius's rhetoric must wrestle with Robert Loius Wilken's contextually sensitive treatment of John Chrysostom's anti-Jewish rhetoric in *John Chrysostom and the Jews: Rhetoric and Reality in the Late Fourth Century* (Eugene, OR: Wipf & Stock, 2004).

Chapter 2 Types, Terms, and Paradigms

1. Of the many recent works on the subject, Kevin J. Vanhoozer, ed., *Dictionary for Theological Interpretation of the Bible* (Grand Rapids: Baker Academic, 2005) and Daniel J. Treier, *Introducing Theological Interpretation of Scripture: Recovering a Christian Practice* (Grand Rapids: Baker Academic, 2008) provide good introductions.

2. R. R. Reno, series preface to the Brazos Theological Commentary on the Bible.

3. Ibid., 11–12.

4. Vanhoozer, "Introduction," 20–22, in *Dictionary*.

5. The term is Frances Young's in *Biblical Exegesis and the Formation of Christian Culture* (Peabody, MA: Hendrickson, 2002), 40.

6. See chapter 6 for a discussion of Athanasius's letter to Marcellinus on the Psalms, which focuses more on the transformative effects of reading Scripture. The commentary on Psalms attributed to Athanasius is now generally regarded as coming from another hand. See J. den Boeft's review of M.-J. Rondeau, *Les commentaires patristiques du psautier* (IIIc–IVc siecles), in *Vigiliae Christianae* 41, no. 4 (1987): 294, where he notes that the commentary is pseudo-Athanasian. See also Christopher Stead, "St. Athanasius on the Psalms," *Vigiliae Christianae* 39 (1985): 65–78.

7. This is acknowledged by Thomas F. Torrance, "The Hermeneutics of Saint Athanasius (Part 1)," *Ekklesiastikos Pharos* 52, no. 1 (1970): 446–68; see also Christopher Stead, "Athanasius als Exeget," in *Christliche Exegese zwischen Nicaea und Chalcedon*, ed. J. van Oort and U. Wickert (Kampen: Kok Pharos, 1992), 183.

8. This challenges the assessment of Johannes Quasten, who wrote that "Athanasius had a predilection for the allegorical and typological interpretation of the Psalter in contradistinction to the more jejune exegesis predominant in his dogmatico-polemical writings" (Quasten, *Patrology*, vol. 3 [Westminster, MD: Newman, 1960], 38, quoted in Stead, "St. Athanasius on the Psalms," 76). Athanasius does not confine his typological exegesis to the Psalms in the *Festal Letters*. The difference between the exegetical focus of the anti-Arian polemics and the letters has to do with the difference of intent. In the first, Athanasius is using Scripture to tear down Arianism and to build a positive Christology and theology; in the second, he addresses his congregation as their pastor.

9. Like many of the church fathers, Athanasius finds a type of the cross in Deut. 28:66 ("your life shall hang . . . before you"). See Gregory T. Armstrong, *The Cross in the Old Testament according to Athanasius, Cyril of Jerusalem, and the Cappadocian Fathers* (Tübingen: Mohr, 1979). Interpreting Deut. 28:66 in this way looks fanciful, but there is more to it than is first apparent. The curses of Deut. 28 culminate with the threat of exile, a curse that Jesus suffers on the cross.

10. Aaron's robes are described as "garments . . . for glory and for beauty" (Exod. 28:2). Would Athanasius press the analogy to say that the Son's investiture with flesh is investiture with the jeweled robe and ephod of humanity?

11. See also, "And as a wise architect, proposing to build a house, consults also about repairing it, should it at any time become dilapidated after building, and, as counseling about this, makes preparation and gives to the workmen materials for a repair; and thus the means of the repair are provided before the house; in the same way prior to us is the repair of our salvation founded in Christ, that in Him we might even be new-created. And the will and the purpose were made ready 'before the world,' but have taken effect when the need required, and the Savior came among us" (*Discourses* 2.77).

12. It is commonly recognized in recent scholarship that the debate between Arianism and orthodoxy is a debate about the meaning of Scripture. See Lewis Ayres, *Nicaea and Its Legacy: An Approach to Fourth-Century Trinitarian Theology* (Oxford: Oxford University Press, 2004), 3. He notes also that philosophical concepts, when used at all, were not a replacement for exegesis but a means for elucidating the text of Scripture (277). See also Young, *Biblical Exegesis*, 31.

13. While I have made an attempt to use gender-neutral language where appropriate, when interacting with Athanasius's works I have generally followed the wording used by Athanasius. It should be understood that masculine wordings are being used generically and are intended to encompass all of humanity.

14. Athanasius also points to qualifying purpose clauses in Jesus's statements about his "coming," citing John 6:38–40; 12:46; 18:37; 1 John 3:8 (*Discourses* 2.54).

15. Similarly, "Solomon, though a son, is called a servant, so, to repeat what was said above, although parents call the sons springing from themselves 'made' and 'created' and 'becoming,' for all this they do not deny their nature" (*Discourses* 2.4).

16. It might be possible to add Athanasius's use of "touchstone texts," such as 1 Cor. 1:24, John 10:30 and 14:10, to which Athanasius frequently returns and which serve as an internal canon that measures the right reading of the rest of Scripture. On this, see James D. Ernest, *The Bible in Athanasius of Alexandria* (Boston: Brill, 2004), 120.

17. For discussion of this concept in Athanasius, see Ernest, *Bible in Athanasius*, 142–51; Ernest, "Athanasius of Alexandria: The Scope of Scripture in Polemical and Pastoral Context," *Vigiliae Christianae* 47, no. 4 (1993): 341–62; Torrance, "Hermeneutics of Saint Athanasius (Part 1)," 459–68; Hermann Josef Sieben, "Herméneutique de l'exégèse dogmatique d'Athanase," in *Politique et theologie chez Athanase d'Alexandrie*, ed. Charles Kannengiesser (Paris: Beauchesne, 1974), 106–10.

18. Young, *Biblical Exegesis*, 43. Torrance, "Hermeneutics of Saint Athanasius (Part 1)," 461, agrees that Christ himself is the *skopos*.

19. The force of this rule has been discussed by scholars writing about the hermeneutics of Athanasius. See especially Ernest, *Bible in Athanasius*, 136–41, who attributes the phrase to Allen Clayton. See also Sieben, "Herméneutique," 195–214; Charles Kannengiesser, "The Bible in the Arian Crisis," in *The Bible in Greek Christian History*, ed. and trans. Paul Blowers (Notre Dame: University of Notre Dame Press, 1997), 217–28; Kannengiesser, "The Athanasian Understanding of Scripture," in *The Early Church in Its Context: Essays in Honor of Everett Ferguson*, ed. Abraham J. Malherbe et al. (Leiden: Brill, 1998), 221–29; and Torrance, "Hermeneutics of Saint Athanasius (Part 1)," *Ekklēsiastikos Pharos* (1970–1971), in four installments. For all its virtues, Torrance's series imposes a Barthian framework on Athanasius. Torrance detaches the *res* of revelation from the word of Scripture in ways that I think Athanasius would have rejected, and he attempts to explain his use of biblical paradigms while holding to Barthian scruples about natural revelation, scruples that Athanasius was far from sharing (see chap. 4 of the present work). See also the comments on Athanasius and Scripture in Thomas Molnar, *Thomas F. Torrance: Theology of the Trinity* (Farnham, Surrey: Ashgate, 2009), 44–52. Though not focused exclusively on Athanasius, Michael Slusser, "The Exegetical Roots of Trinitarian Theology," *Theological Studies* 49 (1988): 461–76, is a fascinating exploration of "prosopological exegesis" and its impact on developing trinitarian theology. I am skeptical that the tripartite rule functions as "a permanent concern of the Alexandrian interpreter" (Kannengiesser, "Athanasian Understanding," 227) and suspect that it is anachronistic to plunder the writings of Athanasius for "methodological" insight. The controls on his exegesis are typically more theological than methodological, and common sense plays a more important role than any rules.

20. This kind of appeal to context is common in the *Discourses*. It is clear from the context that Peter's words about the exaltation of the Son in Acts 2:36 refer to the incarnate Son (2.15.12; 2.15.15–17). If "house" is a metaphor in Prov. 9:1, should not the verb "create" also be taken

metaphorically (2.19.46)? The claim that the God of Israel is "one" was directed at polytheistic idolaters who surrounded ancient Israel (3.24.7).

21. John Behr, *Formation of Christian Theology*, vol. 2, *The Nicene Faith, Part 1* (Crestwood, NY: St. Vladimir's Seminary Press, 2004), 208–10. Khaled Anatolios, *Athanasius: The Coherence of His Thought* (London: Routledge, 1998), 71, agrees that the tripartite rule is a christological standard, highlighting the crucial event of the incarnation.

22. See Anatolios, *Coherence*, 98–100; Torrance, "The Hermeneutics of Saint Athanasius (Part 2)," *Ekklesiastikos Pharos* 52, no. 2 (1970): 99–103; Ernest, *Bible in Athanasius*, 151–59.

23. For an extensive discussion of Athanasius's use of this image, see the lovely little classic by Jaroslav Pelikan, *The Light of the World: A Basic Image in Early Christian Thought* (New York: Harper & Brothers, 1962).

24. I will take up the issue of impassibility more fully in chapter 5, in discussing the Word's participation in the passions of the flesh. For now, it is sufficient to quote Donald Fairbairn: "In the mind of the early church, impassibility implied that God could not be adversely affected or damaged by anything we might do. We cannot ruin the fellowship within the Trinity or disrupt the purposes of God or cause his will to fail. But this does not mean that God cannot choose to enter our world by becoming human, to live a fully human life and to suffer as a man for our sakes." Likewise, "God's immutability means that his purposes do not change and that his love for his people is unchanging. . . . He is constant in his love toward us, and this is a drastically different concept of immutability than that of Greek philosophy" (*Life in the Trinity: An Introduction to Theology with the Help of the Church Fathers* [Downers Grove, IL: InterVarsity, 2009], 176–77). Given these definitions, it is clear why Athanasius thinks of both immutability and impassibility in connection with temporality: for creatures, living in time means decay, weakening, corruptibility, the leakage of determination and devotion to life's projects. Not so for God; to be timeless does not mean that he is incapable of interacting in time but rather refers, on the one hand, to his capacity to enter time without suffering time's ravages and, on the other hand, to his ability to act in time without growing and advancing. Since God is wholly and eternally complete, since he has already from all eternity reached the infinite summit, the *telos* of existence, his entry into time is not an opportunity for self-improvement.

Chapter 3 The One God

1. Karl Rahner, *The Trinity*, trans. Joseph Donceel (New York: Crossroad, 1997). Lewis Ayres wisely points out that reports of trinitarian revival have been regularly announced since the beginning of the nineteenth century, noting that the difference this time around is that theologians are aiming not only to revive a forgotten orthodoxy but also to correct and purify what many have come to regard as a flawed tradition (*Nicaea and Its Legacy: An Approach to Fourth-Century Trinitarian Theology* [Oxford: Oxford University Press, 2004], 407).

2. Rahner, *Trinity*, 22.

3. This point is noted by David Bentley Hart, *The Beauty of the Infinite: The Aesthetics of Christian Truth* (Grand Rapids: Eerdmans, 2004), 156.

4. Ibid., 168.

5. For Hart, theologians can avoid this danger only by insisting on divine apatheia. Without the doctrine of apatheia, the doctrine that God is perfectly God and perfectly beautiful and joyful and infinitely satisfied without creation, there is no distinctive Christian aesthetic: "God is good and sovereign and wholly beautiful, and creation is gift, loveliness, pleasure, dignity, and freedom, which is to say that God is possessed of that loveliest (and most widely misunderstood) attribute, 'apatheia'" (ibid., 157).

6. Ibid., 158–59.

7. This is precisely the perspective of Athanasius. See chapter 5 below.

8. Hart, *Beauty of the Infinite*, 160.

9. I explore these issues more fully in chapter 5.

10. See especially Catherine Mowry LaCugna, *God for Us: The Trinity and the Christian Life* (San Francisco: Harper, 1973).

11. This from Karen Kilby, "Perichoresis and Projection: Problems with Social Doctrines of the Trinity," *New Blackfriars* (October 2000): 2. I am working from a PDF version of the article in which the pagination does not match that of the published version.

12. Ibid., 4–7. In addition to Kilby, see Sarah Coakley, "'Persons' in the 'Social' Doctrine of the Trinity: A Critique of Current Analytic Discussion," and Brian Leftow, "Anti Social Trinitarianism," both in *The Trinity*, ed. Stephen Davis et al. (Oxford: Oxford University Press, 2001), 123–44, 203–5. Coakley disputes the claim that the Cappadocians can be enlisted in support of a "social trinitarianism." Leftow questions how social trinitarianism can claim to be both monotheistic and orthodox.

13. Rahner, *Trinity*, 106–7.

14. Ibid., 23.

15. John Behr, *Formation of Christian Theology*, vol. 2, *The Nicene Faith, Part 1* (Crestwood, NY: St. Vladimir's Seminary Press, 2004), 3–4.

16. Ibid., 6–7.

17. This is the approach of some of the best scholarship on Athanasius, notably Khaled Anatolios, *Athanasius: The Coherence of His Thought*, Routledge Early Church Monographs (London: Routledge, 1998).

18. This point, often noted with regard to Athanasius, is made pithily by Thomas F. Torrance, "The Doctrine of the Holy Trinity according to St. Athanasius," *Anglican Theological Review* 71, no. 4 (1989): 397: "Within his supreme incarnational perspective, soteriological and ontological factors were always combined in Athanasius's development of the Nicene doctrine of God." I would only add the qualification that, for Athanasius, these are not really separate factors "combined," but simply facets of the bright jewel that is Christ.

19. Peter Widdicombe, *The Fatherhood of God from Origen to Athanasius*, Oxford Theological Monographs (Oxford: Clarendon, 1994), 160–61. The quotations cited are listed by Widdicombe.

20. Jon M. Robertson, *Christ as Mediator: A Study of the Theologies of Eusebius of Caesarea, Marcellus of Ancyra, and Athanasius of Alexandria* (Oxford: Oxford University Press, 2007), 187; Ayres, *Nicaea and Its Legacy*, 112–13.

21. Edward Gibbon, *History of the Decline and Fall of the Roman Empire*, vol. 3 (London: William Pickering, 1827), 237.

22. For discussion of the philosophical background and the shift in which the Arian debate is caught up, see Rowan Williams, *Arius: Heresy and Tradition*, rev. ed. (Grand Rapids: Eerdmans, 2001), 215–29. Discussions of Athanasius's views are found in Widdicombe, *Fatherhood*, 188–93, and Anatolios, *Coherence*, 50–51, 56, 104–9.

23. This terminology is used early in the *Discourses* but does not appear later in either this work or other writings of Athanasius. See Widdicombe, *Fatherhood*, 193.

24. Alwyn Pettersen, *Athanasius* (London: Geoffrey Chapman, 1995), 246. For further discussion of the term, see Widdicombe, *Fatherhood*, 188–204; Anatolios, *Coherence*, 102–7, 141–46. This terminology makes it impossible for Athanasius to fall into the dangers that Rahner warns of, for if Son and Spirit are as integral to the meaning of the word "God" as goodness and justice, it is meaningless to construct a treatise on "the one God" except as a treatise on the Trinity.

25. On the debate about will, see C. Stead, "The Freedom of the Will and the Arian Controversy," in *Platonismus und Christentum: Festschrift für Heinrich Dörrie*, ed. H.-D. Blume and F. Mann (Münster: Aschendorff, 1983), 245–57. Anatolios (*Coherence*, 121) nicely points out that the issue is really about not the origination (*a quo*) but the termination (*ad quem*) of creation. Being and will are one in God, but this does not mean that being and the *things willed* are one.

26. Williams, *Arius*, 228.

27. For discussion of Athanasius's innovative use of *theotēs*, see Robertson, *Christ as Mediator*, 152–62.

28. A point noted in ibid., 145.

29. A lively recent translation is that of Edmund Hill, *The Trinity* (Brooklyn, NY: New City Press, 1991).

30. A portion of the first letter is translated in Khaled Anatolios, *Athanasius*, The Early Church Fathers, (London: Routledge, 2004), 212–33. See also the discussions in Thomas G. Weinandy, *Athanasius: A Theological Introduction* (Aldershot: Ashgate, 2007), 103–19, esp. 114–17; Behr, *Nicene Faith*, 231–49; and Theodore C. Campbell, "The Doctrine of the Holy Spirit in the Theology of Athanasius," *Scottish Journal of Theology* 27, no. 4 (1974): 408–40.

31. While the term "perichoretic" may be anachronistic, more Cappadocian than Athanasian, it captures, I believe, the substance of Athanasius's thought.

32. Thanks to my student Stephen Long for the research assistance he provided in establishing this point.

33. Anatolios, *Coherence*, 53.

34. Hart, *Beauty of the Infinite*, 168–69.

35. Ibid., 169.

36. Robert Jenson, *Systematic Theology*, vol. 1, *The Triune God* (Oxford: Oxford University Press, 1997), 121.

37. I am dependent here on Thomas Weinandy, *The Father's Spirit of Sonship: Reconceiving the Trinity* (Edinburgh: T&T Clark, 1995), and Mark A. McIntosh, *Mystical Theology: The Integrity of Spirituality and Theology* (Oxford: Blackwell, 1998).

Chapter 4 Beginnings

1. God creates to demonstrate his love (*Against the Pagans* 41). Paul Kolbet ("Athanasius, the Psalms, and the Reformation of the Self," *Harvard Theological Review* 99, no. 1 [2006]: 91) notes that, for Athanasius, God creates out of *philanthropia*, his love for men that are not yet created.

2. Khaled Anatolios, *Athanasius: The Coherence of His Thought* (London: Routledge, 1998), 48. See also George Bebawi, "St. Athanasios: The Dynamics of Salvation," *Sobornost* 8, no. 2 (1986): 27, who distinguishes the Augustinian theory of "privation" from the Athanasian notion of evil as movement toward nothingness.

3. See Thomas Weinandy, *Athanasius: A Theological Introduction* (Aldershot: Ashgate, 2007), 24. Athanasius's construal of the Creator-creature relation is central to the argument of Anatolios, *Coherence*; see in particular 33–35, 39.

4. Anatolios, *Coherence*, 123.

5. Ibid., 53.

6. Jon M. Robertson provides a useful brief outline and discussion of the treatise in *Christ as Mediator: A Study of the Theologies of Eusebius of Caesarea, Marcellus of Ancyra, and Athanasius of Alexandria* (Oxford: Oxford University Press, 2007), 139–51. I am using the text of E. P. Meijering, *Athanasius: Contra Gentes; Introduction, Translation and Commentary* (Leiden: Brill, 1984).

7. Anatolios, *Coherence*, 28.

8. John Behr, *Formation of Christian Theology*, vol. 2, *The Nicene Faith, Part 1* (Crestwood, NY: St. Vladimir's Seminary Press, 2004), 171.

9. One of the strongest statements of this notion comes from *Against the Pagans* 41: "All created nature according to its own structure is fluid and dissolvable" and "lest it experienced this and the universe were dissolved again into non-being . . . having made all things and having given creation its substance through His own eternal Word, He did not leave it to be carried away by its nature and be afflicted, lest it be in danger of disappearing again into non-being, but as a good God He governs and establishes through his own Word, who is also God, the whole world, in order that creation illuminated by the leadership, providence and ordering of

the Word could remain in existence, since it participated in the Word out of the Father and is helped by Him to its existence."

10. Athanasius's use of the Stoic image of the world as "body" has sometimes been taken as evidence of his debt to Stoicisim. More likely, Athanasius makes rather unsystematic use of images and metaphors from the general philosophical culture around him and does not intend the image as the Stoics understand it.

11. Conversely, if creation's diversity makes up for lack in each part, and God has no lack, then God is in himself, as one God, all that the creation is in its multiplicity. The light of God is the infinite light of sun and moon and stars and all else.

12. G. D. Dragas (*Saint Athanasius of Alexandria: Original Research and New Perspectives* [Rollinsford, NH: Orthodox Research Institute, 2005], 29) picks up on this image, describing creation as a choir in which each thing sings according to its nature. Athanasius highlights the interdependence of created things also in *Against the Pagans* 27. He attacks the worship of creation by noting that no part of creation is self-sufficient: "If somebody takes the parts of creation by themselves and considers them separately, e.g., the sun alone, the moon separately, and on the other side separated from their mutual connection the earth and the air, the warm, cold, dry, and wet substance, then he will find that absolutely nothing is self-sufficient, but that they are all in need of each others' help and that they subsist through each others' support." He illustrates again using sun, moon and stars, earth and water, the four elements.

13. This paragraph summarizes a number of the points made by Anatolios, *Coherence*, 62–67.

14. The question here is not about sin but about the state of creation before Adam's fall. The question might be put this way: did God rig the world so that Adam, because of his created instability, had an inherent tendency toward sin, toward turning from God? If the creation is good, then it cannot include constraints that encourage sin. Sin must, of course, be possible, but it must not be inevitable.

15. Athanasius supports the conclusion that evil is non-being with a number of arguments, mainly negative. The only alternatives to the privation view are (a) evil is a substance but God did not make it, (b) evil is a substance and God did make it, or (c) some other creative being made evil (*Against the Pagans* 6). The first and last deny that God is Creator of all, the second that he is good. Only the privation view of evil is consistent with Athanasius's doctrine of creation *ex nihilo* and the consequent strict distinction between Creator and creature.

16. Athanasius's exposition of this point makes it difficult to avoid the conclusion that the incarnation would have happened without sin, despite his explicit tying of the incarnation to the fall. If the world is tipping toward corruption in itself and needs to be brought to stability, then that can only happen if the Word that sustains all creation forges a deeper bond with creation. For further discussion, see below, chapter 5.

17. For discussions of Athanasius's own treatment of nature/grace, see Dragas, *Saint Athanasius*, chap. 2; Anatolios, *Coherence*, 55; Khaled Anatolios, *Athanasius*, The Early Church Fathers (London: Routledge, 2004), 40–42.

18. For a superb summary of the debate and Henri de Lubac, who lived at the heart of the storm, see Fergus Kerr, *Twentieth-Century Catholic Theologians: From Neoscholasticism to Nuptial Mystery* (Oxford: Blackwell, 2007).

19. Michael Horton, *God of Promise: Introducing Covenant Theology* (Grand Rapids: Baker, 2006), 100.

20. Ibid., 96.

21. Ibid., 93.

22. Ibid., 92–93.

23. Ibid., 89.

24. Ibid.

25. Ibid., 84.

26. Ibid., 91.

27. See Alister McGrath, *Iustitia Dei*, 3rd ed. (Cambridge: Cambridge University Press, 2005), 38–55. O'Donovan's discussion of book 19 of *City of God* is published in Oliver O'Donovan, *Bonds of Imperfection: Christian Politics, Past and Present* (Grand Rapids: Eerdmans, 2004), 48–72.

28. For an argument that civic and spiritual were much more closely integrated in Calvin, see J. Todd Billings, *Calvin, Participation and the Gift: The Activity of Believers in Union with Christ* (Oxford: Oxford University Press, 2007), 177–84. Billings makes a plausible case that civic order is a theological concern for Calvin, but even in his account, justification and justice meet only at the margins.

29. These are the two opponents against which Matthias Scheeben directed his work on nature and grace. This will be discussed in more depth later in this chapter.

30. Instructive as it might prove, in this chapter I do not examine the politics and polemics of the twentieth-century debate itself, which Fergus Kerr characterizes as an outbreak of *rabies theologica*. My aim is more narrowly theological, and I examine the differing formulations of three Catholic theologians.

31. I have relied on the discussions of Scheeben in R. R. Reno, *The Ordinary Transformed: Karl Rahner and the Christian Vision of Transcendence* (Grand Rapids: Eerdmans, 1995), 95–101, and Hans Urs von Balthasar, *The Glory of the Lord*, vol. 1, *Seeing the Form*, trans. Erasmo Leiva-Merikakis (San Francisco: Ignatius, 1982), 104–17.

32. Joseph Scheeben, *Nature and Grace* (1861; repr., St. Louis: Herder, 1954).

33. Ibid., 49, quoted in Reno, *Ordinary Transformed*, 96.

34. Ibid., 16, quoted in Reno, *Ordinary Transformed*, 97.

35. Ibid., 42–43, quoted in Reno, *Ordinary Transformed*, 98.

36. Ibid., 27.

37. Ibid., 25–26.

38. Ibid., 30–31.

39. Ibid., 206, 296.

40. Ibid., 102–3.

41. Ibid., 109.

42. Ibid., 195.

43. Reno, *Ordinary Transformed*, 99–100. On Aristotelian premises, one must be one substance or another, but cannot be two at once. If Scheeben maintained his Aristotelianism and posited the human as a natural being, he would lose the supernatural; if man is a supernatural being, then nature would be absorbed and lost. Yet Scheeben wants to maintain both nature and supernature—what Reno calls an "amphibious" or "mixed" existence—and to do that he breaks out of the substance metaphysics at crucial points. Adoption thus involves a substantial change in the adopted sinner, but Scheeben roots this substantial change, against all Aristotelianism, in a "juridical act" that "preceded and created the new substance."

44. Scheeben, *Nature and Grace*, 330.

45. Henri de Lubac, *Brief Catechesis on Nature and Grace*, trans. Richard Arnandez (San Francisco: Ignatius, 1984), 33.

46. In his *Dogmatik* and other writings, Scheeben develops his christologically based "connubial" theology that highlights a marital union of God and humanity, Christ and Mary, the two natures of Christ. Out of these marriages emerges the marriage of grace and nature, of reason and faith, of body and spirit, of philosophy and theology. Nature, Scheeben claims, must be "in-formed" by grace, and, typically, Scheeben describes this in-formation as a kind of begetting, an implantation of divine seed in the womb of nature, which alone enables nature to be fruitfully energized. This christological center also marries the pure nature and supernature that Scheeben breaks apart in his earlier work. He recovers the patristic notion of the divine nature as an "information" of the human nature in Christ. According to Hans Urs von Balthasar (*Seeing the Form*, vol. 1 of *The Glory of the Lord: A Theological Aesthetics*, ed. Joseph Fessio and John

Riches [San Francisco: Ignatius, 1989]), "As far as Christ's human nature is concerned, this means that its 'natural' reality has a wholly 'supernatural' foundation. And for Christ's total person the reverse holds: the supernatural miracle of two natures constituting one person is 'natural' in the sense that in this union all nature's organic, moral, and matrimonial relationships find their highest form and fulfillment and indeed their ultimate ground." For Balthasar, Scheeben ends with a "total healing of the sharp fracture with which Scheeben's theology had begun" (114).

47. De Lubac, *Brief Catechesis*, 34–35.

48. Henri de Lubac, *Augustinianism and Modern Theology*, trans. Lancelot Sheppard (New York: Herder & Herder, 2000); *The Mystery of the Supernatural*, trans. Rosemary Sheed (New York: Herder & Herder, 1967).

49. Matthew Levering points out that the issue is complicated by the fact that Thomas writes differently about these issues in different places in his vast writings. "Later interpreters have had trouble interpreting him on this point not due to ill-will or rationalism, but because of the divergence in what he says at various places" (personal communication, February 17, 2010).

50. Thomas Aquinas, *Summa contra Gentiles* 3.57, quoted in de Lubac, *Mystery of the Supernatural*, 11.

51. Scheeben, *Nature and Grace*, 57.

52. Quoted in Reno, *Ordinary Transformed*, 117n55.

53. Ibid., 69.

54. Ibid., 69–70.

55. Ibid., 77.

56. Ibid., 42. De Lubac does concede that the terminology of natural/supernatural is not the most felicitous language to capture God's self-gift in Christ. Quoting Vahanian, he writes, "One can certainly say that, just as the word *nature* 'fails to indicate clearly the logic of freedom, so too the word *supernatural* does not fully express the reality of the communication that God makes of himself in Jesus Christ.' These words, therefore, do not suffice to express the 'personal and historic relationship' in which 'the Christian mystery' consists." Yet he believes that "there would be more than one difficulty in trying to eliminate their use completely" (*Brief Catechesis*, 40).

57. Ibid., 42.

58. Ibid., 52, quoting Medina.

59. Ibid., 61.

60. Henri de Lubac, *Catholicism: Christ and the Common Destiny of Man* (San Francisco: Ignatius, 1988), 313–14. Thanks to my student Brad Littlejohn for pointing me to this reference.

61. De Lubac, *Mystery of the Supernatural*, 239–40.

62. Ibid., 105.

63. Anatolios, *Coherence*, 55.

64. See chapter 5.

65. See the superb summary in Anatolios, *Coherence*, 130–33, and Anatolios, *Athanasius*, 64–66.

66. De Lubac, *Brief Catechesis*, 49.

67. John Milbank, *Theology and Social Theory*, 2nd ed. (Oxford: Blackwell, 2006), 224. More fully, in neither Rahner's description of the supernatural existential nor in his account of the natural *Vorgriff* "does self-transcendence denote the encounter with a concrete, recognizable other. Rather, in both cases the 'intrinsic' experimental side is reducible to a self-striving *conatus* away from finite limitations, while the infinite object sought for—*esse*, which the supernatural existential identifies as God—is still extrinsically separate as a 'formal object.' Our 'entitative raising,' insofar as it is a meeting with God, still appears to be something externally and authoritatively confirmed by the arbitrary *fiat* of a positive revelation" (224).

68. De Lubac, *Brief Catechesis*, 140.

69. Ibid., 83, 119–20.

70. David Bentley Hart, *The Beauty of the Infinite* (Grand Rapids: Eerdmans, 2004), 196.

71. Karl Rahner, *Nature and Grace: Dilemmas in the Modern Church* (Lanham, MD: Sheed and Ward, 1964), 136–37. It is the "definition" of created spirit that it cannot be "'defined,' i.e., 'confined,' like sub-human beings."

72. De Lubac concedes that the terminology of "nature" and "supernatural" may not be the best way to express the content of Catholic theology, and he points to Paul's distinction between "soulish" and "spiritual" existence as a biblical equivalent (*Brief Catechesis*, 27).

Chapter 5 Middle

1. The latter position is briefly defended in T. D. Barnes, *Athanasius and Constantius* (Cambridge, MA: Harvard University Press, 1993), 12–13. See also Jon M. Robertson, *Christ as Mediator: A Study of the Theologies of Eusebius of Caesarea, Marcellus of Ancyra and Athanasius of Alexandria*, Oxford Theological Monographs (Oxford: Oxford University Press, 2007), 139n3, for the view that the treatise was written during Athanasius's first exile, around 336.

2. Written as a companion piece to the apologetic *Against the Pagans*, it is part of Athanasius's defense of the rationality of the cross.

3. Throughout this chapter I use the anonymous translation of *On the Incarnation*, rev. ed. (Crestwood, NY: St. Vladimir's Seminary Press, 1996).

4. I examine the role of the Word in preserving the original creation from corruption in the previous chapter.

5. That is, there is no "tension," as sometimes popularly thought, between God's justice and mercy. Such a tension is impossible in any case. Given the assumption that God is simple, his attributes are all identical to his essence, and each attribute is therefore ultimately identical to every other attribute. We must speak of this in qualified terms: God's mercy is just, his justice merciful. For God, there are not two things mutually qualifying each other, but only God the Father, the Son, and the Spirit, who is wholly just-merciful, just as he is wholly good, holy, love. Athanasius locates the tension not among God's attributes but within the apparently irresolvable commitments that he has made to creation: the threat to punish sin, which cannot be empty, and the resolve to preserve his creatures.

6. This runs contrary to a thread of popular evangelical and Reformed piety and theology. In stressing the gratuity of God's grace, it is often said that, after Adam's sin, "God could have condemned the entire human race to eternal hell. That would have been a proper display of His justice." Heinrich Heppe states this position succinctly: "After man had impaired the covenant entered into with God [in Eden], it was in God's power to punish him immediately with eternal damnation" (*Reformed Dogmatics: Set Out and Illustrated from the Sources*, rev. ed. [London: Allen & Unwin, 1950], 371). Athanasius takes the question back to creation: God showed a commitment to creation by the sheer fact of creating, and it would be unworthy of God's goodness and faithfulness for him to take back that commitment.

7. Athanasius almost invariably links the incarnation to sin, as God's faithful response to the destruction wreaked by Adam's fall and the evils of his descendants. Yet much of the machinery is in place for the view later developed that the incarnation would have occurred without sin. First, Athanasius insists that human beings, while made sinless and good, are yet liable to corruption, and thus not perfected. If the human race is to be stable in its reception of God's gifts, to remain (*menein*) in God's love, it must be delivered from created corruption to incorruption. Second, Athanasius everywhere insists that only God is unchangeably himself. Creatures, which originate from nothing and are "in transit," cannot be stable without divine help. Third, the only path that Athanasius leaves open for human beings to rise from corruptibility to incorruption, from instability to stability, from changeability and liability to fall into a state of impeccability, is through union with the stable, incorruptible, unchangeable, sinless God. Within Athanasius's system, it is hard to see how this stability and incorruption could be communicated to human beings extrinsically, from "outside." The grace of human perfection, even in a sinless world, must come to man through God's union with flesh, so that the grace that

perfects human creatures can become intrinsic to humanity. Therefore, even in a sinless world, Adam and his children would have reached perfection through the incarnation of the Word.

8. Christopher Stead states that "the great majority of scholars now agree that the two books against Apollinaris are not from his hand" ("The Scriptures and the Soul of Christ in Athanasius," *Vigiliae Christianae* [1982]: 233–50). On the authenticity of the treatise, see George Dion Dragas, *Saint Athanasius of Alexandria: Original Research and New Perspectives* (Rollinsford, NH: Orthodox Research Institute, 2005), chap. 5, as well as an analysis of Dragas's position in Stead, "Review of *St. Athanasius contra Apollinarem*, by George Dion Dragas," 250–53. See also John R. Meyer, "Athanasius's Use of Paul in His Doctrine of Salvation," *Vigiliae Christianae* 52, no. 2 (1998): 152–59. Arius is commonly charged with being an Apollinarian himself, but see the contrary view of William P. Haugaard, "Arius: Twice a Heretic? Arius and the Human Soul of Jesus Christ," *Church History* 29, no. 3 (1960): 251–63. Grillmeier takes the comparative absence of attention to the human soul of Christ as evidence for a Word-flesh model in Athanasius's Christology; he argues that the human soul of Jesus plays no theological role in Athanasius and that this is the key point of his Christology (Aloys Grillmeier, *Christ in Christian Tradition*, vol. 1, *From the Apostolic Age to Chalcedon (451)*, trans. John Bowden, 2nd ed. [Atlanta: John Knox, 1975], 308). The treatises against Apollinaris address a number of issues: there is a polemic against those who consider the flesh of the incarnate Son to be as uncreated as the Word himself, and an insistence that the flesh of Jesus suffered, accompanied by the equally strong insistence that he did not suffer in his divine nature. The writer offers several arguments supporting belief in Jesus's human soul: he has to be soul in order to share our life and death; without a soul, his death is not the same as our death; if the soul is not renewed by union with the Word, then it can only be saved by "imitation." This last point highlights the inner connection between Arian Christology and Pelagian soteriology. For the texts, see *Later Treatises of St. Athanasius* (Oxford: James Parker, 1881), available in full at Google Books.

9. Grillmeier argues that this text does not mean what it appears to mean, but his argument depends on a tendentious reading of the passage (*Christ in Christian Tradition*, 318–26).

10. Khaled Anatolios, *Athanasius: The Coherence of His Thought* (London: Routledge, 1998), 73.

11. J. N. D. Kelly, *Early Christian Doctrines* (San Francisco: Harper, 1960).

12. See also Gen. 2:19; 9:4–5, 10, 12, 15–16. Later in Genesis, *nephesh* is used to describe human persons (12:5, 13) and eventually something closer to the soul as the seat of thought, desire, and intention (e.g., 23:8; 27:4).

13. Grillmeier, *Christ in Christian Tradition*, 315.

14. Grillmeier (ibid., 317) claims that the term *organon* summarizes the whole of Athanasius's Alexandrian "word-flesh" Christology.

15. R. P. C. Hanson, *The Search for the Christian Doctrine of God: The Arian Controversy, 318–381* (Grand Rapids: Baker, 1988), 448. Grillmeier makes a similar claim, with particular emphasis on the supposed absence of a human soul in Christ: "Athanasius displays a general tendency to weaken the character of certain of Christ's inner experiences which might be attributed to a human soul so as to dissociate the Logos from them from the start. Thus Christ's anguish was only 'feigned,' and not real anguish; his ignorance was no real ignorance, but only an *ignorantia de jure*, which was proper to the human nature from the start. Not only does such a qualification relieve the pressure on the Logos itself, but it also raises the possibility of representing the *sarx* of Christ as the subject of such affections as we should properly ascribe to the soul. As a result, we have Athanasius's remarkable procedure of making the 'flesh' of Christ the physical subject of experiences which normally have their place in the soul" (*Christ in Christian Tradition*, 315). For a sharp refutation of Grillmeier, see Anatolios, *Coherence*, 70–73.

16. T. F. Torrance, "The Hermeneutics of Saint Athanasius (Part 3)," *Ekklesiastikos Pharos* 52, no. 4 (1970): 238, claims that Athanasius was combating the dualism of Christ and his works that he inherited from the Alexandrian tradition. See similar points made by Frances

Young in "A Reconsideration of Alexandrian Christology," *Journal of Ecclesiastical History* 22, no. 2 (1971): 113; and *Biblical Exegesis and the Formation of Christian Culture* (Peabody, MA: Hendrickson, 2002), 44.

17. So Anatolios, *Coherence*, 140. Anatolios argues that the center of Athanasius's Christology is the fact that humanity, in its complete range of experience, is predicated of the Word because the Word has appropriated it.

18. This is central to Robertson's entire argument in *Christ as Mediator*, but see the summary on 213–14.

19. The discussion in this paragraph depends on ibid., esp. 206.

20. Anatolios, *Coherence*, 146.

21. John Behr, *Formation of Christian Theology*, vol. 2, *The Nicene Faith, Part 1* (Crestwood, NY: St. Vladimir's Seminary Press, 2004), 186. As Behr goes on to note, this also undercuts the "blood transfusion" interpretations of Athanasius. If "incarnation" means simply the Word becoming flesh, then Athanasius's claim that we are saved through the incarnation sounds like a claim that we are saved by an infusion of divine stuff into a corruptible world. But if "incarnation" includes the life, death, and resurrection of the enfleshed Word, then Athanasius is saying that we are turned from death through the work of the Word, not merely by the presence of the Word.

22. Young, *Biblical Exegesis*, 44.

23. Khaled Anatolios, *Athanasius*, The Early Church Fathers (London: Routledge, 2004), 141, makes the same point. See also Robertson, *Christ as Mediator*, 145, citing Andrew Louth.

24. See Alvyn Petterson, *Athanasius* (London: Geoffrey Chapman, 1995), 66: "Ignoring God is to God's dishonor insofar as people who properly were created to live not only through God but for God now no longer live to God's glory; but it is to their ruin. What then looks like God's jealousy for himself is in fact God's jealousy for humanity's godly well-being."

25. Arius, at least, did not teach this view. As noted in chapter 1, Arius himself believed that the Son, though a creature, was endowed from the beginning of his existence with all the perfections that a creature is capable of possessing. His glorification is thus not an advance from a low position. Yet Athanasius's attack, though strictly inaccurate, is responding to Arian language and its use of Scripture. The Arians, after all, did use texts like Phil. 2 to rebut the orthodox claim that the Son was always with the Father and always shared full deity with the Father.

26. For my discussion of Hegel, I am indebted to Anselm K. Min, "The Trinity and the Incarnation: Hegel and Classical Approaches," *Journal of Religion* 66, no. 2 (1986): 173–93. See also William Desmond, *Hegel's God: A Counterfeit Double?* (Aldershot: Ashgate, 2003); Cyril O'Regan, *The Heterodox Hegel* (Albany: State University of New York Press, 1994).

27. Min, "Trinity and the Incarnation," 184.

28. Ibid.; translated from Hegel, *Die absolute Religion* (Hamburg: Felix Meiner, 1966), 91.

29. Ibid.

30. Ibid.

31. Ibid., 186. Though Hegel is using the language of traditional trinitarian theology, his views are finally closer to Plotinus, who posits an original "One" who proliferates into multiples that are then reabsorbed by the One. Hegel's main difference with Plotinus lies in his conception of "sublation," according to which the Other or others are not simply reabsorbed but reabsorbed into the One without losing their otherness.

32. Ibid., 189.

33. Hegel, *Die absolute Religion*, 190.

34. Min (quoting from Hegel), "Trinity and the Incarnation," 190.

35. Ibid., 191.

36. Ibid.

37. Hegel, *Phenomenology of Spirit*, trans. A. V. Miller (Oxford: Oxford University Press, 1977), 476.

38. Hegel, *Lectures on the Philosophy of Religion: The Lectures of 1827* (Berkeley: University of California Press, 1988), 468.

39. Richard Bauckham, "Jürgen Moltmann," in *The Modern Theologians: An Introduction to Christian Theology since 1918*, ed. David Ford and Rachel Muers (Oxford: Blackwell, 2005), 153.

40. Jürgen Moltmann, *The Trinity and the Kingdom* (Philadelphia: Fortress, 1993), xvi.

41. Jürgen Moltmann, *The Crucified God: The Cross of Christ as the Foundation and Criticism of Christian Theology* (Philadelphia: Fortress, 1993), 324.

42. Veli-Matti Kärkkäinen, *The Trinity: Global Perspectives* (Louisville: Westminster/John Knox, 2007).

43. Ibid., 109.

44. Moltmann, *Trinity and the Kingdom*, 173.

45. Ibid., 174.

46. Moltmann, *Crucified God*, 222.

47. Moltmann, *Trinity and the Kingdom*, 106.

48. Ibid., 109.

49. Bauckham, "Jürgen Moltmann," 215.

50. We might put it this way: God is the same God eternally. He is eternally the God who responds to my anguish at time X and to my elation at time Y. From all eternity, he is the God who responds to my frustrations and worry about a writing deadline at 9:39 on December 22, 2009, and he is the God who will respond, as the eternal God, to my elation once this writing project is safely to bed several weeks later. He is unchangeably the God who went to the cross on Good Friday, unchangeably the God who brought the Son from the grave by the Spirit three days later. I am indebted to my friend David Field for his formulation and for several very helpful conversations on these points. The particular illustration is, I admit, slightly autobiographical.

51. Robert Jenson, "*Ipse Pater Non Est Impassibilis*," in *Divine Impassibility and the Mystery of Human Suffering*, ed. James F. Keating and Thomas Joseph White (Grand Rapids: Eerdmans, 2004), 119.

52. Ibid., 120.

53. Ibid., 124.

54. Behr, *Nicene Faith*, 227. See the similar analysis of Anatolios, *Coherence*, 152, 155.

55. Ibid., 228.

56. Robertson, *Christ as Mediator*, 209.

57. Anatolios, *Athanasius*, 80.

58. Behr, *Nicene Faith*, 227.

59. Anatolios, *Coherence*, 134.

Chapter 6 End

1. Athanasius writes of predestination only in this brief section of the second of his *Discourses*, and despite the inherent interest of this evidence of a pre-Augustinian and Eastern (!) theology of predestination, little has been written on the subject as it pertains to Athanasius. See F. Stuart Clarke, "Lost and Found: Athanasius's Doctrine of Predestination," *Scottish Journal of Theology* 29, no. 5 (1976): 435–50. Clarke calls attention to Barth's quotation of the passage in *The Doctrine of God*, vol. 2 of *Church Dogmatics*, trans. G. W. Bromiley et al. (London: T&T Clark, 1957), 108–9. Clarke argues that much of the Augustinian tradition is quasi-Arian on predestination, since it does not consider that the Son is a full participant in the act of election and is the "foundation" of the Father's choice. Instead, the Father is conceived of making a choice "secretly," and the Son is seen as the agent who carries out the decree. This is a mischaracterization of the best of the tradition, however. For the Reformed tradition in particular, see Richard Muller, *Christ and the Decree: Christology and Predestination in Reformed Theology from Calvin to Perkins* (Grand Rapids: Baker Academic, 2008).

2. Khaled Anatolios, *Athanasius: The Coherence of His Thought* (London: Routledge, 1998), 138, notes that human beings are in the Father through the work of the Spirit.

3. Virginia Burrus, *Begotten, Not Made: Conceiving Manhood in Late Antiquity* (Stanford, CA: Stanford University Press, 2000), 42.

4. Throughout this chapter, I use the anonymous translation of *On the Incarnation* published by St. Vladimir's Seminary Press (rev. ed., 1996).

5. For intriguing reflections on Athanasius's notion of the cross as payment of a debt, see M. C. Steenberg, *Of God and Man: Theology as Anthropology from Irenaeus to Athanasius* (London: T&T Clark, 2009), 177, 182–83. The debt, Steenberg argues, is to the natural order itself; because of the corruptibility of created nature, all are "due to die," all owe a death. There is a double payment in the cross: All human death is consummated by the death of the Son; he brings to a climax the history of death that is the history of our race. At the same time, the Son pays that debt, but because he pays it with the very flesh of the Word of God, he pays for all. The obligation of death is discharged and overcome.

6. *Festal Letter* 5.1, quoted in David Brakke, *Athanasius and Asceticism* (Baltimore: Johns Hopkins University Press, 1995), 192.

7. In several places, Athanasius draws the line between Creator and creature as a contrast between nature and mimesis: "The Word has the real and true identity of nature with the Father, but to us it is given to imitate it" (*Discourses* 3.22; cf. *Discourses* 3.19). Thus his Christology and trinitarian theology form the foundation of his ethical exhortations and practice.

8. The entire discussion here is indebted to Brakke, *Athanasius and Asceticism*. Brakke convincingly argues that Athanasius's revisions of Alexandrian spirituality were part of a "political" program to build and strengthen the church in Alexandria and throughout Egypt. The strategy was two-pronged: Athanasius maintained sharp boundaries between orthodox and heretical bodies (Arian or Melitian), and he worked to unify the various subgroups within Egyptian Christianity (ascetics like the solitaries, monks, and virgins, on the one hand, and common Christians, on the other). On the one hand, he enlisted the support of ascetics against heresy (see the excoriating speech of Antony against the Arians in *Life of Antony*) and presented ascetic practices as a model that Christians might emulate; on the other hand, he did not believe every Christian should be an ascetic and thus articulated a moderated asceticism for the married, working Christians of the city.

9. Brakke, *Athanasius and Asceticism*, 181.

10. See ibid., 171–73.

11. Quoted in ibid., 184. Brakke quotes from a fragment he identifies as a "Canonical Letter." Athanasius gets the reasoning exactly backward. If the new covenant intensifies requirements for ritual purity, it is difficult to make sense of the purification of meats to which both Mark (7:14–23) and Luke (Acts 10–11) testify. The apostles do not look at the food restrictions of the Old Testament and say, "How much more . . ." Rather, the whole system of purity is transposed into a new key, so that defilement becomes not a ceremonial but a moral concern. Not marital sex but sexual immorality defiles.

12. I am relying on the translation of Robert Gregg, published in Athanasius, *The Life of Antony* (San Francisco: Harper, 2006), 16. Page references are to this edition.

13. Quoted in Brakke, *Athanasius and Asceticism*, 189.

14. On this epistle, see M.-J. Rondeau, "L'épître à Marcellinus sur les Psaumes," *Vigiliae Christianae* 22 (1968): 176–97; Holly Taylor Coolman, "The Psalter for the Formation of Souls: How to Repent; How to Give Thanks; What One Must Say When Being Pursued," *Word and World* 21, no. 3 (2001): 227–34; Paul R. Kolbet, "Athanasius, the Psalms, and the Reformation of the Self," *Harvard Theological Review* 99, no. 1 (2006): 85–101. G. C. Stead, "St. Athanasius on the Psalms," *Vigiliae Christianae* 39 (1985): 65–78, concludes that the *Expositiones in Psalmos* attributed to Athanasius is not in fact from his hand, largely based on the repeated use of the non-Athanasian phrase *to prosōpon tēs anthrōpotētos*, "the 'person' of the humanity."

15. Gregg, *Life of Antony*, 86.
16. Ibid., 91, 92.
17. Ibid., 93.
18. Ibid., 94, 95.
19. Ibid., 112.
20. Brakke, *Athanasius and Asceticism*, 167, quoted in Kolbet, "Athanasius, Psalms," 94. See also Rondeau, "L'épître à Marcellinus," 188.
21. Gregg, *Life of Antony*, 112.
22. Brakke, *Athanasius and Asceticism*, 159. The texts cited in the discussion here are drawn from this work, 159n78.
23. The Greek title of the *Vita Antonii* includes the term *politeia*: "*Bios kai politeia tou hosiou patros hēmon Antōniou.*"
24. Anatolios, *Coherence*, 29; John Behr, *Formation of Christian Theology*, vol. 2, *The Nicene Faith, Part 1* (Crestwood, NY: St. Vladimir's Seminary Press, 2004), 171.

Epilogue

1. "Worded" is Anatolios's translation. See *Athanasius: The Coherence of His Thought* (London: Routledge, 1998), 142–43.

Selected Bibliography

Unless otherwise noted, I have used the translation of Athanasius's works from the nineteenth-century collection of *The Nicene and Post-Nicene Fathers*, second series, vol. 4, *Athanasius: Select Works and Letters*, edited by Philip Schaff and Henry Wace. Available online at www.newadvent.org/fathers/index .html. Slight changes have been made throughout to bring the translation into conformity with contemporary American usage.

Khaled Anatolios has a good selection of freshly translated texts in his *Athanasius*, and at various points above I have also used Robert Gregg's translation of *The Life of Antony and the Letter to Marcellinus*; E. P. Meijering's translation of *Against the Pagans*, published in *Contra Gentes*; and the anonymous translation of *On the Incarnation*. For Greek texts, I have relied on the collection of Athanasius's works found in Migne's Patrologia Graeca, available online at Google Books. To find links to specific treatises, go to cyprianproject .info/PG.htm and scroll to vols. 25–28.

Anatolios, Khaled. *Athanasius*. The Early Church Fathers. London: Routledge, 2004.

———. *Athanasius: The Coherence of His Thought*. Routledge Early Church Monographs. London: Routledge, 1998.

Armstrong, Gregory T. *The Cross in the Old Testament according to Athanasius, Cyril of Jerusalem, and the Cappadocian Fathers*. Tübingen: Mohr, 1979.

Athanasius. *On the Incarnation*. Rev. ed. Crestwood, NY: St. Vladimir's Seminary Press, 1996.

Ayres, Lewis. *Nicaea and Its Legacy: An Approach to Fourth-Century Trinitarian Theology*. Oxford: Oxford University Press, 2004.

Barnard, L. W. "Edward Gibbon on Athanasius." In Gregg, *Arianism*, 361–70.

Barnes, Timothy D. *Athanasius and Constantius: Theology and Politics in the Constantinian Empire*. Cambridge, MA: Harvard University Press, 1993.

Bebawi, George. "St. Athanasios: The Dynamics of Salvation." *Sobornost* 8, no. 2 (1986): 24–41.

Behr, John. *Formation of Christian Theology*. Vol. 2, *The Nicene Faith*. Crestwood, NY: St. Vladimir's Seminary Press, 2004.

Brakke, David. *Athanasius and Asceticism*. Baltimore: Johns Hopkins, 1995.

————. "Canon Formation and Social Conflict in Fourth-Century Egypt: Athanasius of Alexandria's Thirty-Ninth *Festal Letter*." *Harvard Theological Review* 87, no. 4 (1994): 395–419.

Burrus, Virginia. *Begotten, Not Made: Conceiving Manhood in Late Antiquity*. Figurae: Reading Medieval Culture. Stanford, CA: Stanford University Press, 2000.

Campbell, Theodore C. "The Doctrine of the Holy Spirit in the Theology of Athanasius." *Scottish Journal of Theology* 27, no. 4 (1974): 408–40.

Clarke, F. Stuart. "Lost and Found: Athanasius's Doctrine of Predestination." *Scottish Journal of Theology* 29, no. 5 (1976): 435–50.

Coolman, Holly Haylor. "The Psalter for the Formation of Souls." *Word and World* 21, no. 3 (2001): 227–34.

Den Boeft, J. Review of M.-J. Rondeau, *Les commentaires patristiques du psautier* (IIIc–IVc siècles), *Vigiliae Christianae* 41, no. 3 (1987): 293–96.

Dragas, G. D. "The Homoousion in Athanasius's *Contra Apollinarem I*." In Gregg, *Arianism*, 233–42.

————. *Saint Athanasius of Alexandria: Original Research and New Perspectives*. Rollinsford, NH: Orthodox Research Institute, 2005.

Ernest, James D. "Athanasius of Alexandria: The Scope of Scripture in Polemical and Pastoral Context." *Vigiliae Christianae* 47, no. 4 (1993): 341–62.

————. *The Bible in Athanasius of Alexandria*. Boston: Brill, 2004.

Fairbairn, Donald. *Life in the Trinity: An Introduction to Theology with the Help of the Church Fathers*. Downers Grove, IL: InterVarsity, 2009.

Gregg, Robert C., ed. *Arianism: Historical and Theological Reassessments*. 1985. Reprint, Eugene, OR: Wipf & Stock, 2006.

————. "Cyril of Jerusalem and the Arians." In Gregg, *Arianism*, 85–109.

————. *The Life of Antony and the Letter to Marcellinus*. San Francisco: Harper, 1980.

Gregg, Robert C., and Dennis E. Groh. *Early Arianism: A View of Salvation*. Philadelphia: Fortress, 1981.